WESTERN WOMEN WHO DARED TO BE DIFFERENT

By
Gail Hughbanks Woerner

www.WildHorsePress.com

Copyright © 2014
By Gail Hughbanks Woerner
Published By Wild Horse Press
An Imprint of Wild Horse Media Group
P.O. Box 331779
Fort Worth, Texas 76163
1-817-344-7036
www.WildHorsePress.com
ALL RIGHTS RESERVED
1 2 3 4 5 6 7 8 9
ISBN-10 -1940130344
ISBN-13 - 978-1-940130-34-7

Illustrations by & Courtesy of Gail Gandolfi

TABLE OF CONTENTS

1. Polly Burson - *A Wild Ride* 7
2. Temple Grandin - *The 'Mother Teresa' of Autism & Animals* 37
3. Connie Douglas Reeves - *A Century of Keen Perception* 59
4. Imogene Veach Beals - *Premier Rodeo Historian* 85
5. Patricia Wolf - *The World Champion of Western Couture* 110
6. Claire Belcher Thompson - *Eastern Legacy, Western Attitude* 137
7. Violet Hnizdil Christopherson - *Gun Totin' 6th Grader* 154
8. Anna Lindsey Perry-Fiske - *The 'Gem' of the Pacific* 170
9. Lois Herbst - *Who Says a Woman Can't Be President?* 195
10. Adeline Powell Long - *Grit & Gumption* 216

Introduction

Several years ago at the National Cowboy Symposium, held annually in Lubbock, Texas, I was invited to be on a panel composed of western women. The Symposium is held for four days and includes musicians, poets, songwriters, authors, and more. There are a half a dozen stages scattered around the Convention Center where these people perform all during the day. Various meeting rooms are used for panels to discuss or talk on western-related subjects. Meanwhile across the street a Chuckwagon Cook-Off is held.

Rhonda Sedgwick Stearns, of Newcastle, Wyoming, was the moderator of a panel of western women which included me as well. She phoned me a month before the event and requested each of us to talk about a woman in our life who influenced our western way of life. I hung up the phone and my first reaction was, "I can't do that. There were absolutely no women who influenced my western way of life." My love of the west was greatly inspired by my Grandpa Hughbanks, who was a cowboy, and other cowboys I met through him.

I had been brought up on a ranch in northeastern Colorado with my parents, and my paternal grandparents. I was an only child, and an only grandchild. Most of my time was spent with my Grandpa and we generally rode horses doing some kind of ranch work. We counted cattle, moved cattle, doctored them, branded them, and moved them some more. I also helped cut, row and stack hay. My Grandpa always had numerous horses on the place.

When I was eight-years-old, a little buckskin mare arrived at the ranch and he told me she was *MY* horse. It wasn't until I was much older I learned many of those horses before her had been possible choices for me; unknown to me, but Grandpa wanted 'just the right one'. *Peaches* was her name and she and I became inseparable. She had colts every couple of years and Grandpa taught me how to train them to a halter, then to a saddle, and eventually to ride. I never got bucked off. When I looked back on that training I realized he taught me the patience and practice it takes to gentle break horses.

My family also went to all the rodeos and horse races in Colorado and Wyoming. Grandpa knew many rodeo contestants, jockeys, and trainers. I loved listening to these men talk about horses. My Grandpa was a great story-teller and some days I would hear him tell the same story to several groups of men, and laugh as hard the last time he told it as he did the first time. "Nope, there was absolutely no woman who influenced my western way of life!"

Rhonda mentioned on the phone one of the panel members, Georgie Sicking, was influenced by a woman she never met. When I came up with no woman I could possibly think of that influenced me, I realized I was going to have to be more creative. I considered my mother and my Grandmother Hughbanks, but they weren't cowgirls. They left all the outdoor activities to my Grandpa and my dad. My great-grandmother, Adeline Long, had lived on the ranch, but she died when I was six-months-old.

But wait! I vaguely remembered hearing stories about my Great-Grandmother. She had been quite a pioneer and had ventured here, there and yon, in her life, with my Great-Grandfather, who was ill. They also had six children. When I got to thinking about cousins and my Grandma talking about her, it was evident they had a great deal of respect and admiration for her. Could this be the woman that had indirectly influenced me, through my family? After extensive research, I had to admit she had a definite influence on me. I have included her story as one of the chapters, as she truly did dare to be different.

The women depicted within these pages have had lives like no other. However, reading of their experiences, antics, and accomplishments, may encourage someone to look beyond the present, venture forth into the unknown, and try to accomplish what they have been told is impossible. If this should happen, just remember one thing. These women had a passion for what they did and what they accomplished. If you decide "to be different", make sure your passion is on fire!

Turn the page and get ready to read about women who dared to be different.

A Wild Ride
The Polly Burson Story

After interviewing Polly in 2003 and spending several days with her I knew her story had to be told in her own words. Therefore this chapter is written in the first person.

    The Author.

"My earliest recollection was of my mom, hopping mad and saying, 'We don't need your help. I can take care of me and Polly just fine.' With that she grabbed me by the hair, tossed me on her hip, jumped on the back of the horse and we were gone. As best I know, it was my Dad she left, but I don't remember that much. I was nearly three.

After her outburst we left my Grandfather's home in Ontario, Oregon, and she and I rode until way after dark. I finally fell asleep, sitting in front of her on the horse, and never knew when she finally stopped. We slept under the stars; snuggled up next to my mom, with a saddle blanket over us, I was plenty warm.

The next morning we got back on the horse and continued going. By mid-morning I was hungry. Just as I started to cry mom said, "Look Polly-wog, look over there on the horizon. We're almost there. I can see the barns – and the racetrack is right on the other side. I'll get you some food there."

Mom was right, just as soon as we rode up to the barn a man, named Jerry, came toward us. "I was hoping you'd come," he said, as he reached for the reins.

Mom dismounted and pulled me down into her arms. She told him we were starved and he took us to the cook house. Several other men called my mom by name and seemed glad to see us.

The cook said she didn't have much available. It was too late for breakfast and too early for lunch, but she fixed us big pieces of homemade bread with lots of butter on it. She had the remains of a pot of oatmeal and fixed some for me, with heavy cream. It tasted so good.

The cook was a heavy-set woman, and her apron covered her front. The apron had smears of food here and there. You could tell she often wiped her hands on it. She had things cooking in every pot on the stove. When she smiled you could see she had several teeth missing. She held a match in the corner of her mouth. She winked at me and sprinkled a bit of sugar on my piece of bread, and in the oatmeal.

Mom said, "Sure grateful to you. My Polly-wog hasn't eaten since noon yesterday."

The cook was putting wood in the stove, with her back to us, but she waved her hand at us and without turning around said, "Glad to do it."

After we finished our bread and oatmeal my mom lifted me by my hair, grabbed me around the waist, and put me on her hip. We went outside where Jerry was waiting. He walked us over toward an older man, dressed in dark pants and matching coat. He had on a big Stetson hat and was smoking a cigar. He had squinty eyes and a big nose. As he looked my mom over he said, "Jerry says you're a good rider. What kind of race track experience have you had?"

My mom told him she had been riding several neighbors horses in races at the county fair and once in a while two cowboys would bet on a couple of fast horses in matched races. She said she was always asked to ride one of the race horses.

"Did you ever come in first," the man asked as he blew smoke from his cigar up in the air? I was fascinated with the smoke as it curled slowly up to the sky and disappeared.

My mom looked at him indignantly and said, "Hell yes! I always won, if the horse had anything I could work with."

That afternoon he put her on a couple of horses and she galloped them around the track. Meanwhile Jerry sat with me and we watched her ride. Jerry had a nice smile and treated me well. Apparently 'cigar-man' liked what he saw my mom do. He hired her to gallop horses for the next week. He said they would then decide if she was good enough to ride in a race the following week.

Jerry showed us to the bunkhouse which was not far from the track. A dozen cots were lined up on both sides of the room. There were a couple of tables with an assortment of chairs around them. A potbellied stove sat at the side of the room with split wood stacked beside a bucket of coal. A deck of worn playing cards and a cribbage board sat on the table. The cards looked like they had been used plenty. There were some hooks on the walls and various coats and tack were hung there. A couple of tin wash basins and a bucket of water were on a narrow table, just inside the door, as was a tin cup tied to a string, next to the bucket.

Jerry took us to the far end of the room and pushed two cots together. They were made of canvas and had a couple of old wool blankets on each one.

"There isn't a full house of hands right now, and the guys sleep up toward the front. I know it's not the best for you and the girl, but it'll get you through until you can make some money and get something better," said Jerry.

My mom thanked him and she sat me on one of the cots. We had a saddle, a saddle blanket, a change of clothes and a sweater for me and a coat for mom. She thanked Jerry and he said, "I'll leave you two alone so you can get settled. The guys won't be back here until evening."

The first thing mom did was start a fire, heat some water in a pail and give me a good cleaning. It had been a couple of days and we both needed it. She rubbed so hard I thought she'd take my hide off. After my bath she used the water to clean herself as best she could.

Mom loved working with the horses and worked hard to be able to ride race horses. But she had a problem. Me! What could she do with me when she needed to be galloping the horses? I was too young to know this or care at the time. Jerry took care of me when he didn't have work to do, and the cook was swell to let me sit in the middle of the kitchen, if it was in-between preparing meals. She'd give me a big wooden spoon to play with and some pots. Once in a while she'd dip the spoon in batter if she was making something with a little sugar in it. I'd lick it off and that was really a treat. I seldom cried, which was a good thing, as cowboys don't like to hear a kid cry. I think I learned that early.

My mom was loving, but firm. Often she would put me on the old mare, *Maggie Mae*, we rode in on. Then she would park her in a stall. She was so gentle. After awhile I would fall asleep and tumble off the old mare on to the hay. She would never move a muscle, except her jaws as she munched hay, and would stand over me until I woke up, or my mom came back to get me.

It wasn't long before mom was riding flat races and relay races for 'cigar-man' with the squinty eyes. There were races just about every weekend and new horses were always coming to the track to see if they could outrun 'cigar-man's' horses.

Before mom got mad and left home, taking me with her, I spent a lot of time at my Grandpa's place when mom would be working. She was so good with horses and was always out in the corral, or on a race track. I'd spend time with my aunts and uncles. Grandpa and Grandma Bertha had my mom and eight other children. Grandpa had big herds of horses and cattle up until World War I. He had two good remount studs and made a decent living selling horses to the army. He had lots of wranglers to help him break the horses and get them ready to sell. He also had lots of help for Grandma; in the big house he'd built for his family. Although everyone in the family was taught how to work and had chores, he had a cook and someone that looked after the girls.

When World War I broke out most of Grandpa's workers went to war. The army quit buying horses and my Grandpa had to let the rest of his workers go as he didn't have enough work to keep them busy. His income really changed and he didn't make near the money he had before the war. Trying to raise nine children was tough. He moved everyone to town so the children could attend school.

My mom married my dad, Marvel Shelton, when he came back from the war. He had worked for my Grandpa before the war. I don't remember much about him and wasn't very old when she left him. I had a brother, a year and a half younger than me, and when they broke up he stayed with my dad. My mom told me my dad's family had money. They didn't want me, but they wanted my little brother because he could continue the Shelton name.

Mom must have had some gypsy blood as she was always ready to go. She was tough, and a heck of a cowgirl. She would grab me by the hair and say, "C'mon Polly-wog," and off we'd go. I knew she loved me a lot and she always knew how to make a go of it. Oh, I won't say it was always ok and that we never had any trouble. There were days we got a little hungry, but my mom could always come up with some way of making money.

Mom worked for 'cigar-man' for a while but she eventually married a racetrack man and we lived in a small place a couple of miles from the track.

He worked for 'cigar-man', too, but he owned some of his own racehorses. We had the racetrack man for several years until mom divorced him. I don't know why, except I think he wanted mom to quit racing 'cigar-man's' horses, and just ride his horses, and mom said no. She was making more money with 'cigar-man' than she was when she rode his horses.

He insisted she quit, so she quit him. No one told my mom what to do. From there we travelled from one rodeo to a racetrack and back to a rodeo 'cause my mom had a reputation for being one of the best jockeys around that northwest country. She got good mounts, and she always got paid in advance. Whenever she won they always gave her what she called her 'win' money. That money she usually used to buy something we couldn't normally afford.

Rodeo Kid

She still had one big problem. ME! The older I got the less satisfied I was to sit on *Maggie Mae's* back or in one place while she worked. I had learned how to shimmy down the old mare's leg and run off. Mom finally rigged a harness to put on me when we were at a rodeo or the race track. When she was jockeying in a race she would put that harness on me, find a nearby tree, and tether me to it so I'd stay put.

Well, it wasn't long before some of the cowboys realized what she was doing. Cowboys love to play jokes so they would undo the harness and let me run free. I'd be so happy to be loose I'd do whatever they told me to do. They'd point at some unsuspecting cowboy and tell me to go call him a 'son-of-a-bitch.' When I did, and the unsuspecting cowboy would look at me in horror, this little bitty kid saying such a bad word, the cowboys would laugh and laugh. I always enjoyed hearing those cowboys laugh so it took very little encouragement for me to follow their instructions.

Of course, at the time I had no idea what I was doing. My mom would come back from a race and the cowboys would tell her what I'd done. Then I'd get my butt whipped. The cowboys always laughed when that happened, too. She'd be so mad at those cowboys, but it didn't do much good, cowboys just love to play pranks. Whenever they saw me tied to some tree or fence they knew my mom was busy. She tried all kinds of things to keep them from getting me out of the harness. I think she finally got a padlock.

We were at Hayward, California, at the Rowell Ranch Rodeo, located in the East Bay Hills of Almeda County, about fifty miles from the Pacific

Western Women Who Dared to Be Different

Little Polly, tied to a tree, watched as the bucking bulls head straight toward her.

Ocean, and not too far from San Francisco. At the beginning of the rodeo the grand entry riders would race down a steep hill, from the corrals, in to the arena at full speed. It was always very impressive and a great way to start the rodeo. Mom tied me to a limb on a big oak tree near the arena during the rodeo. I'd sit down and play in the dirt awhile, and then I'd walk around in a little bitty circle. I felt like I went hundreds of miles on that line.

After the rodeo, my mom hadn't come to unharness me yet, and the cowboys turned the bucking bulls out of the catch pen, to run them back up the hill to the corrals. All those big old snuffy bulls headed right for me and that tree. By the time they got to me they were running at a fast pace. I just stood and watched them coming. I heard my mom scream. There was no place for me to go. I just stood frozen. Just as they neared the tree those bulls split and went on both sides of me and the tree. I didn't get a scratch, but it was a close call. I guess I was scared. I sure should have been. My mom was sure mad at those damn wranglers.

We moved from rodeo to rodeo and it didn't take much. We lived in a tent, but so did a lot of other cowboys and cowgirls. There were no cottages or motels we could afford. The rodeo people were like one big happy family.

Eventually as I got older I think I got smarter. The cowboys had to pay me to do their little joke of calling someone an "SOB." On one occasion I saw some Indian teepees not too far from the rodeo grounds. I wandered down there to see what I could see and found some young Indian kids my age to play with. I seldom got to be around anyone my own age. When mom finished her race she came back to where she had tied me. The harness was there, empty, and by then the cowboys had all wandered off.

She was frantic and ran around calling my name and looking for me all around the rodeo grounds. She asked several cowboys where I was and no one seemed to know. She finally came to the Indian village and found me playing with my Indian friends. She was so happy to find me I think she forgot to whip me.

When I was about seven years old my mom married a man named John Drayer, who was a good bulldogger and steer decorator. I liked John. He was a good man and took good care of my mom and me.

There weren't many kids my age around the rodeo, but once in a while we would be at a rodeo where Tin Horn Hank Keenan was the hired rodeo clown. He had a son that was called Little Tin Horn Hank, and he was about my age. He always wore his blonde hair down to his shoulders in golden ringlets. I'd always ask him, "Are you a boy?"

He's reply by saying, "What do you think? Are you a girl?"

One year my folks stayed in the Red Bluff, California area and John and my mom decided I should go to school. Little Tin Horn Hank attended the same school. I wasn't the only one who wondered if he was a boy or a girl. He wore pants that zipped up the side and the teachers didn't know where to send him to the toilet. When he had to go to the bathroom he'd go to a corner gas station. I think he had a good time keeping everyone guessing.

I used to spend time with a big black man named Jesse Stahl when mom and John were at a rodeo. Jesse was a good bronc rider as well as a steer wrestler. He always wore old work shoes, even when he was competing. He loved to go fishing, but he had no fishing license. If we were sitting on the creek bank fishing and he'd hear rustling in the bushes, he'd hand me the pole. If it was a game warden he could say he wasn't fishing, that I was. Kids could fish free in those days. Jesse was lots of fun and I enjoyed his company. He'd always rub citronella all over my hands and face to keep the mosquitoes from biting me. He'd tell me stories about his rodeo days and what he would do to impress and wow the audience. He would bulldog a steer and ram the steer's horn into the ground and that way he could hold him there. He called it 'hoolihaning.' He also rode mean bucking horses and told me how much he enjoyed it and how thrilling it was. He would always say, "When dey quits buckin', I kick 'em in the ribs and they starts all over ag'in!"

Jesse was more of an exhibition performer than a cowboy in competition, because in those early days black cowboys weren't allowed to ride during the rodeo with the rest of the competing cowboys. When I'd go home after one of our fishing trips, or a visit with Jesse, my mom always knew I'd been with him.

"You've been with Jesse, haven't you," she'd ask? I could never understand how she knew that, until she told me she could smell the citronella.

When I was nine we showed up at a rodeo and there was a calf-riding competition for kids. Six of us entered and I was the only girl. Jackie Williams, one of the boys that entered was a friend of mine. His mom was a relay racer, like my mom. The rules were that if you rode your calf and didn't fall off they would give you a calf to raise. The cowboys helped me get ready, cause I was always their pet. I was in the back of the chute on my calf when they opened the gate. My calf charged out, jumping over all the boys and their calves, but I didn't. I fell off and every one of those calves ran over me. The cowboys all ran to see if I was hurt. I just got up and dusted myself off. Everyone laughed, but I was disgusted 'cause I didn't win a calf.

Cussin' Kid

By the time I was ten I had developed a pretty foul mouth. My earlier days spent with the cowboys, always teasing me, and getting me to say cuss words was part of my upbringing. I thought I was 'cute' because it always got a rise out of the cowboys. I didn't have the sense to know cuss words were unacceptable. Or when to keep my big mouth shut!

My mother didn't correct me much for my bad language. Maybe it was because I had done it for so long she had just become used to it. I know she didn't approve. But I didn't stop cussing. I was pretty much a regular tomboy with a strong vocabulary. As I got older those foul words weren't near as cute, but I still thought I was hilarious.

Vera McGinnis was a famous early day trick rider and a very versatile rodeo performer. She was also a good friend of my mom. She could Roman ride, trick ride, race relay horses and also rode broncs and bulls. She was a beautiful lady and was often introduced at a rodeo as "Queen of the Rodeo."

When Vera heard me rattle off a variety of cuss words she became quite concerned. I could tell when I let go with a long string of 'em she was not impressed. Although she was shocked at my vocabulary she must have felt I had some saving graces. She told my mother she thought I would make an excellent trick rider. She offered to teach me to trick ride if my mom would let me spend the winter with her. She also told my mom she would work on my use of profanity. I'm sure my mother was ready for a break from me. Off I went to live with Vera and her new husband, Homer, at their winter quarters near Roscoe, California.

Vera never had children, nor did she have much understanding of children, but I stayed with her and Homer for six months. I don't remember that she ever gave me one day of trick riding instruction. I did take her trick riding horse, *Tiny*, for a ride every evening and led another horse, named *Honey*, for exercise. They lived on a hill and I would ride the horse and lead the second one around the forested hills to a nearby orchard.

Occasionally there were some local kids near the orchard playing ball. I longed to play with kids my own age but seldom had the chance. One day the kids asked me to play with them. I tied up the horses and played for awhile, until I felt I had better return. I really missed being with other kids my age.

When I returned from my evening ride Vera called me in to her bedroom and asked me what I had done that day. I thought it was strange for her to ask as she had never asked me before. I suddenly remembered that shortly after I arrived her husband, Homer, took me aside and said, "Polly, if you really want to get along with Vera don't ever lie to her." His sage advice popped in to my head.

"I tied the horses up and played ball with some kids at the orchard," I told her. She just grinned and said, "That's nice. I hope you had a good time."

Later I learned from Homer whenever I took the horses on a ride she watched me from her bedroom balcony with binoculars. I'm sure glad I didn't lie to her.

Vera was very well read, she was intelligent, and she taught me a lot, especially manners—and, of course, that my bad language was unacceptable, and why. At the time I'm sure I was not aware of everything she taught me, but later in life I realized how valuable that period of my life had been. I will say I wished many times she hadn't been the champion that she was. I got very tired of polishing her eleven silver loving cups that she had won at various rodeos.

My mom finally came to the McGinnis ranch and got me. My stepdad, John had found a trick riding horse for me. It was the ugliest little horse you ever did see. I didn't know trick riding from nothing, but I practiced and did what I'd seen other trick riders do. Dad Drayer tried to help me but he wasn't a very good teacher. I also began riding some relay races, just like my mom. Whenever I ran out of money I'd 'hash' in a café. Someone always needed a waitress somewhere.

Although Vera never trained me as a trick rider I met two gals who were trick riders, Dorothy Morrell and Bonnie Gray, and they taught me some tricks. Any trick where a rider hits the ground during the trick is called 'groundwork.' I became known for riding in to the arena full speed in a hippodrome stand, which is standing as straight as possible at the front of the saddle. It is very impressive and I loved doing it.

Better Trick Riding Horses

We were at Pendleton Round-Up and my mom saw an Indian riding a beautiful little white horse in the parade. It had good confirmation and held its head in just the right way to be impressive. She commented to me that the horse looked like it would make a good trick riding horse. After the parade my mom searched until she found who the Indian was that owned the horse and that he lived about 20 miles out of town. That evening we drove out and found the Indian's place.

My mom told him she was interested in buying his white horse. We looked him over by the light of the car and mom decided he was a good buy. I paid the Indian $50 for him, money which I had been saving. I trick rode on him for five or six years. He went 'bad' in the shoulders and I gave him to a friend, Bill Clemens. Bill was a good horseman and told me the horse had rheumatism and we should leave him on the desert for a while and let him 'sweat it out'.

Another good cowboy, Clay Carr, told me he thought he had 'sweenied.' That is when the hide grows to the bone. Carr said if you put a quarter in a slit in the skin, it might correct the problem. Bill tried it and called him 'The twenty-five cent horse.' Nothing worked. But every kid in the area wanted to feel the quarter under the skin on the 'twenty-five cent horse.'

How did I learn to trick ride? Well, I watched all the other trick riders at rodeos. I decided what I wanted to do, and how to do it, then practiced and practiced and practiced. I made a hell of a lot of mistakes, but I kept at it.

I saw Tad Lucas do a trick and I decided I wanted to master that trick. Tad Lucas was one of the best trick riders of the day. When she rode she seemed to do every trick with ease. She made everything she did look so easy. The trick I had seen her do was a showy trick. It was a head stand at the horse's shoulder.

Dick Griffith, who won lots of trick riding championships, showed me how to do that trick. He also helped me learn the 'split through the neck routine.' Dick would always come forward and help me if he saw that I didn't have a trick just right. I always appreciated his willingness to help me.

Not every performer was that generous with their knowledge in those days. Often they were very secretive and felt that if they taught anyone else a trick they performed, especially if it was considered their specialty, their popularity might be diminished. They also felt teaching someone else was just more competition for them.

I will admit there were lots of trick riders in those days. There were some who were great and some were good and then there were some that just showed up. Junior Brady (Buff Brady, Jr.) was a trick rider. He wouldn't come and offer help but if I went to him and asked him for help he'd always oblige me. I always appreciated those guys.

On My Own

Eventually I went out on my own. My mom and dad settled down in California and I headed out to rodeos where ever I could get hired. I bought a horse, named *Pierre*, from Lucyle Richards. He was a real stout horse and I learned I'd better have a good hold on him when I rode him. Lucyle was known for riding her trick riding horses very fast.

The next rodeo after I bought *Pierre* was in El Paso, Texas. The arena was small and hard for a trick rider to work in. In fact, Dick Griffith who was appearing there with me made them take the gates off at both ends of the arena just to make enough room for the trick riders to be able to perform.

I would practice on *Pierre* outside and when I came in the arena it was all I could do to keep from hitting the fence he was so speedy and strong. Once I learned how to ride him, at breakneck speed, we thrilled a lot of ro-

Jockeys getting instructions from a 'finger-waving' gent. Polly right in front. *Photo courtesy of the Dickinson Research Center, National Cowboy & Western Heritage Center, Oklahoma, City.*

deo audiences.

When trick riders perform they often have cowboys delegated to hold up a rope on the inside of the arena to keep the rider's horse running between the outside wall or fence, of the arena, and the rope. The rope would keep the trick rider's horse from veering to the left, into the middle of the arena, during the trick. Trick riders always ride counter-clockwise in the arena.

It was 1939 at the rodeo in San Francisco and I was trick riding. George Mills was one of the cowboys delegated to hold the end of the rope for the trick riders. The Russian Drag is when you hook your feet in the saddle, and lay on your back, with your head and shoulders lying over the horse's hips and tail. Your hands are over your head barely touching the ground.

When I was in the Russian Drag position I could feel dirt hitting me in the face when I went around the far end of the rope. I couldn't figure out how that was happening. Somehow I finally realized George was kicking dirt up in my face, on purpose, as I'd go by him. I guess that was his way of letting me know he liked me. So Romantic!

We met at the rodeo in San Francisco and it seemed every rodeo I was hired for, there was George. George was a bareback rider and had just started working as a rodeo clown and had done a little bullfighting, but not much. He'd been to plenty of rodeos around his home area in Colorado, but was just beginning to rodeo around the rest of the country. He wasn't very romantic but we always had lots of laughs.

One day I was jockeying at Bay Meadows Race Track, in 1939, and got paid $25. George and I decided to get married. We got to looking for a justice of the peace and finally found him in an automotive garage. Can you imagine how romantic that was – getting married in a greasy, oily, old garage. My race earnings, $25 paid the judge to marry us and paid for the wedding ring George gave me. George bought a tent, a Coleman stove and bed for $5. That was our first living quarters. I was hoping for something a little more elaborate. I was raised in a tent and was hoping to 'move up in the world' but with George it didn't happen.

In addition to my trick riding I continued to ride relay as often as I could. I made extra money whenever I could which always came in handy, and we called it our 'drinking money.' At Cheyenne in '39, I won the *Denver Post* Relay Race and got a trophy. I rode Frankie Burns' horses and he had some fast ones. Coming down the home stretch on the third and last horse was so fast it would part your hair. God! That was a lot of fun!

When I married George I also inherited Hank Mills, George's younger brother. He also rode bareback horses, and he traveled with us most of the time. I'll say we had some adventures. George had been traveling with Jimmy Nesbitt before we got married. Nesbitt was the famous rodeo clown who was hired for all the big rodeos, including Madison Square Garden. In 1938 Jimmy was clownin' the 'Garden' and got hurt. George stepped in and subbed for Jimmy, doing his rodeo clown chores, until Jimmy could get back to work.

Two years later George was hired to clown at Madison Square Garden. Here he was just starting to clown and he gets hired for the biggest rodeo in the country. That was a lot of weight on his shoulders, and he was very unsure of himself. We talked about his clowning and he was afraid the cowboys would think he wasn't any good and laugh at him. I said to him, "George, who is paying your salary? The cowboys? Be as funny as you can be, that's the best you can do."

Frank Moore was the manager of Madison Square Garden and he paid George's salary. Obviously, he did quite well as he was hired to clown Den-

Polly with George and Hank Mills after winning the Girls' Relay Race at Cheyenne Frontier Days, July 24, 1939. *Photo courtesy of the Dickinson Research Center, National Cowboy & Western Heritage Center, Oklahoma, City.*

ver and many of the top rodeos across the country. George was a good bullfighter and a very funny man.

One of my first years at the Madison Square Garden Rodeo in New York City, I entered the trick riding competition and came in next to last. My old horse would always lean to the wall and the judges would count off for that. Dick Griffith was competing in the men's trick riding competition. He was the best male trick rider, in my estimation, and always did a fantastic job. Bernice Dossey, another trick rider, and I were watching him compete and we saw him do something he'd never done before.

When he finished his trick ride I said to Bernice, "What did he just do?"

She laughed and said, "He made a mistake but covered it up and 'sold' the trick to the judges."

Dick Griffith was the master!

Work and Play

Everyone in the rodeo, cowboys and cowgirls, had a great time when we were in New York City at the Madison Square Garden Rodeo. We didn't look like the typical New Yorker in our boots, fancy western clothes and Stetsons, so we all got lots of attention. I'll admit some of the things we did in our western clothes and big Stetsons didn't do a lot of good for the reputation of the cowboy or cowgirl.

I remember one night, very late, George and I, Buster Ivory and Gene Rambo, were going back to our rooms at the Belvedere Hotel, near Madison Square Garden. We'd had a little too much to drink. It was an hour or so before dawn. Next door to the hotel was a little all-night grocery store and pharmacy. Just as we walked past, someone noticed the milkman's old nag, harnessed to the milk wagon, standing quietly in front of the store. He was waiting for the milkman to return from inside the store.

Rambo grabbed me and hoisted me up on the horse's back. Apparently the nag was dozing. It startled the sleeping horse and she bolted! Away we went, with me trying to stand on her back. We went about a block before I could settle her down. The milkman came tearing out of the store and was not real happy with cowboys that early morning. He ran down the block to retrieve his horse and wagon. Rambo, George and Buster laughed hysterically, and so did I. We always had such a great time.

In 1943 George and I were hired by Everett Colborn to work the Houston rodeo. I made $250 and George earned $450. We were making decent money for the times. Houston was a big rodeo and it meant we could stay in one place for a while. Most rodeos were two or three days tops, then we'd have to travel to the next one. We spent more hours traveling from one place to another than we did at any rodeo. At least in big cities, rodeos usually lasted more days and it gave us a little rest from traveling.

I must have loved George a great deal, or was just plain stupid, to put up with all the antics he and his brother, Hank, pulled. They were the meanest two men I have ever known, including those cowboys that encouraged me as a child to call an unsuspecting cowboy an "SOB." How I got through it alive I'll never know.

Often we would travel from one rodeo to get to the next during the night. We'd each take a turn driving for an hour or so, then about 1a.m. we'd stop at some little 'hash house' and get a cup of coffee to keep us awake. George and

Mayor of New York City, Fiorello "Little Flower" LaGuardia meets with trick riders performing at Madison Square Garden Rodeo in 1942. (Left to Right) Mary Parks, Bernice Dossey, Mayor LaGuardia, Polly Mills (Burson) Tad Lucas and Faye Blessing. *Photo courtesy of the Dickinson Research Center, National Cowboy & Western Heritage Center, Oklahoma City.*

Hank would sit on either side of me, in some old booth, stirring their coffee again and again, until the spoon was real hot. Then at the same time, they would put those burning hot spoons on my neck. Not only did it hurt like hell, I went around most all the time I was married to George with blisters on my neck from their little jokes.

Sometimes when we'd stop I wouldn't sit with them, because I knew what they'd try and do. Then when I'd get mad they would get totally silent and not talk to me for hours. They were flat mean! I'm surprised I remained sane and in one piece after traveling with them for so long. They did the most hateful, mean-spirited little pranks. I finally divorced George in 1944.

The next year I met Wayne Burson, a bronc rider and steer wrestler. He also had connections in Hollywood and had done some stunt work in movies. Wayne had been at a rodeo back east in St. Paul and a bucking horse had smashed his leg in the chute and broke it. I had to go and get him. His leg was in a cast from his hip to his foot for some time. Wayne and I ran in to George and Hank at a rodeo and Wayne still had his cast on. We stood there making small-talk, which pleased me, to think those two could be civil to Wayne, since I had divorced George.

I didn't know what George might say or do when he saw me with Wayne.

Word had gotten around the rodeo circles that Wayne and I were going to be married, and I was sure George had heard it. All was fine and we had a cordial conversation until George started to walk away and dropped his lit cigarette down Wayne's cast. Wayne said it burned like hell and he couldn't get to it inside his cast. Later Wayne said when it began to heal it itched like crazy.

George married Sis Merritt later. She was a daughter of King Merritt, from Laramie, Wyoming. King was a well known roper who also held some 'high dollar' ropings that brought all the best ropers to Wyoming to compete. Merritt was well respected in the rodeo world and his entire family roped. Word came to me later that Merritt told George, "If you treat my daughter the way you treated Polly, I'll kill you!"

Whenever I was in California, and went through Los Angeles, before I married Wayne, I would try and stay with Doff Aber's wife, who was a good friend of mine. Doff was a good rodeo cowboy and she was a script girl. She knew all the producers and directors and she had encouraged me to try and get some work in movies doing stunts.

She said the pay was great, and with my background in rodeo, the stunts would be a snap. I tried, but it seemed to be a catch-22 situation. They always asked if I had a Screen Actors Guild card, which I didn't. If you didn't have a card, you couldn't work. You couldn't get a card without working experience in the movies. I would try to get an appointment with a studio when I was in town, but the studio would never call me to come for an appointment until I was out-of-town working a rodeo somewhere. By the time I got back to L.A. and answer the call, the job would be filled.

Stunt Work

Wayne competed in rodeos from time to time but he also worked in the movie business. He had been in movies with Jimmy Wakely and doubled and done stunt work for Roy Rogers. Often he would stay home because of his movie work when I had a rodeo trick riding job in some distant town. One day Wayne answered a telephone call from Jack Grant, a Republic Pictures casting director.

"Wayne, can your wife do a high fall," Grant asked?

Wayne didn't hesitate and told him, "Sure she can."

When I arrived home and he told me I finally had a job in a film, I asked him what they wanted me to do.

Polly performing as a stunt woman.
Photo courtesy of the Dickinson Research Center, National Cowboy & Western Heritage Center, Oklahoma City.

"You have to do a high fall," Wayne said.

"What's a high fall" I asked?

He grinned and said, "Oh, you just fall about 75 feet in to a net."

I laughed and said, "Why don't you get a wig and do it yourself. You accepted the job. The farthest I have ever fallen was off a horse, and that's about five feet. I wouldn't call that a high fall."

Wayne had accepted the job for me, so whether I thought I could do it or not really didn't matter. I went to work on my first movie stunt job.

It was 1945 and the movie was *The Purple Monster Strikes*. It was for Iverson, a director who made early day serials, and I doubled for Mary Moore, the actress. She was married to Clayton Moore, who later became *The Lone Ranger*. I was working with Babe DeFriest, who I had known because she used to ride relay horses, but was a top stuntwoman now. She showed me the cliff from which we were suppose to fall.

I looked down over the edge of the cliff. It was at least 75 feet to the bottom. I said, with a quiver in my voice, "I don't think we can get there from here – and live."

Babe told me they were going to build a platform and have a fireman's net on it about 25 feet down. That was supposed to ease my mind, like falling 25 feet was no big deal. I told her, "Hey, I don't bounce!" But since I was new in the business I went along with it.

When it was time to roll the cameras I was instructed to fight with Babe on the top of this rock. Get over to the edge and go over and down in to the net. Babe told me to hold on to something because I would be right at the cliff's edge. I don't know if Babe pushed me, the wind blew me off the cliff, or if I jumped, but I made it!

That was one of those one time shots. Thank God! It was a good take and everyone was pleased. I made $150 and thought I was in 'high cotton.' I had just come from working a rodeo at Livermore and made $50 a day, plus driving there, taking my horse and pulling a trailer. I immediately thought movie work was great. I had finally found my 'gravy train.'

But, my gravy train blew up! I didn't get another call for work in a movie for another month. After that month-long dry spell the phone started ringing. I began getting jobs at Republic Studios. I did some shows with Dale Evans, before she and Roy got married. I think it was two shows, maybe three. They had another girl that was her stand-in and would be her double in all the horseback riding scenes. I only did the stunts.

I'd been in the movie business about six months when Paramount Studios called me for work. Unfortunately I had all ready taken another job with Republic. Jack Grant, the casting director that hired me for my very first stunt, knew this was going to be a good break for me. Somehow he got Republic to release me from the other job. Stunt people did not have agents; they acted in their own interests. You get jobs by what your ability is, and your last job.

The 'good break' Grant wanted me for was to double for Betty Hutton in *Perils of Pauline*. He was right on the money, because the movie was a big hit.

In the beginning I thought it was a one-day job. They used an 'old-timey' crank camera. They had hired another stunt woman before me to do the stunt, but they didn't like what she did. I really don't know why they hired me, as I had such a 'smart mouth.' It's a wonder I didn't run everyone off.

The director said, "Polly, do you want to transfer from a horse to the train?"

My 'smart-mouthed' answer was, "No, I'll just hand the conductor a quarter and get on."

He ignored my remark and went right on. Later I came to realize he liked my pertinent 'smart-mouthed' ways. Plus the cowboys who were working stunts on this picture wanted me on this job. They got around me and protected me, and my 'smart-mouth,' from getting in to trouble.

The directions for my main stunt in the movie were as follows: The Indians were chasing me. I have to rare up my horse, run down a steep hill, turn back, standing up in the saddle, and shoot at the Indians. I keep coming down the hill at full speed on my horse; ride up next to the moving train. Jump on the train from my horse, shoot at the Indians again, killing about three of them, cross the top of a box car, then another box car, then cross a coal car, get on the train engine and walk around to the front of the engine and stand on the cowcatcher.

They had given me a little mare to use. I never liked mares. In the spring, mares always 'dreamed of little hoof prints around the stable,' and they'll kick the hell out of you. But that was the horse they wanted me to use, and I will admit, she did it just right.

When we completed the scene and everything had gone well, I thought we were finished. The director, George Marshall, wanted us to do it again. We did the whole thing again, and as far as I could tell we did it exactly the same, without a mistake. Then he requested that we do it a third time. Each time we did it exactly as we had the time before and I didn't understand why he kept making us do it over.

Finally, after the third take, without a mistake, I walked up to Mr. Marshall, and said, "Are you having fun?"

He laughed and told me, "Polly, all my life I have wanted to be an engineer, and I was just enjoying the heck out of it." He put his arm around me and laughingly said to his assistant, "Put Polly under contract, she is going to double for Betty (Hutton, the star). We don't have any horse stuff for the next six weeks, but how do we know what else Polly is capable of doing? Isn't that right, Polly?"

"Yes, Mr. Marshall," I responded meekly. I had not realized he was the engineer in the train, so not only was he enjoying watching the scene, he was driving the train.

"The crew members will help you. If you will listen to what they tell you and do what they want, they can help you a lot," he advised. He was so right, and I did listen to what they suggested and they were always right.

The film, *Perils of Pauline*, truly was my big break. Later during the filming there was a scene where Pauline, while in London, was to run up, grab the cord on a heavy curtain of a theatrical stage, grab another cord, then fall back about twenty feet in to a mattress. For some reason they originally thought they needed a guy to do that trick. They used one stuntman, who put on her blonde wig and costume. He broke his leg while doing the stunt. The second guy didn't get it done right either. The stunt guys I was working with nudged me and said, "Polly, this is your job."

"Mr. Marshall, can I try it," I asked?

I got it done the way Marshall wanted it the first time I tried it. The stunt guys would give me a push out on to the stage and I'd grab the cord on the way up. It worked perfectly.

Mr. Marshall ordered, "Put Betty's clothes on Polly."

I stayed at Paramount for a year. I fit several of their star actresses in size – Susan Hayward and two or three other stars. Then I went to Universal Studios. I did work at other studios, but mainly at Universal. I doubled for Maria Montez and was a good likeness to Yvonne DeCarlo, by both size and coloring.

One show I worked was called *The Creature from the Black Lagoon*. I doubled for a girl on a river boat in the African jungle. In the film a big monster —and he was big! He looked like a great big lizard on hormones— comes creeping around, grabs me and pulls me in the water. Then the film shows him dragging me to shore. The monster was played by James Arness, who later became the television star, Matt Dillon, of the popular *Gunsmoke* series. He and his brother, Peter Graves, who I worked with later, were both wonderful fellows.

Viva La France

My mother's gypsy blood rubbed off on me because I never could stay in one place very long. Bobby Estes, a good rodeo friend of mine, had put together a rodeo to go to France in 1956. He had the contracts all signed. He called me and asked if I wanted to go and trick ride on the tour. I told him I was ready. I packed and had my horse ready to go right then!

It all went beautifully. We opened in Paris to standing-room only crowds. On May 1 was called May Day, a Communist holiday in Europe, we were told to cancel the rodeo, and cautioned not to leave the hotel. They said it was dangerous for us to be seen on the street. Bobby cancelled the show for that night. The following night we opened, but the Communists started telling people not to take their children to the rodeo. They told everyone their children would have nightmares, our crowds began to dwindle.

Our group of cowboys and cowgirls had a meeting with the officials from the Palace of Sports, the group who had hired us. They said they would pay to send us all home right away. They still had some funds but not enough to complete the tour.

I spoke up and suggested we all work for 'half-pay' for two weeks and see if we could raise enough money to get home on. There were 38 of us on the tour and 112 head of stock to consider. Bobby was broke. Everyone really wanted to stay and thought that was a good idea.

We left Paris and went to Toulouse, in the southern part of the country. It was a cattle and bullfighting area of France and we were well received there. Then we went to Leone and made five shows. We finally wound up in Marseilles. We were contracted to go on to Lisbon, Portugal, but it would have been a 'tough go.' Everyone decided to give it up and head home.

The sponsors had $50,000 left and they put everyone on a charter plane and flew out of there—except me, Bobby Estes and a man from Missouri. Estes and the man from Missouri were going to go home on a Dutch freighter, with 55 head of horses we had brought with us, including my trick riding horse. I asked Bobby if I could go home on the freighter with them and the horses. I told him I'd probably never get back to Europe and I'd like to stay and see some of the country. Bobby said that was fine with him. He said I had two weeks to enjoy the country, before they would sail.

I skedaddled all around Europe. Seeing the sights and really enjoying it. I went to Milan, Italy, then the Riviera. One day I put on a beautiful one piece black satin bathing suit and walked out on the beach. Men had on little colored jock straps and women had hardly anything on, except little pasties. Everyone looked at me like I had crawled out from under a rock. I might as well have had on my bathrobe.

Then I went to Monte Carlo. That cost me a few bucks. But I wanted to go where the 'high rollers' went. I did, but it cost me $100 just to get in, but I got some of their chips.

Next was a visit to Venice. While there I decided I'd better call back to

Bobby Estes in Marseilles, and check on my trick riding horse. Bobby said, "I'm glad you called, we're leaving in two days on a French freighter. If you still plan to go with us you'd better get back." The only way I could reach my destination in time was to take a train. It was so crowded I had no seat, so I stood all the way to Marseilles.

I arrived on time. We boarded the freighter and headed home. It was what they called a 'victory ship,' built by the Kaiser. We were told these ships had a tendency to 'break in-two' in rough weather. That sure didn't make us feel too secure. We did hit a couple of storms. One storm off the Azores was really bad. Before the storm all the horses were getting hungry and stamping their feet and making noises. Then all of a sudden they stopped. There was not a sound. It was eerie. Those horses knew before we did that the storm was coming.

The ship tossed around during the storm so bad I went to the kitchen and got a butcher knife. I decided that if the ship did 'break in-two' and went down I was going to go to the horses and cut them all loose. I didn't know if they could survive out there in the ocean, but at least they wouldn't be pulled to the bottom of the ocean in a sinking ship because they were tied. Fortunately, I didn't have to use the knife. The Captain said he was surprised I didn't fall down the stairs in the storm and kill myself with the knife.

The trip was quite an experience. I was the only woman on the freighter. Only two of the crew spoke English. Some days during the trip I played poker. Since I didn't know the language I didn't know what the hell they were doing but they kept giving me money to play. The Captain spoke English as did his First Mate. The First Mate had been a Captain, but had his ship taken away from him. During the trip home I found out he'd been the Captain on the *Andrea Doria*, when it was rammed by a freighter, and sunk.

I recalled hearing about the *Andrea Doria* tragedy when I was in Hollywood. Ruth Roman, the actress, and her son were aboard when the accident happened. The son was taken and put on a rescue boat and she was put on a different rescue boat. She was absolutely frantic not knowing where her son was, or if he was alive or dead.

I got a big kick out of joking with the First Mate. He would get drunk and I'd talk about 'this old boat.'

He'd interrupt me and say, "Mademoiselle, theese ees a ship!"

In spite of some bad weather the trip was fun. We finally arrived and docked in Houston.

Divorced, But Didn't Know It

While I was gone I was divorced. How did that happen? Apparently my husband, Wayne, took his new girlfriend to Mexico. I later learned a couple can go there, get a divorce with each one signing the document, and you are divorced. Apparently she posed as me, signed my name, and Poof! We were divorced. I could have 'wrecked' them because it was illegal in the United States, but I decided they deserved one another. I just left it alone. A year later I did divorce him legally in the United States.

The following year Harry Knight and Verne Elliott, great rodeo producers, had a rodeo going to Belgium and they asked me to go with them. I turned them down. Instead I went with a rodeo tour to the Far East. I didn't know the man in charge, but I knew people who were going and I thought it would be all right.

We opened in Manila. The promoter had advertised that we had a certain famous actor with us. This actor's movies were playing in Manila. When this 'wanna-be actor/imposter' rode out in the arena, the whole place started booing him. They knew it wasn't the real actor that was advertised. I'm surprised we didn't all get run out of town. From there we headed to Saigon. Our horses were still out in the middle of the ocean somewhere and hadn't arrived yet. The second night we were there we could hear the booming of the guns in Laos.

This old hotel I was staying in had a round elevator in the center. When I heard it coming up to my floor I would run to get it. If I didn't, I might wait forever for the next one. I was rushing and as I rounded a corner I ran right in to Audie Murphy, the well-known actor, and most decorated soldier in World War II. I had worked with Audie years before in Hollywood. I bounced back and when he saw it was me he lit up with a grin.

"Polly, what the hell are you doing here," he asked?

"I guess I could ask you the same thing," I said showing him how glad I was to see him. "Actually, I'm working."

I had worked on a film with Audie in Colorado called, *The Quiet American*. Someone had given him a civet cat as a pet. One morning, on the bus going to our shooting location, he dropped that thing down my neck. I had a fit. I told him I'd get even with him someday, even if I had to follow him to the ends of the earth. Now I was beginning to wonder if this might be it.

He invited me to his suite in the hotel. When he opened his door there sat his stuntman and double, William Willingham, a good friend of mine from Hollywood. His jaw dropped when he saw me. He got up and gave me a great big hug. The three of us visited for quite some time. I told him how we'd been having a rough time and that the rodeo producer obviously hadn't been honest when he booked us in these places. Audie asked me seriously, "Polly, do you want to go home?"

"Yeah, I do. But they won't send me. Plus I can't go until I get my horse and he's out there in the middle of the ocean somewhere," I explained.

"Wait until you get your horse, Polly. I'll give you the names of three people that can get you back home. One contact is in Saigon. One is in Bangkok, and one is in Rome. If you are in any one of those places they can get a ticket for you and your horse," promised Audie.

Next Stop — Bangkok

When I arrived in Bangkok the first thing I saw was a huge statue of the King of Siam. The King that brought Anna to their country. I remember when the movie, *Anna and the King of Siam*, was being filmed, on the Fox studio grounds. They were filming the dance sequence and I wanted so badly to go watch Yul Brynner. It was a closed set, which meant absolutely No Admittance! I knew if they caught me trying to sneak in I could get fired. But I knew so many of the people who worked for the studio, from the secretaries to the guards. One of the guards at the door knew how badly I wanted to watch it and said, "Polly, just walk in calmly behind me and stand in the shadows, don't move." I did exactly what he said, and no one noticed. It was wonderful to watch Yul Brynner and Julie Andrews in the dance scene.

I finally got my horse off the boat in Bangkok. We had a performance there but it was a total disaster, plus I broke my leg. My dear horse, who only had one speed—FAST—had run through a fence, ran in to another trick rider and stepped on me and broke my leg.

When it was time to leave, I decided I just couldn't expect my horse to endure that boat trip home. I owed a local woman some money for room and board. She was a German horsewoman and had admired my horse, so I sold it to her. I made one stipulation in the sale that she not sell the horse ever. She and I kept in touch for years. The horse was all black, and in the sunlight he looked bronze. She taught him dressage and sent me photographs from time to time. He was beautiful. She also was asked by the royal family if the little princesses and princes could ride him. You see, there were no other full-sized horses in that part of the world, except police horses. I'm sure my horse loved the attention and was treated royally.

I wanted to leave Bangkok in the worst way. It was July; the height of tourist season and travel was booked solid. I met a policeman and told him I was ready to 'move on.' He said he could get me an airline ticket. I was suspicious, but I wanted to leave so badly, I gave him my money. Much to my surprise in very little time he returned with a first class ticket. I was so relieved that I had enough money for any kind of a ticket, let alone first class.

My next stop was Singapore, then on to Hong Kong. By this time the only way I could leave was tourist class, which was $750. I was nearly out of money. I put my name on the waiting list at the Kowloon airport. Then I just waited around until they called my name. The first night there I slept in the ladies bathroom. The second day I still hadn't been called and I decided I needed a drink. I still had my broken leg and was on pain medicine and was told not to mix alcohol and the medicine. But after waiting in the airport for days I decided it was time for a drink. Now mind you, my voice is very husky, and people have no problem recognizing my voice.

"I'll have a double scotch," I told the bartender.

I heard someone nearby say, "Not Polly Burson?"

I immediately tried to think, who would I know in Hong Kong? No one came to mind. I turned to look and saw a couple I had met in a bar in Paris on my first European trip with Bobby Estes. We had visited several times in the bar in 'gay old Pareé' and hadn't seen or heard from each other since. We stood at the bar and got re-acquainted. They informed me they had come to Hong Kong to have clothes made for their wardrobe. I told them I was on the list for the cheapest ticket I could get back to the States. My money had finally played out. The husband said, "Give me what money you have, Polly, I can get you on a plane."

I thought to myself, 'All right, you dummy, it worked once, but twice? I must be nuts!' I gave him all I had, and apologized that it wasn't more. He walked off and in a matter of minutes he was back with my ticket. I was amazed when the policeman in Bangkok managed to get me a ticket, and now this gentleman, I'd met in a Paris bar years earlier, had succeeded in getting me a ticket home from Hong Kong. I later learned he was the head meteorologist for Pan American Airlines. I said my good-byes and thank you's and boarded the plane. I had $1.25 when I arrived in the United States.

Back to Work on the Movies

Once I got settled I went back to work on the movies. My leg had healed. Things were fairly routine. I worked on a movie called *The Jayhawkers*, then the movie, *Vertigo*. I kept busy at the studio. We'd work on a set and most days were long.

After work some of us, mainly the stuntmen and women, would go across the street from the studio to a little bar we frequented many nights. I guess we thought we had to 'unwind' and a few drinks would mellow us out. Oh, there were times when we'd stay at the bar and party so late we hardly had time to drive home, put our head on the pillow, before the alarm would go off, and back to the studio we'd go.

I married again to a nice guy by the name of Jerry Gatlin. Jerry was younger than I was and he was lots of fun. We were always doing crazy things. I guess my trips abroad made me realize I had 'salt water' in my veins. One of the crazy things I did was buy a 26-foot cabin cruiser. I was hired to work on a movie that was to be filmed in Mexico. Jerry and I took my boat, went down the California coast 850 miles to Cabo San Lucas. We then went across the Sea of Cortez to Mazatlan, where filming was about to start on a little bitty island off the coast. Everyone was staying in Mazatlan, but me. I had my 'quarters' right there on the island.

There were no facilities on the island. It finally dawned on the fellows making the movie that during the day they had no place for their star, Yul Brynner, to dress or to rest between takes. They approached me about letting Yul use my cabin cruiser each day. They paid me quite well.

It was a great deal. Of course, I had to give up the cruiser for the duration of the filming, but that wasn't a problem. Yul brought a man with him that prepared his lunches each day. He'd take a nap, refresh himself, and be ready for the next take. During the filming Yul and I got to be good friends.

Around the World

By now I'm boat happy. I have crazy thoughts about going around the world on a boat. I had never even stepped on the deck of a sailboat, but I knew that is what I wanted to buy. I spent two years going up and down the coast of California looking for the right sailboat. One I could afford. I finally found what I wanted in San Diego. It was a 42 foot gaff-rigged schooner. I hired a skipper who, I later came to realize, didn't know any more than I did about sailing. He ran up on a sand bar shortly after I bought the boat.

May Boss, a friend and stuntwoman, had a teenage son who I enjoyed named Claytie. We talked about the trip a great deal and it was decided he would go with me. Claytie was fourteen-years-old, and a good swimmer. Of course, I told him if he swam in the ocean he'd have to wear a tether. It would make him so mad to hear I was going to tie a rope on him when he swam in the ocean. He was convinced he could swim well enough to handle any situation. I wasn't so sure.

We got ready to sail. The captain, and my companion at the time, Pat O'Leary, Claytie and I sailed west. We named our boat, *Whistler*. We didn't know enough about sailing to do what we did, but in spite or our ignorance, we made it to Hawaii. We only knew sun navigation, using a sexton. We couldn't navigate by the stars, celestially, which is so important when one is not able to see land. When we got to Hawaii, we ran on a sandbar. At first we didn't realize we had damaged the rudder. Once we discovered the damage we knew we couldn't take off until it was repaired. Claytie decided he had gone far enough and flew back to his mom, May, in California.

Pat and I went on from Hawaii and for five days we didn't have any sun. We saw another ship and they told us to take our sightings from their ship. They said there was an 80 mile drift there. I thought I saw a mast, but it turned out to be a coconut tree on Christmas Island. No one goes to Christmas Island. There is no port there, but that's where we were. During World War II it was a U. S. island, but 5,000 aviators from Australia were now based there. We anchored out about a half mile from shore and stayed there a week or so.

We went on to Niue, but unless the tide was in you couldn't get to the island. We stopped at an island nearby. I had no idea where we were, but a group of us were all huddled in a bar during a storm. In the group were tourists from the United States on their way home. I gave a fellow $5.00 and asked him to call a number, when he got back to L. A., which was my answering service and let her know I was O. K. She, in turn, called many of my friends and told them I was found in a bar in Bora Bora.

We stayed in Tahiti during the storm season. We also sailed to the Cook Islands, Moorea, Rarotonga, and Fiji. The storm season was rough and about 50 or 60 of us with sailboats had to be pulled out. Our boats were beat up pretty bad by the storms and needed lots of repair.

By the time we got to New Zealand we were ready to stay in one place for awhile.

Besides the boat needed more repair. After eight months Pat was ready to immigrate to New Zealand. I was not in favor of moving there. In fact, I was ready to head back to the States. I told him as soon as the boat was fixed I was heading home and he could go with me if he wanted, or he could stay. He came with me and we headed northeast toward Samoa. We got in a hurricane that tore off the mast. I was washed overboard by a giant wave, but managed to climb back on board. I always said that was one of the best stunts I ever did that I was never paid to do. I sold the boat in Samoa. We flew back in December, 1963. I had kept my boat at the yacht club at Oxnard, a nice little farming town, and ended up living there.

Back to the Movies, Again

I went back to work in the movie business again. I was working on a set for the movie, *Earthquake*, when I suffered some pretty bad injuries. I accidentally got hit with a huge rush of water being used in the movie. It messed up my face, broke a couple of bones, and broke my leg. I was laid up for quite awhile. While I was recovering I decided it was time to quit the movie business for good.

Oh I did a couple of movie things after that, but it was time to retire. I had a great time working in movies, but when I'm through—I'm through. There's no turning back.

Polly lived the rest of her life in Oxnard, California, right next to the yacht basin. She died April 4, 2006, at the age of 86, after a brief illness. She received the Golden Boot Award for her work in western movies and was inducted in to The Hollywood Stuntman's Hall of Fame. She was a charter member of the Stuntwoman's Association of Motion Pictures, and later she was named their first honorary life member. She was the first recipient of Tad Lucas Memorial Award, in 1995, given by the Rodeo Historical Society, for a woman who has exhibited the same sort of extraordinary characteristics while upholding and promoting our great western heritage. She was inducted in to the National Cowgirl Hall of Fame in 2002. She was deserving of every award she received.

She had broken many bones and incurred many injuries during her career but considered it part of her job. Her zest for life and athletic abilities allowed her opportunities to do things never done by a woman before. She was the first female stunt coordinator in movies. She was the first woman that did stunt work acting as a man. When she began her stunt career most of the stunts done for actresses were done by small men.

Bob Hoy, a stuntman she worked with early in her career, said her natural athletic ability and her courage made her the best.

Bonnie Happy, president of the United Stuntwomen's Association was quoted as saying, "Polly had integrity. She never said she could do something that she couldn't do."

Stuntwoman, Lila Finn said of Polly, "When Polly tells stories in an inimitable style that even Eddie Murphy might envy I've got to listen. Polly was the preeminent expert on having a good time".

Henry Wills and Frank Pawluc wrote of her, 'She has driven four-horse teams in fast chases, doubled boys and small men, and even donned an Indian brave's costume for a stunt.'

She doubled for stars such as Barbara Stanwyck, Betty Hutton, Ann Baxter, Yvonne DeCarlo, Rhonda Fleming, Dorothy Malone, Ruth Roman, and many others. These people who worked with her knew she was unique in the movie business and tried their best to get her a star on the Walk of Fame, which honors so many deserving actors. They held fundraisers and did everything humanly possible but they failed. Not because she was not qualified, but because the movie industry wants stuntmen and stuntwomen to be 'invisible.' Only actors are eligible.

Regardless of the facts, Polly Burson was truly a woman who dared to be different.

The 'Mother Teresa' of Autism & Animals
Temple Grandin

Temple Grandin has autism. Autism is a neurological disorder that causes abnormalities in the brain. Genetics is the major factor that causes autism, however exposure to chemicals while still a developing fetus can also be a contributing factor. It causes those that have it to be different from other people. Autistics do not like to be touched; they don't interact with others easily; they can be very disruptive by throwing tantrums or worse. Often their parents and teachers are baffled as to how to connect with autistic children. Yet, in spite of Temple's autism, she has accomplished amazing things.

She designs and improves stockyard facilities, more specifically the pens, alleys, squeeze chutes, and dipping vats through her company, Grandin Livestock Handling Systems. Today half of the livestock in stockyards in the United States are in facilities designed by her. Presently, she is a professor at Colorado State University in the Animal Science Department and has been there for 23 years. She also writes books and papers on her designs and lectures world-wide on her stockyard designs.

But that is only part of what this amazing woman does. She writes books, articles and lectures on the subject of autism. How does someone diagnosed with such a brain disorder accomplish this, you ask?

Temple credits her ability to see the need to design better pens and equipment to deal with cattle more humanely in a stockyard environment, because <u>she thinks in pictures</u>. The fact that she does think in pictures, instead of in words like most of us, is a definite result of her autism.

The first time she went to a stockyard she could see the distress and fear in the cattle that were being prepared for slaughter. She knew immediately there was a better way to deal with them. After much research with cattle in that situation she knew she could improve their last days. She wanted the cattle, as well as other animals used for meat, to go to slaughter with ease and have as little stress as possible. It has also been proven that the meat of cattle, not under stress, is better and tastier. Frankly, it is also more humane.

In the autistic person's brain, the frontal cortex is 'overbuilt.' Some other parts of the brain of an autistic person are perfectly normal, such as the visual cortex and the area in the rear of the brain that stores memories. Other parts of the brain seem to have 'forgotten to hook up some of the connections.' This is an extremely simplistic definition of a very complex disorder. Not every person within the autistic syndrome has the exact same problems or the same abilities. They can be severely affected, minutely autistic or somewhere in between.

This makes diagnosing autism in children extremely difficult. Some autistics are extremely talented in certain areas, while in other areas of the same brain there can be major deficiencies. The areas where the deficiencies seem to be are generally dealing with other individuals and learning to interact successfully with others. Simply said, they have a difficult time being social.

Because autism affects people in so many different ways families and educators have a difficult task determining how to aid each individual, in hopes that they can reach their full potential.

Parents of children born with autism are often perplexed with their beautiful child's actions, or lack of action. More likely than not the child does not want to be held, or even touched. Often an autistic child will look past people, even their mother or father. They often get transfixed on some very small thing, such as watching a wheel go round and round or the wind blowing leaves across the lawn. Sometimes they do not speak. Often an autistic child will begin to talk as normal babies do, until they are 18 months to two-years-old and then merely stop talking. Tantrums are common. Their brain just does not process things in the same way the brain of someone who is considered normal.

Here is Temple Grandin's Story

She was born, the first child, to Richard and Eustacia Cutler Grandin, in Boston, Massachusetts on August 29, 1947. Although she appeared perfectly normal it wasn't long before her 19-year-old mother sensed there was something that made Temple different. She was not like other babies the same age. When her mother socialized with other mothers she watched as they talked and interacted with their infants. Those babies, in turn, would smile; make a cooing noise, sometimes even a tiny hand would reach for their mother.

Temple showed no interest in cuddling, talk or any type of toy. She seemed to look past her mother. This made Mrs. Grandin extremely concerned.

By the age of two Temple had not spoken a word or even attempted to speak. Her mother took her darling daughter to a neurologist in hopes the doctor could advise her wisely. Instead he diagnosed Temple as having brain damage.

This was 1949, and very little was known about autism at that

Temple Grandin as a toddler.
Photo courtesy of Temple Grandin

time. Mrs. Grandin tried going to other doctors , but they also suggested that Temple be institutionalized. Temple's father agreed with the doctors. He was convinced that she should be placed in an institution.

Fortunately for Temple, her mother wouldn't think of it, and refused to even consider such an act. Mrs. Grandin was determined to find someone or something that could suggest a kinder and more productive direction for the blonde, blue-eyed toddler.

Most medical doctors in those days were hesitant to define the disorder. Since symptoms vary from child to child, and so little research had been done, they were hesitant to give a diagnosis. Autism had not been studied and researched enough at that time for anyone, including medical professionals, to feel comfortable dealing with such problems.

Most doctors preferred not to get involved. It was an extremely frustrating time for parents of children with autism. They acted differently than normal children. What should parents do? What should they not do? How could they help their child?

In 1943 Dr. Leo Kanner a pioneer in child psychology, had written a pa-per that first talked of autism. Case histories of children with similar symptoms were reported. They all had the need to be alone and the need for a consistent routine, day in, day out.

There were some primary symptoms that signified children 'could be' autistic. These children were generally non-verbal; did not like to be touched; had tantrums; could not function in chaos or tolerate loud noises; had no interest in social interaction; had repetitive behavior and fixated interests. Often autistic children were thought to be deaf, until they were tested, and it was determined they could hear.

Temple's mother refused to accept advice by professionals that gave her no hope for her daughter. She was determined to do everything in her power to see that Temple be given the best quality of life possible.

She refused to put Temple away. She kept her in the mainstream with normal children. Mrs. Grandin found a nanny, which had highly praised credentials and past experience with a child that had traits similar to Temple. The nanny came to live with the Grandin family and worked with Temple daily.

But Temple still had not learned to talk. Mrs. Grandin was referred to a woman who had much success helping youngsters with speech problems. The lady ran a small structured nursery school and Mrs. Grandin enrolled Temple. The school had small classes, not to exceed 12 students. By three and a half, having attended the school for a year of intensive speech therapy, Temple began talking.

The teacher was firm and enforced the rules of the school. If her students had problems with the rules they were dealt with in a calm, but appropriate manner. Generally, the school functioned with little upheaval, no loud noises, and little to no confusion or chaos. Temple handled this quiet, structured environment relatively well.

Her mother admitted that there were times when Temple would get upset and have tantrums. Sometimes at school and other times at home. One time she even smeared feces across the wallpaper in her room. It was not an easy time for the family. Mr. Grandin continued to suggest that Temple needed to be 'put away.' Her mother ignored his statements and absolutely refused to consider it.

Temple was always reprimanded when she had a tantrum or got in to trouble at school. Mrs. Grandin kept in close contact with her teachers to be made aware of Temple's behavior and her ability to learn. Her mother disciplined Temple when she had a tantrum by not allowing her to watch her favorite television program *Howdy Doody*. Eventually Temple realized that she was punished for her tantrums. Instead of having a tantrum she began expressing her frustration by having a good cry. Her mother never disciplined her for crying. Temple had figured it out!

Mrs. Grandin continued her research on autism, although, with the nanny and the teachers at school, Temple was improving. She also searched for people who could and would handle her first-born with understanding, determination, persistence and love.

The nanny spent many hours each day playing 'take-turn' games with Temple. She taught Temple that whether she liked it or not, there were other people in the world to be considered, and she had to learn to take turns. When Temple's younger sister was old enough to participate she was also included in the games they played. The sister was born two years after Temple and had no signs of autism. Structure was still very important in Temple's daily routine. It was also important that she not be overwhelmed with too many different things going on at the same time.

Problem Clothing

There were many instances when Temple would be bothered by things most normal children would not find as a problem. Often her clothing was scratchy, or they might be too tight and uncomfortable. She wore her crinoline petticoat occasionally under certain dresses. It was one of the most irritating pieces of clothing she wore. She described wearing it as, "sandpaper scraping away at the raw nerves." Overly sensitive skin is common to autistic people and can cause additional distress.

Temple has a difficult time getting used to new clothing. For example, even as an adult she needs to wash a new bra numerous times before it feels comfortable. She actually prefers to wear her bra inside out because to her it is more comfortable. The stitching feels like pin pricks on her skin. The change from wearing long pants to shorts in the summer was difficult at first for her. Then as the summer turned to fall she found it difficult to change back to long pants. Most autistic people have a problem with change and prefer to wear the same type of comfortable, soft clothing every day.

Autistic children often seem to fixate on one thing and stare at it for as long as they are allowed to do so. They seem to dismiss the rest of the world around them and go in to a state of simply ignoring the actions going on around them. They will 'zone out' of their environment.

Temple definitely had these times, but either her mother, nanny or her teacher would try to keep these 'zone out' times as brief as possible. When she absolutely had to 'zone out' it was as if she were shutting out the rest of the world. Regardless of what was said to her or what was happening around her she was totally immersed in her 'zone.' One of her favorite 'zoning out' fascinations was at the beach. She liked to sit and let sand go through her fingers and she would watch the process and the tiny grains of sand for long periods of time. It was eventually realized by her mother and the nanny, that Temple needed time when she could just 'zone out.' However, they limited Temple's 'zone out' time to no more than an hour a day. Today, as a mature woman she no longer has the need to 'zone out.'

School

Grade school and high school were the worst times of Temple's life. She had trouble interacting with her classmates and they obviously had trouble interacting with her. Her 'nerdiness,' as she called it, made her think differently and respond to things differently than her classmates. She admitted she was bullied and teased a great deal. Those that bullied and teased her called her "workhorse" (when she applied herself she did work very hard), or "tape recorder" (because she repeated things), and "bones" (she was very skinny). She got in fights with both boys and girls when they teased her. She was kicked out of one school for fighting and disciplined in another school for her actions.

During her early teenage years Mr. and Mrs. Grandin divorced. Temple's mother gained full custody of Temple and her three younger siblings. Meanwhile Temple was at a small boarding school in New Hampshire. The school concentrated on teenagers with special problems. The school had a farm where she was able to observe animals. She was very taken with the animals. She spent most of her time at Hampshire Country School riding horses and working at the barn. She really spent very little time on other things. She worked with horses, kept the barn clean and competed in horseback riding events where she would walk, trot, and canter her horse.

Meanwhile Mrs. Grandin decided to go back to college at Harvard. At first, it was only on a part-time basis. She was the first person that was allowed to take less than a full academic load at the prestigious school. With

Temple as a young girl riding English-style. She competed in horse shows. *Photo courtesy of Temple Grandin*

recommendations from two professors teaching at Harvard she began her studies in a course on Shakespeare and another on creative writing.

Her income had diminished considerably when she divorced. She and her at-home children all studied together during the evenings. Mrs. Grandin graduated from Harvard with a Bachelor of Arts degree in English in 1965.

That same year Temple's mother married Ben Cutler, a Yale graduate that had become a popular 'society' band leader in the New York City area. His sister, Ann Brecheen, lived on a ranch in Arizona. After the newlyweds visited his sister on her ranch Temple's mother told her new husband she thought the ranch would be a wonderful place for Temple to spend some time. Ben agreed with her, as did his sister, Ann.

When Temple's mother told her of the invitation to go to her Aunt Ann's ranch in Arizona, Temple said she didn't want to go. Temple was fearful. She didn't know what to expect and did not know if she would be comfortable there. Her mother knew it would be good for Temple once she got over the newness of never having been to the ranch. Temple gave many reasons as to why she shouldn't go. Her mother was relentless. Temple was going to go to the ranch.

First Ranch Experience

Once Temple arrived at the ranch it took her very little time to become comfortable in the new surroundings. She was fascinated with the animals, and all the necessities required for them to be raised successfully. Aunt Ann introduced her to many new experiences on the ranch. Temple watched in awe as the cattle were put in the squeeze chute to be branded or given shots and to be doctored. She saw that once the cattle got over the anxiety of being moved in to the squeeze chute most of them became very calm. Once they were in the chute and pressure was applied to their sides, to keep them

Temple riding Western-style. She loved spending time with horses.
Photo courtesy of Temple Grandin

confined while they were doctored or branded, they seemed to accept the pressure and completely relax.

One day Temple asked her Aunt Ann if she could get in the squeeze chute. She wanted to see what it felt like to have the pressure against her body. She wondered if it would calm her anxiety like it did the cattle. Her aunt agreed. Aunt Ann cautiously pressed the squeeze apparatus against Temple and gently closed the head restraint bars around her neck. At first she felt panic and tried to resist the pressure. But suddenly a feeling of total relaxation ran through her body. Temple stayed in the squeeze chute for thirty minutes before she asked her aunt to release the pressure.

After she got out of the apparatus she felt extremely calm and at ease for over an hour. Her anxiety had been greatly diminished. In her book *Thinking in Pictures* she says, "This was the first time I ever felt really comfortable in my own skin".

Temple Grandin

Temple at work sawing boards to build her 'squeeze chute.'
Photo courtesy of Temple Grandin

Her Own Squeeze Chute

When Temple got back from her summer vacation on the ranch she returned to school. It didn't take long before she got busy with some lumber she bought at the lumberyard and other supplies. She built a squeeze chute for herself. When it was completed she got in it and applied the pressure; this allowed her to experience the calm she had experienced on the ranch. It was an action that gave Temple a great deal of comfort.

When the teachers at her school heard about Temple's 'squeeze chute' they were baffled and thought it was very strange. Autism was still thought to be caused by psychological factors during that time. Using her squeeze chute on a daily basis kept Temple calm and relaxed. Before she built the squeeze chute she was riddled with anxiety. Intensive exercise was the only solution she had found that would eliminate her anxiety. Temple discovered the squeeze chute she designed gave her the same results as intensive exercise. It has been found that pressure is pleasurable to many autistic people. Often most autistics naturally will crawl under seat cushions and other places where they can experience applied pressure.

In time, the Therafin Corporation, located in Illinois, began to manufacture squeeze machines. In their advertising they said, "For individuals with sensory needs. Applying deep touch pressure produces a calming effect on the nervous system of some hyperactive and autistic individuals." Since then, it has been discovered that the pressure of the squeeze machine does not work with all people in the autistic syndrome.

Temple was 15 when she learned, from her mother and her aunt, that she was different from her school friends, because she was autistic. She knew she wasn't stupid. She was greatly relieved to know she was different than other students for a specific reason that wasn't a result of weakness or lack of character.

Temple is a visual thinker. Her thoughts are in pictures, instead of thinking in words, which is how most of us think. When she discovered that other people didn't think the same way she did, it made more sense to her why she had trouble getting along with other students. She admits in her book, *Thinking in Pictures* she still didn't learn the full extent of her differences until she read many books on the subject of autism, and questioned other people about their thinking and sensory processes.

Temple admitted her mother often made her do things she was extremely uncomfortable doing, especially when doing something the first time. Once she helped her mother renovate a room in their home. During the process they needed some lumber from the lumberyard. Her mother forced Temple to go by herself to get the wood at the lumberyard. Temple came home crying, but had been successful in getting the wood. From that time forward she handled going by herself to the lumberyard with ease. In hindsight, Temple admits that once she did the things that made her uncomfortable and overcame that 'first time' obstacle, it was always easier from then on. She now realizes how important that lesson has been to her. Her mother forced her to do things for herself and not to expect it to be done by others. What a great lesson for all of us to learn.

High school was difficult for Temple. She wasn't much of a student at first. Then she became friends with Mr. Carlock, a high school science teacher. He took a serious interest in Temple. She told him about her squeeze chute. He listened and was not skeptical like so many other teachers had been. Temple told him she wanted to show people that the squeeze chute had real scientific value. Mr. Carlock was quite interested in her creation, but he knew she needed guidance. He explained to her if she wanted to become a scientist she needed to continue her education. Getting her education meant going to college, and she should even consider getting advanced degrees. He also told her that first it was important that she meet the academic requirements of high school.

Once Mr. Carlock explained to her seriously what she needed to do, she set her mind to being a good student. She began to work harder at her studies. Several of the subjects she was required to take were quite difficult for her. Tutors were hired to help her with these subjects. She graduated from Hampshire Country School in 1966.

Temple was accepted by Franklin Pierce College in New Hampshire. At college, Temple quickly learned another lesson. If she wanted her classmates to assist and be interested in her projects she must show an interest in the projects in which they were working. She saw that showing an interest in her peers' projects she had the support from them with her own projects.

Math was her hardest subject. It was explained to her that she had to master math if she did want to continue her education and go to graduate school. In 1970 she graduated from Franklin Pierce with a bachelors degree in psychology, magna cum laude, and was second in her class of 400 students.

Temple Disagrees with the Cause of Autism

Although she had excelled while getting her degree at Franklin Pierce College she had problems accepting her major's premise on autism. During her time in college psychologists thought autism had physiological causes so that is what psychology professors taught. Temple could not agree with that reasoning.

She had autism, had lived it, researched and studied it. She had the knowledge, first hand, of autism and did not believe it was caused by physiological causes. She also had the ability to write and talk about autism in such a way, that families with autistic members, as well as educators and medical personnel dedicated to helping them, could learn so much from her about the autistic syndrome. Nope! She knew autism was not caused by physiological causes.

Temple decided to change her major from psychology to animal science when she went to graduate school. Her interest in animals and her ability to recognize their fears and actions were her motivation. She attended Arizona State University, in Tempe, where she received her master's degree in 1975.

Temple's first job was in 1972 with the *Arizona Farmer-Ranchman* magazine. She was hired to write an article about the pros and cons of different cattle chutes. It was entitled, *The Great Headgate Controversy*. The article was well received and she continued to write for them while she worked toward her master's degree. Her articles also helped her get a job at Corral Industries to design cattle chutes.

Temple went to the Scottsdale Stockyards so that she could witness the cattle being kept and fattened, and ready for slaughter. Upon arrival, she was told "they didn't allow women in the yards." This was a complete shock to Temple. What difference did it make if you were a man or a woman? Stockyards were definitely a man's world and the men working there resented any woman wanting to come in to their 'world'.

Being a Woman, or Being Autistic?

At first Temple had to wonder if being a woman wasn't more of a problem to get to work with animals in a stockyard, than being autistic. She visited other stockyards that weren't quite as chauvinistic as the Scottsdale location but the lack of women in stockyards everywhere was obvious. There were no women in the field at that time.

Temple had a series of happenings meant to discourage her and 'run her off' when she attended Arizona State University in animal science and first entered the business. Bull testicles were found decorating her car. She was given tours that would gross anyone out. She even had to use the men's restroom at Arizona State to change in to her uniform in order to enter the facilities.

Today's women have followed Temple's lead and are definitely included in the world of stockyards. In fact, women are preferred for certain positions in the business, such as handling and doctoring the animals. It has also been proven that women handle the animals more gently. How different things have become in 40 plus years.

Badges

Each time Temple conquered a major challenge in her life she liked to reward herself. When she was hired to write articles for the magazine she felt she had reached an important goal. Then, when she was hired to design cattle chutes she knew she had reached another special goal. Temple had observed that in various branches of the United States military soldiers were awarded pins as they were promoted from one rank to another. They were given different pins or badges that indicated their rank, or a special badge for an unusual feat of valor or accomplishments.

This appealed to Temple. She always wore a green work uniform. She decided to award herself with cattle pins to show her accomplishments and advancements in the field. The first cattle pin she awarded herself was in bronze. When she received her first job she awarded herself a silver pin. When she advanced by meeting another goal she wore a gold pin.

Emil Winnisky, the construction manager at Corral Industries, realized that Temple's green uniform made her stand out. It seemed to bring attention to her, but not in a kind way. He was thoughtful enough to talk with her about selecting appropriate clothing for her job. He even asked a woman staff member to accompany Temple to buy clothing that would allow her to fit in better. Temple bought a western shirt, which was more appropriate and helped her blend in with others working there. She continued to wear her pins.

The next difficult subject Emil was faced with was talking to Temple about her grooming. It must have been extremely difficult for him to approach her about the subject. But he cared enough about her being successful in her job to put his discomfort aside. He decided he should talk to her just like he would talk to his own daughters.

One day, Emil walked up to Temple and handed her a bottle of Arid deodorant and said, "Temple, your pits stink!"

Temple resented his comment at the time, but followed his suggestion and began using the deodorant. In her book, *Thinking in Pictures* she tells of the incident. Today she is grateful he was brave enough to talk to her about such a touchy subject and willing to help her. She realizes most autistic people need guidance with their dress and grooming. It is not unusual for those with the syndrome to have difficulty with certain types of clothing because of their hyper-sensitivity to various fabrics, elastic waistbands, zippers, etc.

Tom Rohrer, the manager, at Corral Industries, became one of Temple's most important mentors in the business world. She admitted that when she met him she still talked too much. He put up with her unusual ways including her incessant talking because she always seemed to be able to figure out how to solve problems in clever ways that no one else could solve. Through Rohrer's lead, other employees eventually recognized her unique capabilities and overlooked her differences.

Later Temple sold Swift Meat Packing a contract for a ramp to be installed at a Corral Industries location. Once again she learned another important lesson. She witnessed several employees doing some sloppy welding. She criticized the welders for their shoddy work in a very tactless way. The manager made her go and apologize to the workers for the way she criticized them. Each mistake Temple made was a learning experience for her. Recognizing the workmanship that was below par was not a mistake. But, the way she chastised the workers was insensitive and not acceptable. With each experience her ability to handle interactions with others improved. She admits now that her development was a series of incremental discoveries.

Her Ability to Recognize Problems

In the very beginning, she studied and researched existing feed yards or cattle yards on ranches. She began by observing the animals and she could see there were better ways to move the cattle through the stockyard to get them to the end result, which was to go to slaughter. By 'thinking in pictures' she was able to see that if the stress level of the animals was lessened they would go through the stockyard process in a more relaxed and comfortable manner. With this discovery she could visually see how to design better dipping vats, better corrals, and more useful and efficient handling facilities. On some occasions she has recommended that her customers tear out all the old corrals and facilities and start over. She has designed stockyards and ranch pens all over the United States and beyond.

Her very first job was to design a better dipping vat. In her study she recognized that cows are afraid of shadows and small things most people wouldn't even notice. A ladder hanging on a barn wall might spook the cows. Even a rope hung over a fence might make them nervous. The reflection in a water puddle could even scare them.

Dipping vats are used in stockyards to rid the cattle of all kinds of parasites and bugs. This means that each cow has to be completely immersed in the liquid to kill the insects and bugs that prey on them. The dipping vat is at the bottom of a path that slants downward at a graduated angle until the animals are completely submerged in the pool of pesticides or whatever eradicating fluids are being used. At the opposite end of the immersing vat is another graduated path leading upward and out of the pool area. To make cattle more relaxed going in to the vat Temple designed a floor that had raised bumps that would keep them more sure-footed. They could walk down the ramp more confidently into the pool.

On her very first job Temple put her designed dipping vat in place. Unbeknownst to her, some cowboys changed her new flooring leading into the pool. They replaced her specifically chosen flooring with a piece of slick metal that caused the cattle to slip and slide. The entering cattle were unable to keep their footing. Two cows slipped into the pool and drowned. When Temple discovered what the workers had done she was furious. When she explained her original flooring to the company executives they were very sympathetic to Temple. The cowboys who caused the death of the two cows were dealt with properly.

Temple reflected that her second project, another dipping vat, had no problems and the process went perfectly. Not a cow was lost or even appeared to be anxious. They went through the process with secure footing in a very calm and easy manner. She couldn't have been more pleased, as was the company that hired her.

Health Problems

Temple's business was going well. She should have been pleased by the success she was having, but something else was horribly wrong. When she reached puberty she began having nerve attacks, colitis and headaches. By the time she reached her late twenties these attacks began happening more frequently. She went to every doctor she could find but they could find nothing physically wrong. She even had a brain scan which proved nothing. Temple had just been elected as the first woman on the board of the American Society of Agricultural Consultants. But personally she could barely function due to her anxiety attacks and other medical problems.

Temple found that stopping whatever she was doing, work or play, and have a quiet period every day was good for her. She had been doing it since she was a teenager. Her mother and she had found that when she stopped for a brief 'time out' daily, she could control her anxiety better. From the time *Star Trek* began on television in the 1960s she had found watching the program was pure relaxation. It gave her a sense of calm, plus the stories always taught good values for her life skills. Although she was busy with her business she continued to take a brief respite each day. She knew it helped her become more relaxed and calm.

A skin cancer on her eyelid was discovered when she was 34. The doctor advised her to have it removed. Inflammation from the surgery started the worst anxiety attacks she had ever had. Temple's heart would pound like it was going to jump out of her chest. She began waking at 3 a.m. every night in fear she was going blind. She was convinced she was on the verge of having a complete nervous breakdown. Because of her determination and always looking for a solution she turned to biochemistry to help with the anxiety she had lived with for so long.

Anxiety to Calm

She went to the library and began her research. She came across information regarding anti-depressant drugs which were known to help control anxiety. She read the symptoms of anxiety and realized she had a number of those symptoms that were on the list. She took the information she gained to her medical doctor and he prescribed a 50 milligram dose of *Tofranil* for her to take each day. Within a very short period of two days she began to feel better. In her autistic-mind Temple compared taking the medication to control her anxiety to a person adjusting the screw that controlled the idle on an old-fashioned car engine.

Three years later she switched to a different anti-depressant called *Norpramin*. It was just slightly more effective than *Tofranil* but had fewer side effects. The medication helped her become a 'true believer' in biochemistry. She said several things changed in her daily life after she began taking the anti-depressant on a regular basis. She stopped writing in her diary and her business improved because she didn't push herself into a frenzy.

"I miss the passion, but I never want to go back to those days," Temple admitted.

She has always avoided taking tranquilizers. She believes, "Medicine that works should be used, if it doesn't work discontinue it. Medication can reduce anxiety, but it will not inspire a person the way a good teacher can."

She does have relapses of anxiety. Now she realizes the relapses are cyclical. They happen in the spring and the fall of the year. She has learned to 'tough it out' during these brief times and continues to stay on the same antidepressant dosage that has worked for her for a number of years. Today physically and mentally she has made great improvements. She recognizes that she walks with her back straighter, she used to have a limp but it has disappeared, and she makes better eye contact with people. What she is doing is obviously working well for her.

Temple went on to further her education at the University of Illinois. She received a doctorate in animal science in 1989. She has been a professor at Colorado State University in the Animal Science Department since 1990. She teaches livestock behavior and facility design. Additionally, she lectures and consults with companies, educators and numerous people in the livestock industry. She continues to design stockyard facilities and equipment for companies throughout the world through her company, Grandin Stockyard Systems. In addition to the U. S., she has designed facilities in South America, Europe, and England and has done a great deal of work in Australia.

Uniquely Gifted to Solve Difficult Problems

When Temple began to be known in the animal industries, it was her ability to be able to solve problems that no one else was able to solve. These problems primarily occurred with cattle in stockyards, but she also worked with other animals as well. One stockyard owner's problem was that his cattle would not go willingly down a narrow alley to the squeeze chute where they were given shots. Shots are mandatory because cattle are extremely susceptible to certain illnesses and diseases. Because they were balking and refusing to go down the alley the workers were using cattle prods to force them to go down the alley. These cattle prods give an electrical shock to hurry them along.

Cattle prods should only be used on rare occasions. The electric shock they give is not harmful, but it does cause an animal to stress. When it becomes a necessary part of the handling of animals, and most animals must be prodded, the reason for the need to use a cattle prod must to be found.

It is a known fact that a cattle prod will cause a cow to become stressed. When a cow is stressed their immune system goes down and they begin to get sick which causes an owner to have to pay veterinarian bills. Cattle also will gain less weight when stressed which means the owner will sell less meat. Less meat and vet bills can greatly affect an owner's profit margin.

Temple was assigned to go to the stockyard and find the reason the cattle were hesitating to go down the alley. Until they needed to go down the alley to the squeeze chute, the cattle were absolutely fine and moved along with no hesitation and no stress. No one working with the cattle, or the owner, could figure out why they hesitated. Since Temple thinks in pictures when she arrived she saw that the animals had to walk inside a barn from their pen into a round holding area. The cattle did that without a problem. Next they were to walk into a curved single-file alley. That is where they balked.

The alley was exactly like many feedlot alleys all around the country. No one could understand the reason they were hesitant to go on without using the prod. Temple saw the problem immediately. It was too dark. They were walking from bright sunlight into a pitch-black alley. When Temple talked with the owner about the cattle and their actions she asked how they reacted on cloudy days, or at night. The owner realized the facility worked perfectly during those times and the cattle did not seem to balk. The cattle, being in bright sunshine, entering a darkened area caused them to stop. Their eyes were not adjusting quickly enough and they were hesitant to enter the darkened area because they could not see. Once lights were installed inside the building to brighten the alley area the problem was solved. The owner had a minimal cost to correct the problem and no more prodding was necessary.

Temple solved the owners problem by seeing what the animals saw. Many things can disrupt an animal, such as smells; changes in routine; and exposure to new things. Temple gets paid for going to a problem-situation and seeing things normal people don't see. She thinks in pictures as do animals.

McDonalds, the famous hamburger haven, hired Temple in 1999 to implement an animal welfare audit she had previously created. McDonalds got their meat from 50 meat packing plants. McDonalds had announced to the plants if they did not pass Temple's audit they would no longer be suppliers for McDonalds. Temple's job was to train their auditors. One of her rules on the audit list was employees could only use the electric prod on 25% of the cattle or less. This meant going in to the plant and finding the things that were making them hesitate to move forward. It was always some small thing like a dark area, a reflection that gave a bright light, or some simple thing no one else could find. The problems were always solved if the 'culprit' could be detected. She trained the auditors to look for sensory problems first, like sight, smell, noise, or movement of objects, and so on.

Temple has studied many animals, not just cattle. In her book *Animals in Translation, Using the Mysteries of Autism to Decode Animal Behavior*, she gives numerous examples of her research and findings.

In one project, she studied pigs being used for breeding. There were two different locations owned by the same company. Both locations had the same goal which was to pick the best breeders based on a series of criteria, and cull the rest. Temple found at one location the pigs chosen were very excitable and hyperactive. At the sister-location the pigs chosen were calm and easygoing. The culling system to determine the best pigs to use for breeding was identical at both locations. It seemed that the excitable ones were eliminated from those kept for breeding at one location. The pigs chosen to breed were calm.

During a further investigation, Temple discovered at one location the scale used to weigh the pigs was a problem. The needle went crazy if the pigs were excitable thus they were more difficult to evaluate. The end result was that the excited pigs got culled. At the other location their scale was more stable and caused no problems. Regardless of the pigs excitability they were evaluated on the stable scales more effectively and more excitable pigs were not culled.

Although there was no intention of culling hyperactive pigs, versus calm pigs, the scale that had a needle that wouldn't hold steady when they were placed on the scale, was the cause of excitable pigs being culled. This is an example of natural selection which causes no problems or harm, and might even be good for the breeding animal. She also pointed out that if the pig wasn't being handled by humans it might never have happened.

Temple has also done a great deal of research with dogs. One example is that the collie head has become thinner and thinner through the years. The collie from earlier times had a wider forehead, but breeders tried to emphasize the long thin nose of the breed, and by doing so bred-out the wider skull. This gives the collie a smaller area for their brain. This breeding for a slimmer nose has caused the collie to be less intelligent than they used to be. Her research is in depth, and covers many breeds. She did find the mutt, or mixed-breed dog, is normally much healthier than purebreds. Hip dysplasia, for which many purebred dogs are treated, can disappear in one or two generations, when removed from the purebred line.

Another interesting difference between mutts (mixed breeds) and purebreds is that the majority of fatal dog bites, 74%, come from purebred dogs. However, purebred dogs are only 40% of the total pet dog population. She thinks aggressive mutts are more likely to be put down than aggressive purebreds. Probably because mutts can be free for the taking, or only a small cost to the owner, whereas a purebred can cost hundreds of dollars or more.

Although she is a professor at Colorado State University, at Fort Collins, she spends much of her time on the lecture circuits. Some of her lectures are on the importance of proper stockyard design. She had her first lecture on her stockyard research and designs in 1974, but as her research continued to add to her knowledge and experience, she received additional requests to speak to groups world-wide. Her lectures on autism also has had a wide array of audiences, from families, educators, medical professionals, as well as a variety of organizations whose purpose is of helping people who are challenged in some way.

Thoughts on Religion

When asked about her religious feelings she recommended that the final chapter in her book *Thinking In Pictures* should be read.

She says, "Accepting anything on faith, alone, because my thinking is governed by logic instead of emotion is difficult for me."

She admits she thinks all religions have a place in the world and one is not better than another. To Temple the use of organ music in church has an effect on her she does not get from other music.

"Science without religion is lame. Religion without science is blind", quoted Einstein on religion, which she included in her book.

Her research and life has taught her there is one thing which separates people from animals. Altruism. The dictionary defines the word 'altruism' to mean; concern for the welfare of others, as opposed to egoism. Humans will protect something, or someone, they believe in, even if it means their life. Animals do not have this commitment.

Temple knows autistic people tend to obsess on negatives. Temple believes it is important to teach autistics positive religious values, to treat others with kindness and respect, be a good citizen, and treat others the way you want to be treated. She points out the old-fashioned values in which anyone can relate, such as the scouting code, 4-H pledge, and Roy Rogers' "Rules of Living" emphasizing politeness and kindness.

Temple Grandin is a mentor for families and educators of people who have autism, Asperger's and other hyperactive disorders. Having been diagnosed with autism and having studied it extensively, Temple's explanations and recommendations are very important. She has the ability to convey information to lay people about the disorders from her own experiences and in simple language anyone can understand. She encourages families of autistic people, and the other disorders mentioned, to concentrate more on the autistic's talents instead of working on their disabilities or areas in which they are lacking.

"Half of Silicon Valley, California, which is the home of many computer-based industries, is autistic," says Temple. To prove her point she adds, "Einstein didn't talk until age three".

She is emphatic that people understand there is no 'quick-fix' for anyone with these disorders. Her advancements and successes in coping with her autism have been a continuing series of realizations. She is the first to admit her inabilities and anxieties. She is always willing to share the discoveries she has made as to what helps and what does not help her to cope and have a good quality of life. She encourages families that might suspect their children might have any of these disorders to be diagnosed as early as possible.

Often families 'put off' finding the answer, and in the meantime the child is left to watch television or play video games. It is important to get the child away from things that merely take up their time. Temple knows they need to 'get out in to the world' so they can discover what interests them beyond toys and television. She is also quick to explain that although there are some 'core symptoms' of autism such as not being social, having repetitive behavior and fixated interests, autistic people don't always respond to the same things the same way. An example of autistic diversity is that her designed squeeze chute does not help or comfort all people with autism.

Temple admits she would never want the world to be free of autistic people. She believes that the talents of many autistic people would be lost, and there would be a big void in our society. She truly knows her ability with animals and what she has accomplished in the world of animal science can

Temple receiving her medallion when inducted in to the National Cowgirl Hall of Fame. (Left to Right) Mary Margaret Richter, Temple and Adelaide Moncrief Royer. *Photo by Rhonda Hole Photography, courtesy of the National Cowgirl Hall of Fame.*

be attributed to her autism and her ability to think in pictures.

The research community and the machinery that is being developed to study the brain has changed so much in the fifty plus years since Temple was born and diagnosed. What will happen tomorrow and years to come will only improve ways of diagnosing and determining the best ways in which to help those in the autistic syndrome live their life to the fullest. Temple will always be there on the cutting edge of discovery and promoting the best way to deal with autism. We can definitely say Temple Grandin is truly an amazing woman who certainly dares to be different.

The honors that have been bestowed on Temple are too numerous to mention. Each one is well deserved.

A Century of Keen Perception
Connie Douglas Reeves

Once in a great while someone is born with an ability to make everyone they meet feel special. I was fortunate enough to meet such a person with this ability, and she did not fabricate the truth. She had an innate ability to recognize talents of those she met and was willing to let them know that they were unique. How often do you meet a person who continually makes others feel important? It is rare, but it's a trait to be cherished and appreciated.

Connie Douglas Reeves was just such a person, and I was one of the lucky ones who knew her. Thousands knew her and I don't hesitate to say they will all readily agree with my assessment. She also had the ability to never forget a name. She would recall what each person's specialty happened to be. I only wish I had known her longer and could have spent more time with this special lady.

When I met Connie she was 92-years-old. One of her former students, Jack Long, whom she had taught in high school in San Antonio, Texas, thought I should meet her. I don't know exactly why Jack thought we should meet, but I will be forever grateful that he introduced us.

Jack, in his 80s, and I drove to her home in Kerrville, Texas in the spring of 1994. He had called her to make sure she would be home and had time to meet with us. She greeted us with excitement and warmth in her voice and immediately I felt I was visiting a long lost friend. Connie was slim, with short white hair, and at first, I was totally unaware her eye sight was dimming. She moved around her home with such ease and announced she had just finished mowing her yard. But in short time she told me her eyesight was very poor. I then noticed her chair was about a foot in front of her television.

As we visited and got to know each other we discovered many similarities in our early lives. We both considered our grandfathers our mentors to all things western and were men we highly respected. We both spent much of our youth horseback. She married a cowboy, Jack Reeves, and spoke lovingly of her time spent on the ranch. I grew up on a ranch and enjoyed every minute of it. When we said goodbye I felt I had truly met someone that would be my friend forever.

That fall I received an invitation from Connie to be her guest at a Women's Week at Camp Waldemar, an exclusive camp for young girls from well-to-do families near Hunt, Texas. Connie, at age 36, (56 years earlier) had been hired by Camp Waldemar to head up the horseback riding division for campers. After the summer campers returned home and were back in school, the camp set aside a week for women to come and either indulge themselves or return to their youth and get out in the sunshine and cool, refreshing waters of the Guadalupe River that flowed through the camp.

It was a rare get away for women, from family, business, the telephone and the stress and frustration we get ourselves involved in during our daily lives. The women who attended were everything from former Camp Waldemar campers and former counselors to professionals, including doctors, attorneys, professors and the like.

During Women's Week, you could sign up for horseback riding, tennis, rowing, archery, and numerous other active sports. There were massages, hairdressers, manicures and pedicures and pure pampering. At various times guest speakers gave sessions on a multitude of subjects, plus a whirlwind of wonderful meals and social gatherings.

The women-campers slept in the cabins in bunk beds, just as the young campers had a few weeks earlier. I felt so privileged to be asked by this wonderful new friend, and signed up without hesitation. I was excited to 'go to camp' but my main excitement was the opportunity to spend days with Connie, in her normal surroundings. I could hardly wait.

I drove to Camp Waldemar from Austin, which only took a few hours. After reaching Kerrville I headed along the Guadalupe River to Ingram where the road narrows and the Hill Country scenery becomes it's most beautiful. A few deer crossed my path making their way to the river for a drink of cool water. The trees hung over the road making it appear as if I was driving through a tunnel of greenery. After arriving in the small village of Hunt, I turned right toward the North Guadalupe River, and passed several other camps along the way. They had also bid goodbye to their campers and were now inactive. Finally, I approached Waldemar and turned in to the grounds nestled in grass under big oak and cypress trees which lined the river banks.

As I drove in to the compound I could see handsome buildings of stone, with a German influence in the design, surrounding a large grassy area which was the athletic field. The cabins dotted the hillside, behind these larger buildings, almost hidden as they were nestled among the heavy foliage of the hill country of Texas. I parked and went to register in the nearest building, which I discovered was the dining hall. I asked for Connie but was told she would be arriving shortly. I was anxious to see her.

Next on the agenda was a sign up sheet for various activities. I signed up for the sunrise breakfast trail ride the following morning. I was told Connie would be leading the group. It wasn't long before Connie arrived and she welcomed me to camp. We visited briefly but everyone who saw her wanted to say hello and talk with her. It was evident Connie was a favorite with everyone. These women had a great deal of affection and admiration for this senior counselor. I couldn't imagine how many young girls she must have mentored while teaching them horseback riding skills in years past.

The first night at camp everyone gathered in the original Camp Waldemar Lodge, the very first building that was built at the camp. We were officially welcomed, followed by much laughter, singing and camaraderie as we all got comfortable in our new setting and with new friends.

Connie introduced me to others attending and various staff members, then it was off to our assigned cabins for the night. I quickly met the women who were assigned to my cabin and we settled in for a good night's rest. I fell asleep early as I had set my alarm for an early hour. I didn't want to be late for the trail ride.

When the alarm beckoned, I was out of bed, into my clothes quietly as the others in my cabin slept on. They obviously had not signed up for this 'before daylight' trail ride. I made my way hurriedly through the darkened camp to the stables where the trail riders were instructed to meet. The staff was busily saddling and preparing our mounts.

The first light of dawn was just thinking about coming up over the eastern horizon. Connie was in her glory, giving orders, and talking to each rider. I knew she was measuring each rider's horseback ability so she could assign the horses appropriately. Finally, as the sun began to peak its beautiful golden head of light above the eastern sky we were all mounted and Connie's high pitched yell said, "Follow the leader."

We rode in single file through the pasture and quickly got on a narrow trail, wending through cedar and oak trees, which led up a hill. We would eventually, at the end of our ride, enjoy a breakfast cooked over an open fire. The cool, clear morning and fresh air was perfect. Connie was mounted on her horse, *Macho*, and she moved back and forth, from the back to the front of this group, checking to make sure each rider was comfortable, stirrups were the right length, and horses were responding properly. There were no problems for the first 30 minutes. Connie rode by me at one point saying, "Are you doing OK?"

I called to her, "I'm loving it," as she disappeared toward the front.

I could hear her ask other riders the same question. She wanted everyone to be at their comfort level so they could enjoy the ride and the beautiful Hill County morning. This was exactly what I needed and to share this ride with such an outstanding horsewoman was so special. I was totally relaxed.

A few minutes later I heard some of the riders in front of me yelling. I couldn't hear what they were saying, but here came Connie's riderless horse, charging back down the trail. *Macho* was wild-eyed and breathless. I knew something was terribly wrong. As he went past me I reached out and grabbed his dangling reins and he stopped. Once he stopped he settled down and stood beside my horse patiently.

His body twitched from time to time. I didn't know why. The other riders and I were stopped for some time and were instructed to stay where we were until we got further instructions. The trail was so narrow between the trees it was not possible for us to move forward to see what had happened. One of the young camp counselors came by me and took *Macho's* reins from me. She told me she was taking him back to the stables.

Meanwhile we waited to be told what had happened. There was very little talking. We knew it must be bad. It seemed like it took forever, but I'm sure it was just a few minutes. Finally, we were told that the riders in the front got too close to an unseen ground hornet nest. The hornets were attacking the horses of some of the riders. When Connie rode up to try and calm the riders' horses, her horse was attacked by many hornets. *Macho* obviously got bitten numerous times. In his panic he reared back and Connie fell off backward and landed right on top of the ground hornet's nest. She, too, was bitten numerous times. She also sustained several injuries, and was unable to get up.

The counselors reacted extremely fast and when they got to her they realized she should not be moved. They gently moved her away from the hornets. A doctor and a nurse were on the trail ride so Connie was well taken care of the minute they got to her. A vehicle was summoned by radio and she was moved back to base camp, then on to Methodist Hospital in San Antonio by ambulance. She was held in the intensive care unit for observation for several days. The injuries she incurred were a fractured arm, several broken ribs, a punctured lung, plus too many hornet stings to count.

Needless to say she did not return to camp during the program. I was not only so very sorry that she had sustained such injuries, but very disappointed that I would not get to spend time with her during the camp. The Women's Week at Waldemar was a wonderful experience, but my hopes of getting to know Connie, at camp, had come to an abrupt halt.

I am happy to say that within six weeks Connie was on an Arizona trail ride with a group of friends. Unfortunately, she was instructed to ride an ATV, not horseback like the others. Her ability to heal so quickly was amazing.

Connie's friends, from Camp Waldemar and elsewhere, traveled to various parts of the world to ride the trails and experience the wonders of the out-of-doors, with her each year. It was one of her greatest thrills in her yearly activities. She was a great testimonial when talking about good genes and someone being 'tough as nails'.

Connie's Life

Connie Douglas was born September 26, 1901, and raised in south Texas, the only child of William and Ada Douglas. Her paternal grandfather, Douglas Ross, was from English nobility, but being the youngest boy in the family he felt there was little future for him in England and immigrated to the United States. He changed his last name to Douglas and became part of the Texas militia. He was stationed on the Mexican border, in Eagle Pass Texas.

Connie's maternal grandparents were ranch-raised in West Texas. Connie always gave her ranching grandfather credit for keeping her mounted with a good horse. She also told me he was the one who taught her 'horse sense' which she always said went far beyond training and working with horses. Connie's father was a District Judge, on the border of Texas and Mexico, but when she was 16 he moved the family to San Antonio and practiced law.

The young horsewoman decided to follow in her father's footsteps and study law. She attended the College of Industrial Arts, in Denton, Texas (which later became Texas Women's University) and concentrated on basic studies. Her mother thought Connie should become an actress because she was always so animated and could talk to anyone with ease. Therefore Connie also became involved in the drama department, which she truly enjoyed. Connie participated in various plays and other venues of the drama department. When she received her Bachelor or Science degree she went on to law school at the University of Texas in Austin. It was her dream to enter her father's law practice upon completion of her degree.

Connie was a very active student at the University of Texas and participated in many extra curricular activities including the drama group and was elected chairman of the Women's Council, a legislative branch of the student body. At the time it was a goal of the University to build a stadium for sports. However additional funds were needed to make it happen. Connie's chairmanship led a campaign to convince local donors for the need to raise funds to build Memorial Stadium. Her responsibilities involved going to civic groups in the Austin area and speaking of the great need for the stadium and asking for donations to help with the cause. Obviously, those working toward the support and construction of the stadium, such as Connie, were successful as the stadium has become the continuing home for the 'spirit' on the UT campus.

Connie Chooses Teaching

When leaving the university she opted not to pursue her legal career. The depression was just beginning and had already affected many of her father's clients who were unable to pay him for his services. Her common sense told her that another lawyer in the family was not going to put more money in the family coffers. She applied for a teaching position at the Main Avenue High School in San Antonio. It was 1925 and she taught speech and english. She also organized and started the first pep squad in San Antonio.

When a new San Antonio high school opened in 1932 she moved her teaching prowess there. The school was named Thomas Jefferson High School. Connie also started another pep squad there called *The Lassos*. The girls in the squad had western-themed uniforms in red and blue, and wore jaunty white cowboy hats and white boots.

She asked Jack Long, who had been one of her students and was a cowboy who often trick roped, if he would purchase enough rope and make trick ropes for each member of the squad. Jack was proud to do so, especially when it was for his favorite teacher. The ropes were made into a short lasso that operated on a swivel that was relatively easy to learn and use.

Connie then got professional trick roper, Johnny Regan, to teach the squad a variety of rope tricks. *The Lassos* were such a unique and enthusiastic support of the Thomas Jefferson football team and other school sports venues it didn't take long before they began to be invited to perform all over the country.

The Lassos performed on a Goodwill and Educational Tour that traveled east to New York City during the World's Fair in 1939, and on to Washington D. C., Philadelphia, Chicago and Niagara Falls. This performing group of 120 gals, all twirling ropes in unison, was such a novelty that Hollywood became interested in them. A film crew was sent to San Antonio in 1940 and made a movie about them. It was called *High School* and featured the popular young movie starlet of the day, Jane Withers.

Horses and More Horses

Connie was a determined young woman and had a tremendous drive. Her teaching position and directing the pep squad wasn't enough. She and friend and suitor, Harry Hamilton, started a riding stable. The Hamilton family owned 100 acres of land on the outskirts of San Antonio which became the stables. Connie and Harry taught horseback riding, showed horses in area horse shows, and stabled other owners' horses.

Harry, who became Connie's fiancé, also taught school. He was involved with many after-school activities, such as coaching football and basketball. These activities kept him from being at the stables as often as needed, but Connie took up the slack.

Connie primarily taught western pleasure classes, but also enjoyed teaching girls to ride English-style. English-style was not the type of riding she had been raised doing, in South Texas, under her grandfather's tutelage. She remembered when her grandfather was teaching her to ride as a very young girl he would say to her, "Don't let me see you bobbing up and down like a 'Bolly' Englishman!"

She did not want to ever face the 'wrath' of her loving grandfather. When she saw her grandfather's car approaching the stables, and she was teaching girls to ride English, she would immediately stop 'posting' and ride western style. She hoped he would not notice. Her utter respect for this important 'giant of a man' in her life never waned throughout her lifetime. If Connie thought for a moment her ranch-raised grandfather's ire might have been directed toward her paternal grandfather, who came from England, she never mentioned it.

It didn't take long for her ability with the equine set and her reputation and knowledge of all things horse-related spread through the area. She began to be asked to judge various horse events. Little did she realize, at that time in her life, where this love of horses and her involvement would lead her.

After a lengthy relationship with Harry Hamilton, Connie ended their engagement and moved on. It was evident they were good friends, and cared for each other a great deal, however neither of them were willing to make a commitment to marriage. In time Connie began searching for other endeavors to fill her time away from her school responsibilities. She raised and trained her own Saddlebred horses at Oak Hill Stables which kept her busy.

Camp Waldemar

Fate sometimes has a way of handling all things. Johnny Regan, the trick roper that Connie had asked to teach *The Lassos* to rope, was also a very good friend and occasional performer for rodeo producer Colonel W. T. Johnson. It just so happened that the Colonel's sister, Ora, built and owned Camp Waldemar. She was a former teacher in San Antonio and built the camp in 1926, with total support from her brother. It was her dream to have a camp for young ladies of means in the Hill Country.

The Colonel loaned Ora ten excellent riding horses from his ranch to begin her horseback riding program at camp. He also enjoyed the responsibilities to find additional horses that were appropriate for her young well-to-do campers. Arabians were often selected because of their gentleness and good nature. He also obtained some Paint horses, which added much color to the program. When the Colonel found horses that would make Camp Waldemar the premier horseback riding camp he spared no expense. He

Connie and *Schoolboy* clear a four-foot jump at Camp Waldemar.
Photo From I Married a Cowboy

made sure they were ridden and tested, for safety of the girls, before making any final decision to buy them.

While looking for broncs and saddle horses for his rodeos he continued to add to the camp herd with suitable mounts. When the camp was not in session the Camp Waldemar horses went with the Colonel to all the major rodeos such as Madison Square Garden in New York, Boston Garden, Chicago and Houston. Johnson also hired Regan, originally from England, to perform his trick roping and bullwhip routines at his rodeos.

In between rodeos, Regan also went to Camp Waldemar where he performed and worked with the young campers. He was well liked at camp. He was small of stature and his witty remarks made him a popular mainstay at camp. He traveled in a large touring car where he kept all his worldly possessions. He went back to England every other year to visit an aunt, otherwise he stayed at the camp or traveled the country visiting and living off friends he had made along the way. Often it would be the families of campers. But everyone enjoyed the Brit as he was a great entertainer.

The horseback riding program became so successful at Camp Waldemar they realized they needed to expand and hire an additional counselor. They needed someone capable of the responsibility of that section of the camp, not just a good horsewoman.

Regan remembered his association with Connie and the pep squad and recommended her to Doris, Miss Ora's niece. Doris took charge of the camp in 1934, after Miss Ora's death, in 1931.

Waldemar, nestled in the hill country, was a prestigious girl's camp that was a must for young girls of wealthy families in and around the state. Connie's reputation as being one of the best equestriennes was well-known throughout the state and her teaching background made her a prime candidate for this position. She was hired at the camp in 1937.

Horseback riding at Camp Waldemar, in those days, involved much more than just learning basic riding skills. Many of the young ladies that attended were taught a variety of talents horseback including trick riding and acrobatics. When families came to camp to gather their girls they were privileged to watch a performance of their daughters. Parents were absolutely amazed at the variety of horseback tricks their darling daughters had been taught.

Camp Waldemar was the dream of Ora Johnson in 1926. She had been an outstanding San Antonio educator and had envisioned having a camp for young women to aid them in improving themselves as a result of "lofty ideals and standards put forth by the camp".

Her older brother, W. T. Johnson, had previously been a banker and was a successful rancher and had accumulated a large number of ranch holdings. He helped her finance her dream and also assisted her by finding the right craftsman to build the magnificent structures that made up the original buildings of the camp. He also had his best ranch foreman, Jack Reeves, at Camp Waldemar during the camp season.

Jack Reeves was one of the best wranglers in the country and W. T. Johnson had hired the cowboy and ranch hand to take care of the main Johnson ranch at Junction, Texas. There wasn't anything about the ranch Jack could not handle. Earlier work experiences had taught Jack everything about horses and ranching.

When Ora built her beloved camp W. T. encouraged her to hire Jack to look after the horses during the camping season. It was most important to

Ora and W. T. that the horses be taken care of by someone who could be responsible to keep the mounts sound and safe for the young girls. Miss Ora was very pleased with Jack, and his abilities at the stables. His primary responsibility was to keep all the horses in good form, healthy, and the tack in tip-top shape. Jack was perfect for the job. When camp was not in session he continued to oversee the Johnson ranch at Junction. He moved the Camp Waldemar horses there during the off season so he could continue to care for them. He also tended to the rodeo broncs and parade horses when they were not being used at rodeos. Ora and the Colonel knew their horses would have the best of care under Jack's supervision.

Connie Meets Jack

When Connie came to Camp Waldemar, in 1937, she was paid $50 for the summer. She and Jack worked side by side. It didn't take long for the blonde horsewoman to learn that Jack was extremely adept and knowledgeable about many things other than horses. He was so different than the men she had dated being a city girl from San Antonio.

Although she knew much about the world of horses and their care, she had never had the opportunity to spend much time on a ranch. She had been raised in the city and an occasional visit to her grandparent's ranch where everything ran smoothly was taken for granted.

Connie would often get Jack to talk to her about his experiences ranching, and she was fascinated. It didn't take very long to realize they enjoyed each other's company. They had much in common in spite of the differences in their upbringing.

Connie had been the daughter of well-to-do people, well educated, and was accustomed to wanting for little. Jack had come from a very poor family, as he had lost his father early in his life, which caused him to learn to work early and help support his mother and six sisters. Luxuries were not a part of Jack's life, nor did he have any need for them.

Connie found Jack extremely refreshing, down-to-earth, and honest. She knew there was much she could learn from him. In time they fell in love. After the camping season ended in 1943 they married.

After their wedding, they drove to the Johnson ranch, near Junction. As they approached they found their house aglow with lights. Everyone that lived for miles around was there to welcome the new bride and groom. The neighbors had brought and prepared a variety of food and drink and a great celebration was held. It was a special surprise to the newlyweds. Late that night Connie and Jack waved good-bye to the last guest. Life was good. Connie was thrilled to meet and visit with her new friends and neighbors.

The first morning Jack saddled the horses and took Connie to the highest point on the ranch where they sat horseback and looked at the country for miles and miles. Jack pointed to various places on the horizon and told Connie about the significance of each place. Some of the places he located were on the Johnson ranch, some were on neighboring land. Connie would become very familiar with all these locations in and around the ranch in time. She would get to know them like the back of her hand.

Although Connie had her ranch wife chores, such as cooking and cleaning, she realized she had much to learn about ranch work, and had no intention of being inside the house much. She was determined to learn everything Jack could teach her about the ranch.

When they first arrived at the ranch there was no electricity; Connie had been accustomed to having electricity when she lived in the city. She had to learn to cook on a wood stove. They read by kerosene lamplight in the evening. They brought ice from the icehouse in town for the icebox to keep necessary foods cold. But all these new chores she mastered quickly because she preferred to be out-of-doors with her groom and as she explained, "If he fixed the windmill, I assisted by handing him the necessary tools. If he was vaccinating the cow herd, I was filling the syringes." Their teamwork required long hours and Connie thrived and enjoyed every bit of it.

Their days on the ranch were full. Connie watched her new husband arise before daylight, and work long days, often past dark. He introduced her to every chore and responsibility he had on the ranch which was fascinating to his new bride.

Connie soon came to realize that a rancher had to be an expert in many things. There was never a day that his work was not interrupted by something unexpected, which caused him to 'switch gears' taking care of the problem at hand, then go back and finish the chore he was in the process of doing. Connie soon realized Jack certainly had the equivalent of a PhD in ranching. Her respect for her groom and his work ethic and knowledge never waned.

Several years later Jack took Connie to the big Madison Square Garden Rodeo in New York City. He had competed there, before he met Connie, as a calf roper. He wanted Connie to experience the thrill of it. It wasn't long after they arrived that she realized how unusual it was for a New Yorker to see someone in a ten gallon hat and red-topped cowboy boots!

Her husband got many stares as they walked down the streets of the city. Connie laughed to herself as she observed these city folks as they stared at the cowboys. Most of the New Yorkers presumed the cowboys and cowgirls were wearing their 'costume.' She laughed to herself as she realized they had no idea that everything a cowboy wears has a purpose when working on a ranch. She thoroughly enjoyed the experience and never forgot that trip with Jack.

Back to Camp Waldemar

During the summer they closed their home at the ranch and moved back to Camp Waldemar. One of the ranch hands was left in charge, and they only returned to check how things were going, for short visits, while camp was in session. With hundreds of girls attending the camp there were many responsibilities for both of them at Camp Waldemar.

Connie was a wonderful counselor and enjoyed her association with all the campers. She generally had a nickname for each girl and was always challenged by their concerns and hesitations with the horses or camp life. Until Connie got to know a camper well enough to hang a 'nickname' on her she called them all "Brats." But they knew it was in an endearing term to Connie and it always made them laugh. Connie's high pitched voice could be heard distinctly from a distance calling, "Now you brats get to know your horse. Give him a pat now and then so he knows you approve. Keep your back straight, keep a leg on each side, and your mind in the middle."

As years passed campers grew to adulthood, married, had families and some became doctors, lawyers and even politicians. But regardless of where life took them no camper ever forgot the special attention paid to them by the blonde horseback riding teacher. She got them to do things horseback they never dreamed they could do. These former campers continued to send their female offspring to Camp Waldemar in hopes they, too, would gain some of the smarts and savvy they had reaped from their association with 'Miss Connie.'

Connie and Jack, in spite of their different backgrounds and upbringing, were happy and content. Connie always said it was the horse and love of the outdoors that made them one. It wasn't long before Connie was also loved by the entire community of Junction. When one lives in the country it is just natural that most everyone shares their best talents with the community.

Junction's Easter Pageant

Junction Texas always put on an Easter pageant that brought spectators from miles around. Various scenes depicting the death and resurrection of Christ were performed at stations in and around town and on the hills surrounding Junction. Connie was asked to direct and guide the program, which she was happy to do. She continued doing it for 17 years. She never lost her interest in drama and her efforts toward being an integral part of the community.

The fact that they were absent from Junction during the summer months when camp was in session didn't seem to matter. All ranchers are so busy in the summer their social activities slow down a great deal. When Connie and Jack returned in September they just took up right where they'd left everything months before.

After 40-some years of marriage Jack began to have health problems. They bought a home in Kerrville which was close to the Veterans Administration Hospital where Jack could get the proper medical care he needed. He eventually succumbed to the dreaded Alzheimer illness that attacks so many bright, intelligent human beings. As the illness ate away at Jack's mental abilities he also was diagnosed with cancer. A slow death always takes a toll on the victim and their family. In the case of the Reeves, Connie agonized over his affliction, but there was absolutely nothing she could do to help her loving husband improve.

Connie Writes Her Grief Away

After Jack's death in 1985 Connie wrote and published a book about her life with him entitled, *I Married a Cowboy*. By the time I met her in 1993 the book was sold out, but Jack Long loaned me his copy to read. She had lovingly written it with her heart and the passion she felt for her husband, her companion, her mentor, and her horseman.

She had written this book to express her admiration for all she gleaned from their experiences. She also wanted those who read her book to know what knowledge and self-taught education Jack had from all he had accomplished. The book truly told how this highly-educated eloquent lady and the cowboy that didn't finish his schoolhouse training truly meshed and became one. Her ability to write and describe her surroundings, especially the country-side and all things out-of-doors, was definitely written by a woman who had a vast vocabulary and a passion for the beauty of the Hill Country. Her true feelings for Jack are evidenced in this book.

Connie had great wisdom. She explained, in her book, she always related so well with young campers because she spoke on an 'adolescent' level and could talk to them in their 'own language.' In time I learned she always had the ability to speak appropriately to everyone, whether she was engaged in conversation with a mature senior, a highly educated person, or a youngster. She had that innate ability to sense what words were appropriate in any given situation. Few people possess this trait.

In her book she described her relationship with Jack through their daily life and the various incidents that happened over the years. She described Jack as the all-knowing teacher who, through his country and community upbringing, and cowboy ways, knew how to evaluate a situation and handle it. It was evident her great love for him, and all she learned from him on the ranch, allowed her life to be complete. She told of the many unusual events that happened to them, including flooding and ice storms, injured animals, shearing the Angora goats five times a year, the crash of an airplane, the sheriff handcuffed to one of their trees, and more.

The pain of losing her 'better half' and seeing him suffer toward the end of his life was no doubt eased by her writing of her life married to a cowboy, which gave her so much joy. But life goes on when we have such a loss and Connie continued her work at Waldemar and considered it a blessing. The camaraderie she experienced with the campers, other counselors, owners, and employees of the camp kept her within a 'family' unit that she loved. She kept the horses in shape and throughout her entire career of being the head of horseback riding, there was never a serious injury to a camper participating in the horseback riding curriculum. All her years with the four-legged ponies, plus her years with Jack the top wrangler, she knew how to keep the riding venue safe.

Reprint of Her Book

On one of my visits to Connie in Kerrville, during her off-season, I mentioned to her I was very anxious to see that her book was re-published. I offered to go to my publisher, Eakin Press, in Austin, if she was willing to let me present the book. At first she was reluctant and I dropped the subject.

Connie was certainly not one to 'toot her own horn' and obviously had not considered having it redone. However many of her dear friends at Camp Waldemar must have agreed with me that it would be a blessing if her book could still be available for those who thought so much of Connie. Each new season of campers that met Connie would love to have her story and it was a shame there were no copies available. Sometime later I received a letter from Connie, written in large print. She wrote,

"I'm thinking seriously of going for a second publication of my little book and something you said gave me the impression that you knew someone in Austin that might be interested. Any helpful suggestions you might give me will certainly be appreciated. Excuse writing. Connie."

When I received the letter I immediately took Jack's only copy of her book to Ed Eakin, owner of Eakin Press, and asked him to read it and see if he would be interested in re-publishing it. It only took a week before he got back with me and said he would very much like to consider it.

A friend brought Connie to Austin, for a visit with Mr. Eakin and shortly she contacted me and thanked me. She said Mr. Eakin was interested but wanted more about her life (before and after Jack). She knew she could not write about herself. She also said he was interested in having many more photographs in the book of her and Jack, but mostly more of her. She admitted her eyesight was so poor it would be almost impossible for her to determine which photographs would be appropriate. She asked if I would come to Kerrville and go through her photos and make those decisions.

When I asked her who would write about her she said, "I'd like you to do it, Gail." I was honored to be asked. I just hoped I would do justice to this fine lady that I admired so much.

I made several trips to Kerrville shortly thereafter. Sometimes we just talked about her life, and she answered every question asked of her. Sometimes we just went through her photos and I picked those I felt most appropriate, beginning with one of her as an infant and so on throughout her life. The portion of the book about Connie was easy. It almost wrote itself. She was such a special person. The photographs told the rest of the story. The 'new' *I Married A Cowboy* was published in 1995. Connie was pleased and sent me an autographed book and a note saying, "Thank you, Gail. You did a marvelous job of making an old woman sound interesting."

The book has sold very well.

An Honor She Deserved

Connie's friends at Camp Waldemar had submitted her credentials for induction in to the National Cowgirl Hall of Fame at some earlier time, but nothing had come of it. Once the book *I Married A Cowboy* was re-published and more about the feisty little lady, with a following that wouldn't quit, she was considered for induction. In October, 1997, she was inducted in to the National Cowgirl Hall of Fame at a noon luncheon at the Worthington Hotel in Fort Worth, Texas.

The banquet room, overflowing with women and some men, who were there to applaud her and the five others being inducted (Lindy Burch, Nancy Bragg Witmer, Marie "Mary" Keen Gress, Nita Brooks Lewallen, and Clara Brown). I was privileged to be invited by Connie to sit at her table, which was a great honor. I knew she had so many friends it was a difficult task for her to decide who she could include. She told me I was the cause of her being inducted, by getting the book re-published.

Connie at her induction to the National Cowgirl Hall of Fame, Fort Worth, in 1977. *Photo courtesy of the author*

I disagreed with her. No one is inducted to the National Cowgirl Hall of Fame that doesn't have the credentials and the history worthy of induction. However, I would like to think that getting the book re-published helped a little.

When she was escorted to the podium and gave her induction speech she brought the house down. Her modesty continued as she said to those former Camp Waldemar campers scattered throughout the room with everyone listening, "I am not here to be honored for what I did, but what you' brats' thought I did".

The audience roared with laughter.

As she continued she made the statement, "I always saddled my own horse."

Which was not only her way of preparing to ride, it was her way of encouraging those in the audience to always work hard and do their part, and not expect someone else to do it for them.

Those six words were so profound that once the fundraising for the new National Cowgirl Hall of Fame took hold and all the while the new Hall of Fame building was being built, her statement became the theme for the 21st century Hall.

There is a "Saddle Your Own Horse" series of talks by various honorees in the Hall open to the public. A talk with Kay Bailey Hutchison about her book, *Unflinching Courage: Pioneering Women Who Shaped Texas*, was a part of this series.

Connie Douglas Reeves was so impressive at this gathering of 'movers and shakers' of the western world, other things continued to happen for her. Late November, 1997, I received another letter from Connie and in her handwriting she wrote,

"Dear Gail, I was decoyed by a friend to have lunch with her at my favorite restaurant, but was surprised to find Marsha (Elmore) and other friends there. The real surprise came when Marsha read the announcement on the next page. Will the snowfall ever quit rolling? You stirred up a lot of excitement! Have a great turkey day. Love Connie."

The announcement Marsha made, written as Connie said, on the next page is as follows:

"On October 31st, 1997, Constance Douglas Reeves was inducted into the Cowgirl Hall of Fame in front of an audience of 700 plus women and men. Her acceptance speech held the audience spellbound and was followed by a standing ovation.

Connie looked beautiful in her western outfit and handmade boots by Justin. Needless to say the 120 Waldemar women, who were there, were very proud.

As a result of this honor and the impression that Connie made at the ceremony, Linda Davis decided to nominate Connie for the National Cowboy Hall of Fame Chester A. Reynolds Award. Linda is a 1995 Cowgirl Hall of Famer and chairperson from New Mexico in charge of selecting the person nominated. The Cowboy Hall of Fame board of directors unanimously chose Connie this week. She will be the first woman to receive the Chester

A. Reynolds Award. Chester A. Reynolds was the founder and first president of the Cowboy Hall of Fame. This award recognizes the person whose contribution has perpetuated the ideals, history, and heritage of the American West.

One more note: Connie's life-size bronze sculpted by Marsha English Elmore now stands at Waldemar.

That a-going, Connie."

I was thrilled for her. The Chester A. Reynolds Award was another great honor. I phoned her immediately after reading her letter. Again she said she knew I had caused it to happen. Again I continued to deny that what little I had done had nothing to do with her being chosen for this honor. The 'right people' had finally found this great lady and were bestowing on her the appreciation for what she had done throughout her life. But it was important to Connie that she let me know she appreciated what I had done.

Another Prestigious Award

I was at her induction in Oklahoma City at the National Cowboy Museum and Hall of Fame on that April, 1998, evening, at the 37th Annual Western Heritage Awards black-tie event. It is held in their wonderful ballroom surrounded by Wilson Hurley trip-tych of dynamic scenes from various western United States landmarks. There is no way you can be in that ballroom without feeling a tremendous sense of pride for our country and those that are recognized for their accomplishments in the western world.

Again Connie asked me to sit at her table which was such an honor. I observed her as she was surrounded by various celebrities from Hollywood that were there for this gala event. I was not surprised when I heard movie star Melissa Gilbert tell Connie,

"When they do a movie about your life I want to play you, Connie."

Chester A. Reynolds, a Kansas City businessman, was the founder of the National Cowboy & Western Heritage Museum. In 1990 this award was started in memory of this forward-thinking man who had such a love of the west. His dreams evolved in to reality in 1955 when the National Cowboy Hall of Fame was founded. The building was completed and opened in June, 1965, and has grown and become one of the most prestigious western museums in the country.

The award in his memory is given to a living person whose life best exemplified the ideals of the American West. Connie was being given the ac-

Connie chats with movie actress, Melissa Gilbert, who told her she wanted to portray her when Hollywood made Connie's movie. Taken at the National Cowboy and Western Heritage Museum, when Connie received the prestigious Chester A. Reynolds Award, 1998.
Photo courtesy of the author

colades she deserved, and not only in front of those of us that knew the wonders of this remarkable lady, but in the presence of Maureen Reagan, daughter of President Ronald Reagan, who's bigger than life-size statue, done so well by artist, Glenna Goodacre, was also unveiled that evening in the Hall. Reagan's dear friend, Charleton Heston was also present.

Following Heston to receive her award Connie extolled the virtues of living a western life-style as she said, "Let the East have their computer wizards, their skyscrapers, their stock market, their pollution. But leave the wide open spaces and the fresh air to the West".

With that familiar twinkle in her eye this statement brought the audience to their feet and once more she received a standing ovation.

Connie continued to receive honors. One that especially delighted her was that of being chosen as one of 94 Texas Women of the Century. She was selected along with Barbara Bush, Ann Armstrong, Lady Bird Johnson, Barbara Jordan and 89 other fine women from Texas.

However, some of the things which happen to a new "celebrity" aren't always what you would expect. Connie was asked to be on the Rosie O'Donnell television show, which meant going to New York where the show was taped. However, once she found out the star of the show, O'Donnell was allergic to horses, Connie politely declined their offer. They wanted her to sit on a plastic horse and trick rope. Connie's response was, "It was kind of a disappointment, but she's a damn Yankee!"

Cowgirl Hall of Fame's Grand Opening

The Cowgirl Hall of Fame in Fort Worth was finally ready to have their well advertised opening celebration for their brand-new 21st-century Hall of Fame and Museum in 2002. The location, near the Will Rogers Stock Show & Rodeo complex to the museum's east, and other important museums, such as the Fort Worth Science and History Museum, Amon Carter Museum, was physically set perfectly considering the inductees and their families were generally involved in all things western, including rodeos, cattle, horses, and the arts.

The day was kicked off with a morning parade of cowgirls riding horse-

Jimmie Gibbs Munroe, Connie and Jerry Ann Portwood (honorees) cut the ribbon to open the National Cowgirl Hall of Fame in Fort Worth, 2002. *Photo courtesy of the author*

back, or in buggies, stagecoaches, wagons, and walking. Connie was there and mounted her horse by stepping from the bed of a pickup into the saddle. She had incurred a leg injury years ago. (She was kicked by her horse, *Dr Pepper*, and it shattered her thigh bone. This injury left her unable to swing her leg over the saddle.)

This problem has never dampened her spirit for riding horseback, and it sure wasn't going to stop her on this special day. She'd been using a 'step up' for years. The injury had left her with one leg shorter than the other, but no one ever saw her limp. She rode between Pam Minick and Jan Youren, two other Cowgirl Hall of Fame honorees. At the end of the parade all attending honorees of this fabulous museum were seated in front of the entrance where a wide blue ribbon stretched out in front of them.

Connie sat between Jimmie Gibbs Munroe and Jerry Taylor Portwood. On closer observation one noticed that each cowgirl had a pair of scissors in her hand. When they were instructed to "Open the Museum" each did so by cutting the ribbon in front of them. The museum was officially open!

That afternoon I enjoyed going through the new facility with Connie, and friends, Marsha Elmore and Jan Cannon. We took photos as Connie stood in front of her photograph and biography as an honoree in this 21st century facility.

The board of directors of the new hall invited the Hollywood Disney Studio graphics people to help with the building and make sure the museum was current with all the innovations and newest technical features that were available. A touch of a finger on the list of honorees can bring up each one, for visitors to review. Films were continually being shown in the in-house theater and various darkened areas of the museum.

We also went to an area where a plastic bucking bronc was on display, allowing visitors to mount it, have their photo taken, which could be picked up in the gift shop before leaving the museum. The good sport that she was, Connie, was the first one on and the photo taken shows her dramatic preparation to attempt to ride this 'wild cayuse'. Connie was willing to mount a plastic bronc in the National Cowgirl Hall of Fame for the fun of it, but was smart enough to decline riding a plastic mount for an allergic 'city girl' for a New York television program! What a momentous day it was for me to share these memories with Connie.

Connie thanks all that attended her 100th birthday party.
Photo courtesy of the author.

Connie Celebrates Her 100th Birthday

On her 100th birthday Camp Waldemar invited Connie's friends to attend a '100th Birthday & Cowgirl Fiesta' in her honor. The day was perfect and the weather complied. The parade grounds in front of the camp buildings were immaculately manicured for the occasion and teaming with guests. Of course, Connie arrived on her favorite horse, *Dr Pepper*, wearing a red straw cowboy hat, and red with black trimmed western shirt.

Her speech to everyone there was, "It is my pleasure to live in happy surroundings all these years. Thank you, Waldemar, for giving me 66 summers and great pleasure of happiness in a miniature Garden of Eden, with four legged horses and smiling-eyed little 'brats.' It's the biggest compliment anyone could give me. I love all of you."

A large ice sculpture of a horse head, surrounded by 100 red roses was a fitting centerpiece for the occasion. A song written for Connie by Allison Kerr entitled *Connie's Song* was performed and in part she sang; "a lady on two feet, a legend on four" and "she's got horse sense and cow sense, and good Texas pride." It was evident everything done by these women who loved Connie so had created everything for this day with their hearts.

More Honors

Connie was surprised to receive a letter from the senior vice-president of The Freedom Forum in Arlington, Virginia, congratulating her on being selected as a 2002 *Al Neuharth Free Spirit of the Year* honoree. The award annually honors individuals who have stirred the public's hearts and souls by demonstrating the human capacity to dream, dare and do. The letter went on to say, "Your recognition as a Free Spirit Honoree is for being a 101 year old "cowgirl" who was inducted into the Cowboy Hall of Fame and for continuing to teach kids to ride horses. The honor is given to you as a unique individual "Free Spirit" with the hope that you will continue to perpetuate that ideal."

The Freedom Forum, which promotes free press, free speech, free spirit, was to hold this event at the National Press Club in Washington, D. C. with 102 high school journalism students, plus other honorees and dignitaries. She flew to Washington, D. C. in May, 2003, to receive one of four national Spirit Awards for her continued commitment to educating young people.

Connie and Marsha Elmore, owner of the camp, went horseback riding at Waldemar in early August, 2003, just a few days before the final term of the camp season ended. After walking their mounts for a distance Connie told Marsha she wanted to canter her horse, *Dr Pepper*, a bit. When she gave him the sign he lowered his head and tossed the 101-year-old equestrienne off. She fell on to her neck. Two Care-Flight helicopters arrived on the Camp Waldemar golf course to airlift Connie to Wilford Hall Medical Center in San Antonio. The attending physician was enraged that anyone would let a woman, 101-years-old, ride a horse! He was not aware of her background and history. In days to come, Connie endeared herself to everyone in the hospital from the doctors to the aides. Twelve days later, August 17, 2003, after complications from her injuries, she died of cardiac arrest.

"She had been telling us all summer she was going to go off a horse, and she and *Dr Pepper*, had talked about it," said Marsha Elmore, as reported in the *San Antonio Express-News*. "After she fell, she told us he'd just retired her a little early," Marsha reported.

Connie was survived by six nieces and six nephews, and four generations of Camp Waldemar campers and friends. A service was held at Grimes Funeral Chapel in Kerrville, Texas, and she was buried at Camp Verde Cem-

Celebration of Life of
Connie Douglas Reeves

September 26, 1901 - August 17, 2003

Celegration of Life of Connie Douglas Reeves program, held at the stables at Waldemar, 2003. *Photo courtesy of the author.*

etery.

A memorial service was held at 6:30 p.m. on August 22, a Friday evening, at the Camp Waldemar stables. My husband, Cliff, and I attended the service which was a Celebration of the Life of Connie Douglas Reeves. The service began with a Memorial Ride-In of Liz Pohl, who took Connie's place as head of horseback riding at Waldemar, and Catherine Pipkin, leading Connie's horse, *Dr Pepper*, whose back was draped with a blanket of red roses, with her saddle that held her boots backwards in the stirrups.

Then Allison Kerr, who wrote *Connie's Song*, sang the words that described this remarkable woman. Marsha Elmore made the welcome and Jan Cannon did the affirmation and scripture reading; Words of Celebration and Remembrance were given by Bonnie Lou Campbell, Debbie Norton and Moey Rutledge. Connie's favorite song, *You are My Sunshine* was sung by the children of Waldemar, and Liz Pohl gave the Dedication, then *Taps* was played.

At the bottom of the celebration program was written, "Connie wrote this last passage in *I Married A Cowboy;*

"Let there be no moaning at the bar when the gate is shut on me. My cowboy husband will be waiting there, sitting tall in the saddle on old *Paddy* and holding *Danger Boy's* bridle reins. Together we will ride the beautiful pastures and climb the rugged hills. Maybe we'll find little Johnny Mendoza's bud in the Heavenly garden and smell the fragrance on the flower. 'The joys we share as we linger there, none other can compare.'"

She was a beautiful lady, inside and out, and had an insight in to people that is rarely equaled. She guided with a quiet hand, and yet she never stopped learning and appreciating every opportunity that she was given. She saw so much beauty in our western world, our animals, and the things around her. Connie never felt despair or pain that she couldn't handle. She appreciated her heritage, her journey through life, her friends and the future through those she helped to guide. She never dwelled on the negative and always saw the best in those around her and wasn't afraid to tell them. Those who knew her and were touched by her are blessed. Connie definitely dared to be different.

Premier Rodeo Historian
Imogene Veach Beals

Imogene Veach Beals and I traveled together for 15 years. We gathered rodeo history and attended rodeos and cowboy gatherings from upstate New York, to deep Florida, to sunny California; Pendleton, Oregon; Cheyenne, Wyoming and even Hawaii – just to name a few of our destinations and adventures. I always marveled at how compatible we were, until it dawned on me "Maybe Imy is just easy to get along with and 'goes with the flow.'" Regardless of the reason, she is one of the most fun and delightful women I have had the pleasure to call my friend. At times we traveled long distances and spent weeks together on these trips. We were always ready to get up at the same time, got tired at the same time, and got hungry together. We literally talked our way across country and back and it was primarily about rodeo. Oh my, what a memory this gorgeous lady has for rodeo information and the cowboys and cowgirls that competed and performed. To this day, if I need verification of some obscure bit of information about early day rodeo, all I have to do is call Imogene and she'll have my answer in no time. The Author.

This is Imogene's Story

Monroe and Alta Brown Veach had six children and Imogene was the oldest daughter. She was born July 5th, 1921, near Trenton, in the northern part of Missouri. Her father, Monroe, was a cowboy and had a multitude of talents including making leather goods for horses, harness, saddles, and more. He was also a trick roper, and for a time he put on rodeos in and around that part of the country, using his family as hands.

Imogene was a black-haired darling and always had something 'up her sleeve.' She was her daddy's girl and preferred to be out-of-doors with him rather than to help in the home. In addition to an older brother, Billie, she gained three younger sisters, Mary, Letty, and Peggy. When Peggy came along Imogene was 18-years-old. Younger brother, Ben, also made an appearance after Letty.

Monroe, the patriarch of this family, was born near Trenton, in 1896. His early ambition was to become a cowboy. He left home and went west. He was hired as a cowboy at a large cattle ranch, near Eads, Colorado. In 1919, Monroe built his first leather shop in front of the home place, seven miles from Trenton.

He had just been discharged from the army. He had been assigned and taught to repair leather equipment for the cavalry at Fort Riley, Kansas. The ambitious young man had married his childhood sweetheart, Alta Brown, that year. To learn what cowboys wanted and needed in the way of leather goods, he joined the prominent Fog Horn Clancy Wild West Show as a trick and fancy roper. He stayed with the show for nine years, coming home to his family and saddle-making business between seasons.

As a youngster it was not unusual to see Imogene in her dad's leather shop helping him with some chore. She loved working with leather and learned as much as possible about the business. Of course, there were those days she had to go to school. At first she went to a one-room school at nearby Shott. Shortly thereafter, she and brother, Billie, rode on horseback to school at Tindall.

After about six months Billie quit school, but a neighbor girl, Mevelyn Webster, rode with Imogene. They were good friends and there were times they had to ford the river because the bridge would wash out. If the snowfall was too heavy during the school day and was difficult to get home, the two girls would spend the night with various families in town, and keep their horse safe in a barn.

Sister Letty remembered, "Imogene took me to school with her one day before I was old enough to go. I don't remember if mama was sick or away. It must have been a 'show and tell' day," she chuckled.

Tindall was only a two-year high school so Imogene finished her schooling at Trenton High School, graduating in 1939. She rode in a 'home-made bus' over seven miles of dirt road, and could recall it was bumpy enough to loosen your teeth. During her senior year she lived with a family in Trenton and after school she took care of their daughter. They paid her $3.00 a week, plus room and board.

Letty recalled there was always something going on around the Veach home. The Baptist Church was to the west and the Methodist Church was to the east. The Veach children took in the activities at both churches. On Sunday afternoons all the neighbor children came, some by horseback, to the Veach home. There were always games and fun activities for the youngsters. In the winter a nearby neighbor had a steep hill upon which everyone enjoyed sledding down after a good snow.

Grandmother Nora Veach's sewing machine sat in front of a door, to let the cool breeze in during the summer, recalled Letty. This grandmother taught all the girls to sew.

Letty said, "Imogene and Mary were the best. Mary could make a three piece man's suit as good as any tailor. Imogene could make coats and blazers and always told me to 'use a thimble.'"

Monroe got busier as each year passed, eventually moving his saddle shop into the town of Trenton. The Veach Saddlery was active constantly as there was always much to do. It was also a place where the children could help with some chore that needed to be done. Many other items were made in the shop other than saddles.

As Imogene got older she began weaving cinches and stitching boot tops on a treadle sewing machine. She also began doing more intricate leatherwork. Monroe would draw the design for fancy boot tops on the leather, and then turn them over to her to be sewn.

Saddles were the primary item in the busy shop. During the 1940s, Fred Lowry, of Lenapah, Oklahoma, a world champion steer roper, won a saddle made by Veach at the Nowata, Oklahoma rodeo, produced by Clyde S. Miller. He was very impressed with it and came to Monroe asking him to make some changes in the style. The changes gave him better comfort when steer roping. The new saddle, with the changes suggested by Lowry, was promoted by Veach Saddlery. Soon they were swamped with other steer ropers wanting the popular Fred Lowry Roper Saddle.

Monroe had also designed and made a trick riding saddle that became extremely popular with the various performers. Even today a Veach-made trick roping saddle is a highly prized item. It is still popular with trick riders, even if they have to buy one that has been used extensively and sorely in need of repair. The cost of repairs on a Veach-made trick riding saddle seems to be more important than a brand new saddle.

Romance Happens

Rodeos were held at various locales in and around Missouri on a regular basis. Monroe seldom missed going to a rodeo. Due to his large family, it was not possible for him to take the entire family. The annual rodeo at Sidney, Iowa, was one of the larger rodeos in that region, and was often compared to the historic Cheyenne Frontier Days, in size and scope, during that era.

Sidney only had a population of around 1,000 residents. Everyone at Sidney worked toward the success of the rodeo, sponsored by the American Legion. Most visiting cowboys had to stay in tents, but some were invited to stay at residents' homes, for a reasonable fee. It was Imogene that Monroe invited to go with him and attend the 1939 rodeo at Sidney. It is possible since she had just graduated from Trenton High School this was his gift to her.

Little did the recent high school graduate realize this rodeo would change her life forever. Imogene met Charley Beals at that rodeo. He was from Newton, Iowa, and was competing in the bull riding, saddle bronc and bareback riding events.

Charley had been with the Clyde S. Miller Wild West Show since 1936 and made $10 a week. He had been raised on a farm and knew he wanted to be a cowboy, not a farmer. Red Dougherty joined the Miller show the same time Charley did and they both joined the Cowboys' Turtle Association. Charley always declared he got a 'rodeo education' while with Clyde S. Miller Wild West Show, out of Waterloo, Iowa. He said that was worth a great deal more than his $10 a week salary.

It was evident there was an attraction between Imogene and Charley. He was immediately drawn to the dark-haired beauty and she to him. They talked, and when he was not competing, he sat near her in the bleachers. Monroe promoted his leather-making business at these events and often went home with orders from the cowboys. Charley had ordered a custom-made belt from Monroe.

Some time later Charley made a trip to the Trenton shop, supposedly to check out the belt being made for him. Letty and Mary decided that maybe Charley was not as concerned about his belt as he was about seeing their sister Imogene again. Whatever the motivation might have been, on January 17, 1940, Imogene became Mrs. Charley Beals.

The couple went to rodeos, where Charley competed, and Imogene cheered him on. Between rodeos Charley worked in Monroe's saddle shop. He was learning the leather business and saddle-making trade from his new father-in-law, and was a quick study.

It wasn't long before Imogene discovered she was expecting. The couple lived in Trenton where their daughter, they named Donna Kay, was born October 24, 1940. How proud they were of their beautiful baby girl!

Charley continued to compete in rodeos and Imogene and Donna went along. They had a tent, and camped at the rodeo, just like most of the other competitors. Everyone cooked their meals over an open fire. After the rodeo it was always fun to meet and visit with other cowboys and their families. In time they made many friends among the competitors. They never once complained, or even considered it a problem to tent at a rodeo. Even when the weather turned bad, if they got wet or cold, so did all their friends. Rodeo people were just one big happy family, and could adjust to just about anything.

World War II Changes Things

World War II definitely slowed rodeo down and things changed for everyone. Both Imogene and Charley were hired by Boeing, sight-unseen. They got jobs with the Boeing factory making airplanes, in Renton, Washington, to work as electricians. They put their belongings in the car and Charley, Imogene and Donna drove from Trenton to the northwest.

Imogene was hired to place the electrical wiring in the airplanes while Charley worked in a different department. They were assigned furnished living quarters which were unused barracks. Although it was 'sparsely furnished,' Imogene's decorating ingenuity came in handy. She took a camping mattress; they used when they camped out at rodeos, and put it on the back of a cot, creating a make-shift davenport. A card table was their kitchen table.

While working on the war effort in Renton they saved as much money as they possibly could. When the war ended they wanted to head home to Missouri with more than a few bucks in their pockets. Many of the people who worked at Boeing spent every cent they made. When they were let go some didn't have enough money to return home. But the Beals' had a dream. Their frugal ways, and the money they saved, would make that dream become a reality.

When they arrived back in Trenton they told Monroe their dream was to open their own saddle shop. They wanted his approval and his advice on where they should consider locating. He told them that most of his orders came out of the state of Oklahoma. They made an investigative trip to Oklahoma and after some careful searching decided Tulsa was the best location. Charley and Imogene opened the Veach Saddlery Company of Tulsa in 1945.

Tom Gray had leased a barn for his Quarter Horses on the Tulsa fairgrounds. He made a deal with Charley and Imogene. He offered Charley four stalls that they could convert in to the saddle shop. Gray had his carpenter box in the doors and windows and the shop was opened. What an exciting day that was for them. Imogene and Charley were determined to make it work.

Their closed-in area made one large room. Charley had bought some used large wooden shelves and benches from the Spartan Aircraft Company. Spartan were selling items no longer needed once the war was over, and the shelves were used by the Beals as room dividers. They also placed the shelves to close off a portion of the back part of the room to be used for their living quarters. Imogene hung a curtain next to the shelves to discourage customers from entering the private area they considered 'home.'

Imogene and Charley slept on a rollaway bed. An army cot was little Donna's bed. Imogene cooked on a hot plate. The bathrooms were in a rock building next to the barn. During events held at the fairground these bathrooms were public restrooms, with numerous toilets and sinks. You won't find many women during that era, or any era, that were willing to consider a horse stall their home. Imogene did, and didn't think a thing about it. She, Charley and Donna were content and happy. The fairgrounds was always having an event of some kind and there was a constant flow of people in and out of their shop. Business was good.

While Charley was getting well-known in the business, Imogene set up her sewing machine in a corner of the shop. Once when Charley was preparing to go to a rodeo to compete, he told his wife he would like to have a western shirt made out of a certain striped material she had on hand. Before he left for the rodeo, Imogene had worked out the pattern, put her trusty sewing machine in to action, and his new striped shirt was ready to be worn. This began a whirlwind of sewing projects for Imogene, but she could always put it aside when it was time to go to the rodeo with Charley.

Meanwhile, Charley competed at as many rodeos as possible. Imogene accompanied him as often as she could, but on some occasions she stayed and kept the shop open. She knew it was necessary, but she always hated to miss a rodeo. When possible her dad and mother would come down from Trenton and keep the shop open and take care of Donna, so Imogene could accompany Charley. There were times when Charley had to travel to rodeos without his family. Gene Peacock or Bill George were cowboys who often traveled with him. Other times Charley might just take daughter, Donna, and Peggy Veach, Imogene's youngest sister, who was just a couple of years older than Donna. The girls always enjoyed one another's company. To this day they continue to find rodeo adventures to go on together.

Appreciation of Arts

Charley met Orren Mixer, a cowboy artist, at the Guthrie '89er Days Rodeo in 1946. The artist was taking photographs of rodeo events in preparation to paint various rodeo scenes. The two cowboys hit it off from their very first meeting and became life-long friends. Orren painted many paintings depicting rodeo and the west. One painting Orren did was of Charley, riding a bull, with well-known rodeo clowns, Hoytt Hefner, John Lindsey and barrelman, Jasbo Fulkerson, in the background. The Beals' bought the original painting from Orren and it hangs prominently in their home to this day. They had prints made from the original and have proudly given them to special friends through the years.

Orren became one of the best horse and animal artists in the country. Proven by the fact he was asked by the American Quarter Horse Association to paint a large painting of a typical Quarter Horse. The AQHA bought the painting, made prints from the original and sold them to Quarter Horse lovers and breeders across the nation. It soon became known that Orren had the ability to paint horses with the correct confirmation and traits of the horse, whether it be a Quarter Horse, an Appaloosa, a Paint, or any other breed. In time, practically every horse breed association came to the artist and had him paint the 'typical' horse of their breed. The friendship that developed between the Beals and Mixer families is a special bond which has never been broken.

After getting established and business was going well, the Beals' were offered a larger area in a former army barracks on the Fairgrounds. The offer came at the right time as Charley's business had grown and their quarters, made of four stalls, were getting cramped. The barracks building had been used during the war.

Now that it was vacant the Beals' shared this building with another family, Clyde and Bertha Roberts and family, who used one wing of the building. The Beals had the other wing. Veach Saddlery was in the front of the building. Both families shared a common bathroom, which contained six sinks, six toilets, and one huge shower room with six showerheads.

Imogene's daughter, Donna, said, "We had no kitchen. Mom used her trusty hot plate and a roaster oven for our meals. We did have a refrigerator. When the Roberts family moved out I used the vacant wing of the building for a roller skating rink. I loved having the 'run' of the fairgrounds and rode my bicycle all over it. After the big October fair and carnival left town I would go over to the midway area to see what trinkets were left behind. I always found something."

Charley continued to rodeo and Imogene had made numerous friends in the rodeo world. One of her best friends was Frances Gasche, nicknamed Frannie. She was a sister to Shoat Webster who became a world champion steer roper. He was from Lenapah, Oklahoma, and shortly after he and his aunt, Kate Lowry, had returned from the big Madison Square Garden Rodeo, he ordered a custom-made shirt from Imogene. He asked his sister, Frannie, who lived in Tulsa, to pick it up for him. Frannie and Imogene became friends on their first meeting. On occasion, Shoat would ask Frannie and Imogene to help him drive to some distant steer roping he had entered.

Imogene has fond memories of the first time she went to the King Merritt Steer Roping in Laramie, Wyoming, in 1949. Shoat had won the steer roping in 1948 that was held at Encampment, Wyoming. Some say it was held there because Laramie was not ready for pari-mutual betting. But the following year the roping was moved to Laramie. Shoat won it again in 1949. No doubt, that had a lot to do with Imogene's memories of being there. It is always thrilling to be rooting for someone who comes out the winner.

There were numerous other trips as well. The gals would help him drive, pulling some of his well-known favorite roping horses in the trailer behind. Shoat won the annual King Merritt Memorial Steer Roping in Wyoming in 1948, 1949, 1953 and 1955. Charley, Imogene and Donna Kay spent many Thanksgiving and Christmas holidays with the Webster family over the years. Their own families lived too far away to travel for the holiday.

The Kentucky Derby

Kate Lowry had tickets to the Kentucky Derby in 1950. Something came up and she knew she would not be able to go. She knew how much Frannie and Imogene enjoyed traveling and gave them her tickets. The girls donned their "Derby" hats and headed to Louisville, Kentucky. They had no reservations, just their strong desire to go to this very famous race. Sometimes desire is all that is necessary. When they arrived they quickly learned all the hotels in the city were full. As fate would have it, the girls met a lady who invited them to stay in her home. They were so appreciative to have a place to sleep.

It so happened that Imogene's friend and former landlord, Tom Gray, had a horse named *Oil Capitol* running in the Derby. It was doubly exciting to go to such an important race when you knew someone who owned a horse running in it.

When they arrived at Churchill Downs the two adventuresome gals decided they should go across the tracks to the barn. Imogene wanted to wish Mr. Gray and his team good luck. Unfortunately, they discovered they didn't have the proper credentials necessary to go there. But never underestimate a determined woman.

It wasn't long until they met a photographer and while talking with him, lo! They discovered he did have the proper credentials. Accompanying him they made it across the infield to the barn. During the race this photographer took their photo as they watched the race and cheered on their choice. They asked him if he would sell them a copy of the photo, he informed them it would be in their local newspaper. He was with the Associated Press.

Their bets were on Tom Gray's horse, *Oil Capitol*, of course. When the race ended three year old *Middleground* had won. Their betting loss hadn't dampened their spirits too badly. When they arrived back in Tulsa they found their photo, taken at the Derby, was indeed, on the front page of the *Tulsa World* newspaper.

Imogene loved to travel and took every opportunity to do so. She and Kate Lowry went on a European tour in 1960. They traveled to the Soviet Union, Switzerland and Germany. In the 1970s Frannie's daughter was in school in Spain so Imogene and Frannie toured Spain. In 1976 they took a trip to India.

The King Ranch

Fred and Kate Lowry wanted to go to the King Ranch in far south Texas. Each year the ranch had an important horse sale and in 1976 they went with Imogene driving them. It was a big affair and many people attended, especially the top horse buyers in the country. The King Ranch had some of the most popular Quarter Horses in the country. They had a great time.

On their way home, Fred mentioned to the ladies that he had been offered an opportunity to take them to the main house for a tour. The main house was an impressive large hacienda that Imogene and Kate mentioned several times while they were there they would just love to get to see the inside of that beautiful home. Fred told them he had turned the offer down. He said he didn't want to 'put anyone out.' The ladies gave Fred a good talking to, for quite a distance, as they traveled homeward. It would have been much better for Fred if he had not told them of the invitation he had refused.

Shoat Webster asked Imogene and Frannie to accompany him again to the annual steer roping in Laramie, Wyoming in 1956. They also took with them two teenagers, Donna, Imogene's daughter, and Frannie and Shoat's nephew, Jimmy Fuller. During this same time Fred Lowry had been operated on for cancer at Mayo Clinic, in Rochester, New York. While in Laramie the group received word that Fred had died. Shoat and Frannie flew back to Oklahoma as quickly as possible to help make arrangements for Fred's body to be returned and to be with Aunt Kate.

Meanwhile Imogene was left in Laramie with Donna and Jimmy Fuller, plus two of Shoat's good roping horses. She loaded the horses and the car and pulling an in-line trailer drove back to Oklahoma with no problem. Donna and Jimmy teased each other most of the way, typical of teenagers, but Imogene ignored their teasing and kept driving until she reached home. A few days later, at Fred's funeral, someone came up to Imogene and said, "I know who you are, you're Imogene. Fred always said you could do anything."

Growing Business, Bigger Quarters

Business at Veach Saddlery kept growing, and it was time to look for more permanent quarters. They rented a brick building on 11th Street in Tulsa, which was the famed Route 66, in those days. The building was owned by Glenclif Dairy, and they just happened to have an ice cream store

Imogene hand-tooling a leather piece for a saddle. Only one of her many talents. *Photo courtesy of Imogene Veach Beals.*

next door, much to daughter, Donna Kay's delight. Again the family made living quarters in the back of the saddle shop. This space, however allowed the family more room.

The Saddlery was one large room, with a bathroom and shower. The Beals cordoned off an area to be Donna's bedroom, and another area to be the kitchen. Imogene fixed meals for the family on her hot plate or roaster oven. They now had a small refrigerator, a table and chairs, and a dish cabinet.

Peggy, Imogene's youngest sister, came to stay quite often as she and Donna were great companions and got along so well. Peggy said, "I can remember Imogene taught us to bake cookies in the roaster oven. When she wasn't baking she could grill on it."

When it came to washing dishes Imogene would take a dishpan to the bathroom, fill it with hot water and carry it back to the kitchen.

By this time Veach Saddlery had a large following and many repeat customers due to the quality of the work and the warm reception everyone was given. Charley designed a bareback rigging in 1946 that became very popular with the bareback riding cowboys. The Beals' rigging continued to be popular in that event into the 1970s. Some of the well-known bareback riders who used his rigging were; Jim Shoulders, Larry Mahan, Jack Buschbom, Casey Tibbs, Johnny Hawkins, Jim Houston and Harry Tompkins.

Eventually a new style of riding bareback broncs was introduced by the Mayo brothers and Jim Houston. They began to lay back on the bronc almost hitting their head on the horse's rump. This style definitely required a different type of rigging. Jim Houston phoned Charley and told him he was working on a new rigging and the reason why. Charley congratulated Houston on his new design and told him he hoped he would be very successful.

Charley thought Houston's phone call was a fine gesture, and one of respect for him. He did appreciate it.

The Saddlery always had many stops by competing rodeo cowboys traveling through Tulsa. Charley and Imogene always enjoyed their visits. The cowboys always knew they could visit, repair a piece of their equipment, and even bunk at the shop before going 'on down the rodeo road.' In 1958 Charley made the official prize saddle for the RCA World Champion Bull Rider. It was won by Jim Shoulders, an Oklahoma world champion, from Henryetta. Imogene remembered it pleased Charley so much for Jim, an Okie, to be the one to receive it.

Sewing, Designing

Imogene was always willing to use her sewing machine for various projects. She had set up an area in the store where she could sew. She did custom sewing of all kinds. She made colorful western shirts for the family, friends and friends of friends, too. Word spread about her talent as a seamstress and her unique western designs. She spent much of her day working at her sewing machine. She even began designing new western apparel. Some of the top rodeo hands, not just Charley, wore her custom-made western shirts. She also made western-style suits for men and women. She even made jockey silks for many of the jockeys living and riding at the tracks in the area. She was especially popular with musical entertainers and rodeo queens because of her flair and creativity in her designs of western clothing.

Western wear, except for blue jeans and denim jackets, wasn't seriously manufactured until the 1960s. H. D. Lee, makers of Lee jeans, approached her about going to work for them to design and create western wear. She declined the offer, but they did use her tapered western shirt pattern when they began manufacturing shirts. Her creations were so popular one prominent Oklahoma rancher sent his private plane to Tulsa to pick up the clothes Imogene designed for various members of his family. The dark-haired beauty, taught by her grandmother to sew, never dreamed her talents would be so popular.

First Real Home

Imogene and Charley finally bought their first house in 1956. It was on East 7th Street, not far from the store. Donna was a junior at Will Rogers High School. Imogene thoroughly enjoyed decorating her first house. The sewing machine was busy day and night getting drapes and bedspreads made.

Donna said, "My mother could make something out of nothing. She always had the ability to make our homes, whether it was a house or the back of the shop, attractive and comfortable; regardless of the circumstances."

Donna graduated from high school in 1958. By this time she had met the man who would become her husband, in October of that year. He was a roughstock riding cowboy named Duke Clark. She met him in Trenton, Missouri, when visiting her grandparents. He was working for her uncle, Billie Veach, in his rodeo producing business.

After Donna and Duke married he worked for Charley in the saddle shop and learned the leather-making trade, too. Of course, he still competed in rodeos. By this time Charley had retired from competition. Now he and Imogene attended rodeos to watch their son-in-law compete.

When Glenclif sold the building Veach Saddlery had occupied, since 1956, another move was necessary. But they didn't move far. Just seven blocks west was the next location, 4702 E. 11th Street. It had been a former Mobil Oil service station, but it made a perfect saddle shop. With the new location they added western wear to their shop. It was 1962.

Imogene began going to Western Wear Market in Denver, Colorado each January to order the next season's clothing. It was a great get-away for her and Charley. The Rodeo Cowboys Association convention was also held in Denver during the same time. It was a great time to see old friends they had made while rodeoing, and meet new friends, too. They always looked forward to their trip to Denver in January.

Among their friends were Gene and Jean Pruitt. Gene was the RCA's editor for the association magazine, *Rodeo Sports News*. Pruitt was a former world champion saddle bronc rider. Imogene and Jean Pruitt were always finding new adventures, in addition to market, in and around the Denver area.

Madison Square Garden

Charley often went to Madison Square Garden, which was the biggest rodeo in the fall. It was also one of the rodeos all the best cowboys tried to make. There were years that Imogene stayed and ran the store while Charley was gone. But several times they got someone in the family to fill in, and Imogene would go, too. New York City was always exciting for cowboys and their families. Dressed in western wear they always caused a sensation with

New Yorkers. Additionally, it was one of the biggest rodeos in the country and it was held at the famous Madison Square Garden.

One year while Charley was at the rodeo at Madison Square Garden Imogene left the city. She took a bus to visit one of their customers in Connecticut that had ordered goods from their shop, had a sizeable bill, but had not paid it. Imogene had sent them several invoices, but they were ignored. While Charley was at the rodeo, Imogene boarded a bus to New Haven, Connecticut, and located the man's business. When she walked in their business and stated why she was there the owner was dumbstruck. He realized she had come in person to collect. He paid her immediately and she left with the money owed them. The bill had been 'Paid in Full.'

Both Imogene and Charley made friends easily. It didn't take *The Ranchman* magazine, published in Tulsa; long to realize Imogene was the perfect person to write a rodeo cowboy column for the magazine. Her column entitled *Boots & Saddles* told various happenings primarily in rodeo, but also included race track and horse world news. Most of the news was information about people and events in and around Oklahoma. She started writing a column for them in 1955 and continued for five years.

Some of the happenings she reported included:

In her May, 1955 column "It's a girl for the Clark McEntire's of Kiowa, Okla. This makes two girls and a boy for Clark and Jackie. They have named the new girl Reba."

"Harry Tompkins was sporting a very pretty pair of new chaps in the very popular color, pink, with a maroon trimming; they tell me Casey Tibbs was wearing a pair of lavender ones the first night of the rodeo."

In her July, 1955 column: "Shoat Webster and Clark McEntire got together for a matched calf and steer roping; they roped six calves and five steers — Grand total was 264.2 seconds for Webster and 221.8 for McEntire."

In the February, 1958 column; "Oklahoma is mighty proud of Jim Shoulders, 29-year-old native. Jim was born and raised in Tulsa and attended East Central High School here. This is the third time he has won the World's Champion title to become the biggest money winner in Rodeo. Jim, his charming wife, Sharon, two daughters and a son live on their ranch east of Henryetta,

Oklahoma. Jim is not only the all-around Champion for the year 1957, but is also the Bull Riding Champion and the Bareback Riding Champion. Duane Howard and Johnny Hawkins gave him close competition in the latter two events. Jim won close to $34,000 and received a RCA point for each dollar won to be declared Champion."

Her reporting became so popular other western-related magazines asked Imogene to write for them, as well. She produced columns for *Hoofs & Horns* magazine, when it was owned by Willard Porter, and for the *Buckboard* and *Rodeo Sports News*.

There has always been a great camaraderie in rodeo between Australia and the United States. Australia held competitions between the Aussie cowboys, Canadian and U. S. arena competitors in the late 1930s and early 1940s. Each country sent a team and those that went always came back with great tales and the competition was always keen.

The Rodeo Cowboys Association invited several competing cowboys from Australia to come and visit rodeos and various rodeo people in the United States in 1959.

When the 'down under' cowboys came Charley and Imogene spent lots of time with them. Some of the Australian cowboys spent hours talking with Charley. Not only did he know so much about riding roughstock, which is called 'buck jumping' in Australia, but he was willing to show them all about saddlemaking, too. The cowboys were fascinated by the saddles, bareback riggings and other tack Charley made for cowboys.

The visiting 'hands' were in the United States for a month. It was not a surprise to hear they gave an open invitation to the Beals, if and when they could ever get away from Veach Saddlery long enough to go to Australia. It was a trip they were anxious to make, especially after making such good friends with so many of the boys. They looked forward to going, once they retired.

On one visit, Aussie, Ron Doherty, fell in love with a gal from Oklahoma and decided to stay in the states. He eventually became a U. S. citizen, lives in Oklahoma, and continues to be a long-time friend of the Beals.

Ambassadors of Rodeo

Imogene and Charley were always interested and concerned about the rodeo world and were committed to helping it grow and prosper in various ways. They were important 'ambassadors' for the sport of rodeo. They were among the first people to join the Rodeo Historical Society when it was formed. They always worked diligently to get others to join and become members. Both served on the board of directors of the organization, and their loyalty to it has never waned. Through their efforts, and others with the same commitment to keep the history of the sport alive, the organization has thrived and continued to grow.

Donna and Duke Clark had three boys; Derek, Doug and Drew. The boys were brought up on rodeo and had many rodeo experiences in their granddad's saddle shop. It is not surprising that all three have been long-time competitors in professional rodeo.

Derek chose the saddle bronc event and qualified for the National Finals 15 times. He also sat on the PRCA board of directors for years in various capacities. His grandpa Charley told him once that when you retire from competing in rodeo the main thing you have from your time in rodeo are memories, good friends, and lots of photographs. Derek always considered this bit of advice important and took it to heart.

Doug took to the other end of the arena and competed in roping events. Duke was an excellent horse trainer, and Doug followed in his footsteps as well. Although Doug's time is divided between training roping horses and competing, he has a string of important wins in major rodeos. He was the 1995 all-around champion at Cheyenne Frontier Days. He won the steer roping event at the 2005 Pendleton Round-Up, and went on to make the Steer Roping National Finals that year, which is only for the top 15 steer ropers in the country.

Drew also competes in roping, but stays closer to home and primarily competes at rodeos in Oklahoma, Missouri and Arkansas. Drew presently operates the Veach Saddlery/Drew Clark Custom Saddles business located on the Clark-Beals Ranch near Colcord, Oklahoma.

Their life has never been dull. Imogene and Charley had a successful business in Tulsa, for which they were well respected. They collected a bevy of friends, both locally and in rodeo that lived all across our nation. Anything either of them could do to promote the sport of rodeo they were always willing to do.

Family has always been important to the couple. In fact, Imogene hosted the second International Vietch-Veatch-Veach-Veech Reunion, in 1977, in Tulsa. (Doesn't matter how you spell it, they are all related) The event has developed in to quite an annual affair for the Veach family members. The reunion is held annually and is hosted by a family member and held in different locales across the country. Imogene, her sisters, and daughter, have missed very few.

Imogene and daughter, Donna Kay, took a trip to Scotland, England and Wales, with the Veitch Historical Society members in 1983. They visited the family's ancestral home in Peebles, Scotland. After this, the two left the tour, and went by train to Cardiff, Wales, to visit a cousin of Charley's mother, Faye Jones Beals. Imogene never hesitated to venture forth on her own to learn more, especially about her family or rodeo.

A Tulsa Parade of Homes in 1966 was a must for the cowgirl. She always enjoyed seeing new innovations and ideas on decorating. With her unique style and creative mind she always found new ways to improve and add to their western-style décor. One of the houses in the Parade of Homes, on South Lakewood Avenue, grabbed Imogene's attention. She liked everything about it. In fact, she thought it was perfect!

When she got back to the saddle shop she told Charley about the house. He told her if she could figure out how to pay for it she could buy it. It didn't take long and she had it all worked out. By trading the house they lived in at the time, she could purchase it. Once the sale was made she pulled out all her decorating abilities and ideas and the Beal's new home turned in to a real western showplace.

Often Imogene would take her aging dad, Monroe Veach, on trips to various places. Sometimes her sisters would accompany them. It was usually to see a rodeo friend, or go to a specific rodeo, or to visit a saddle-making pal. Her father thoroughly enjoyed these trips, as did the daughters.

Finally, Charley and Imogene decided to retire from the saddle shop. It was 1984 and both still had their health and wanted to travel. They were still making memories, especially in the world of rodeo and with rodeo friends. The closing of the saddle shop, after forty years of business, was bittersweet. They had made so many connections and good friends. They would surely miss the flow of people in and out of their shop ordering, buying or just stopping by to visit. But it was time to have the freedom to do things they had put off. They liquidated the Veach Saddlery Company of Tulsa and sold the building.

Donna and Duke had moved to the family ranch near Colcord, Oklahoma, in 1973. Charley moved the remains of the saddle shop to the ranch. That way if he got the urge, or was asked to make a saddle, he still had a place to do it. Many of the numerous rodeo photographs that they had displayed in the Tulsa shop were moved, too. The history of the sport and those cowboys are shown in those old photos.

To the Outback!

The Beals had kept in contact with the Australian cowboys who had visited 20-odd years before. They began making their plans to visit Australia. They took a six week trip in 1986. Robin Yates and his family were their hosts. While there they went to the Mount Isa Rotary Rodeo, which was one of the best in the country. It amused Imogene that the rodeo stopped when a fight broke out between two fellows in the stands. It was stopped so all the spectators could watch, and enjoy the fight, too.

Yates took them many places, including the Lightning Ridge Opal mines, which was high on Imogene's list of places to visit. They also attended horse shows and visited a race horse farm. Since it was not smart to drive at night in the country, because the kangaroos were plentiful and one on the road could cause a serious wreck. This hazard often caused them to spend the night at various places on these excursions.

Yates had opened the Robin Yates Western Saddlery when he returned from the States in 1959. He claimed Charley had taught him enough while there that he felt confident to open his shop. It had become very successful. Charley received several orders for saddles from Australia after the cowboys had visited and returned home in 1959.

George Williams, an Oklahoma cowboy, had gotten well-acquainted with Charley and Imogene, in his young life. You might say they were much like parents to the young cowboy. He traveled to Australia before the Beals trip, and had been asked by Ellen Willoughby, at Wurabarra, South Australia, if he could find her a pen pal back in the States. When he returned he asked Imogene if she would write to Ellen. Of course, Imogene was most willing. The two women had corresponded for several years before the Beals' trip.

Ellen had extended an invitation for them to visit her and her family when they came. The Beals boarded a train in Sidney and rode for 28 hours across the country to Ellen's home, called Broken Hill. Ellen met the train and they stayed with her and her husband for several days. Ellen's sons were wranglers on movie sets which were made in their area. At the time of the Beals' visit they happened to be working on the movie *Robbery Under Arms*.

While visiting at Broken Hill the Beals' received a telephone call from the United States. In those days receiving a phone call when visiting a foreign country always gave everyone a concern that something tragic had happened back home. Charley went to the telephone in trepidation. Their grandson, Derek, had called to tell them he had won the saddle bronc competition at the big Cheyenne Frontier Days rodeo! He was so proud of his accomplishment, and although his grandparents were half a world away, it was important to him, and worth the expensive phone call, to share his success with them. They were his greatest fans. They were overjoyed to hear the news.

Rodeo Historical Society

The Rodeo Historical Society began in 1968. It started at the National Cowboy & Western Heritage Museum, located in Oklahoma City. It was formed 'to preserve and collect information regarding the history of professional rodeo.'

Charley and Imogene joined immediately upon hearing about it, but were only able to attend meetings on weekends, because of the Saddlery. After their return from 'down under' they continued to attend RHS events. This is where I first met them. During the National Finals Rodeo in Las Vegas the Rodeo Historical Society held several days of activities for members in 1987.

At a RHS social, I met them, and told them I was doing research for a book on the history of the rodeo clown. Charley was kind enough to introduce me to retired rodeo clowns, stock contractors, world champions and just about everybody attending. I have been eternally grateful for this gesture. It was evident he was well respected by all rodeo people. His support of my rodeo writings have been invaluable to me in meeting everyone connected with the sport.

The couple also attended as many cowboy reunions, rodeos and family get-togethers, around the country as possible. Charley was honored as the Saddle Maker of the Year by the Boot & Saddle Makers RoundUp in 1992. Paul Bond, of Nogales, Arizona, was honored as the Boot Maker that same year. This organization began in 1989, and was held at Burnet, Texas. Burnet was considered a central location, for most members, and many supplier displayed new innovations at this gathering. It was also an opportunity to meet and get to visit with some of their suppliers, as well as their contemporary craftsmen. It was at this gathering in 1992 my husband and I invited them to come and stay at our home in nearby Austin. This was the beginning of a lifelong friendship between our families.

The Rodeo Historical Society, in Oklahoma City, inducted Imogene's father, Monroe Veach, posthumously, in to the Hall of Fame in 1993 for his many contributions to the sport of rodeo. Beyond his saddlemaking skills he had produced rodeos, performed trick roping and continued to attend rodeo events. He died on Christmas Day in 1986. These honors are bestowed on the very elite in rodeo. It was a tremendous thrill for Imogene and her sisters, Mary, Letty and Peggy, to accept in his honor at the National Cowboy & Western Heritage Museum.

June and Buster Ivory, were good friends of the Beals. They were both very active in rodeo for years. June had grown up competing in barrel racing, and then became a top rodeo secretary. Buster was a roughstock competitor, like Charley, as well as being involved with the Rodeo Cowboy Association as secretary-manager for four years. He was also the National Finals Rodeo stock superintendent for the first 26 years. The Ivorys even took a rodeo tour to Europe one year.

In 1994, the Ivorys and the Beals traveled the west visiting various stock contractors, past and present, as well as their descendants, to gather information about their stock contracting rodeo experiences. A book was being planned by the Professional Rodeo Stock Contractors Association and they had asked these couples to do their fact-gathering. The two couples knew practically every stock provider in professional rodeo which made it a most delightful adventure. The book, *100 Years of Stock Contracting*, was published in 1997. The results of their travels and research is contained in a large 12" by 16" book chocked full of information, including photographs of the rich heritage of this essential part of rodeo that provides the best bucking and roping stock in the world.

The Ranch

The Clark-Beals Ranch, near Colcord, Oklahoma, where Duke and Donna had settled in 1973, is a short hour and a half east of Tulsa. While Imogene and Charley still had the Saddlery open it was an ideal get-away for them. For years Charley's aged parents also lived in Colcord, and when they

Imogene and Charley during the 50th Wedding Anniversary Party held in Tulsa, OK, 1990. *Photo courtesy of Imogene* Veach Beals

began having medical problems Donna looked after them.

Imogene and Charley celebrated 50 years of marriage January 14, 1990. Family and friends held a 50 Year Wedding Celebration for them at the Winning Colors Club Room at the Fairmeadows Race Track in Tulsa. The room was packed with well-wishers and those that had been friends for years. It was evident this couple was highly regarded by many – and rightly so. They both gave so much to their many friends, in rodeo and in their community.

Charley passed away December 27, 1994, after a year-long battle with cancer. The 'rodeo family' and the Veach-Beals-Clark loved ones all rallied at his side. Imogene handled this tragedy as well as could be expected. She had been his dark-haired darling, his companion, his business partner, and his loving wife for 54 years. The years ahead would change a great deal for this strong woman.

Imogene continued to live in Tulsa in the house on South Lakewood Drive that she and Charley enjoyed for the next few years. There were some things she just couldn't face without Charley. Going to the National Finals Rodeo in Las Vegas and helping June and Buster Ivory, Bobby and Phyllis Clark and Harry Tompkins with the Cowboy Reunion was especially difficult, and she stopped going for a few years.

The reunion is a very successful three day gathering of 'the competitors of yesterday'. At this gathering of old-timers with bent, crippled legs and wrinkles galore, many stories were shared and retold over and over again. Visits among cowboys and cowgirls who hadn't seen one another in 'a coon's age' are cherished. It was one of the highlights for Charley each year. Imogene just had to let a little time pass before she could consider going again.

Imogene horseback holding the flag at a Veach family gathering held in Kansas City, 1996. *Photo courtesy of Imogene Veach Beals.*

It was just too painful. But she kept busy and in time she did return to see and visit with long-time friends.

Donna and Duke lived in a house on the ranch near Colcord that had been built many years before. With time and wear the old house had many problems that they knew had to be improved or replaced. They encouraged Imogene to move from Tulsa to the ranch. They wanted her to be nearer to them. They knew their present house was not big enough for the change.

The three decided a new house needed to be built at the ranch. Imogene kept very busy designing and working on the plans that would satisfy both Imogene's needs, as well as Donna and Duke's needs. This took much thought as well as design. Lots of communication back and forth, plus a few compromises between the three that would live there. The house was completed in 1997 and Imogene sold her Tulsa home and moved – lock, stock and barrel, to the ranch.

The house is perfect for this trio. It is one story, set in a pastoral setting, with horses grazing behind and to one side of the house. Imogene's every need is in one wing, which includes her study, with shelves loaded with rodeo-related books, scrapbooks, and memorabilia, plus her television, comfortable chairs and a fireplace. She spends hours each day in her study doing research, reading, writing letters and cards to friends. She also finds information for various museums regarding early-day rodeo when asked. She has continued to be a great source of historic information for reporters, as well as other historians about rodeo, Oklahoma, and the people she has known.

The common area of the new ranch house, such as the kitchen, dining area and living room are in the middle. The opposite end of the house is Donna and Duke's bedroom and private area. The compatibility of this family has little need for separation as they are very close, and yet extremely considerate and thoughtful of one another. They also know and respect each person's need for their own space. The décor is just what you would imagine – western paintings, many done by Orren Mixer, and a plethora of rodeo memorabilia. It is perfect for this family immersed in the western way of life. Imogene continues to use her decorating talents and she still re-vamps clothes to fit the times.

Her move to the country was easy. There were many visits made to family and friends. This is also when she started traveling with me to rodeos, and other western events, which often involved gathering material for my books on the history of rodeo.

She and Charley had been collecting rodeo magazines, rodeo programs, books, photographs, and friends for more than 50 years. Every trip or visit she and I made just added more to her collection. Two of her grandsons, Derek and Drew, live on or near the ranch. Doug lives just a few hours away near Wayne, Oklahoma. Imogene has had the good fortune to have much contact and time with her entire family including grandchildren and great-grandchildren.

Our Travels and Adventures

As I stated at the beginning of this chapter, Imogene and I traveled to many rodeo-related destinations with the desire to gather historic and present-day information from cowboys and cowgirls, interview as many as possible, as well as learn more about the history of the sport.

On one of our trips to Cheyenne Frontier Days we decided to stay in the long-time popular Plains Hotel in Cheyenne. It had been under renovation for some time, and they had hoped it would be completed before Frontier Days began. Those ten days in July was the biggest celebration of the year in the Wyoming capitol and the town would be overflowing with spectators. Although we had reservations they hadn't quite finished their construction. Our room, on the second floor, was completed but down the hall workmen could be seen and heard working at a frenzied pace in and out of unfinished rooms. Every day, when we left our room to go to the rodeo we made sure our room was locked. Every evening when we returned the door to our room would be standing open. None of our belongings were ever taken or

Imogene and author taken at the Rodeo Historical Society Rodeo weekend at the National Cowboy & Western Heritage Museum in Oklahoma City in 2012. *Photo courtesy of ownbeyphotography.com.*

moved. I'm sure it was just workers doing their daily tasks. Since we suffered no loss, we thought it rather humorous.

One afternoon we stopped by the Plains Hotel bar for a drink. Imogene is a 'teetotaler' so she enjoyed a coke while I had a drink. We were joined by a cowboy we knew and as we sat at the bar talking with him, he said to Imogene, "May I tell you something?"

Imogene said, "Of course." Not giving it much thought.

He said, "You are the most beautiful lady I've ever seen, and ma'am, I mean that as a compliment. I'm not getting fresh."

Imogene thanked him, and quickly changed the subject.

The following morning at breakfast I told her I was going to have to quit traveling with her. When she looked at me in shock, not knowing why I had said that, I told her she got all the compliments and I was getting an inferiority complex. She knew I was joking, and we had a good laugh over it, but frankly at her age, (which was well over 80 at the time) she is always well-dressed, of course always western, and every hair is in place, and she has beautiful skin. She truly is a most beautiful lady, both inside and out.

On another of our 'adventures' to Pendleton Round-Up in 2005, we had seats in the media booth, which is adjacent and above the bucking chutes. Round-Up has a tradition; at the last performance, the winner of each event is announced then rides in to the arena on horseback and goes in front of the main grandstand, where dignitaries wait to present them with all their winnings. That year, Imogene's grandson, Doug Clark, won the steer roping. When his name was announced as winner we waited for him to appear.

The wait seemed to be too long. Where was he, had he gone back to his rig unaware he had won? I thought Imogene was going to 'leap over the railing' where she was standing and go collect his winnings for him. Finally, he appeared. Talk about a proud grandmother, Imogene was thrilled to be there to see him accept his rewards.

Our trips together have been much fun and we met so many people, mainly rodeo competitors and their family members, plus fans. We never encountered any serious problems and have traveled mostly by car or by SUV. Imogene's grandson, Derek Clark, told some of his rodeo friends, when he was competing, he never knew when or where his grandma would show up. Competing cowboys and cowgirls have a 'fast track' to get to as many rodeos as they can in a short period of time. Especially if they are working toward making the top fifteen, in their event, and be eligible for the National Finals Rodeo. Derek decided his grandma was on a 'fast track,' as well.

Imogene's 'bucket list' was complete when her beloved Charley was inducted in to the Rodeo Historical Society Hall of Fame in 2010.

What an amazing life Imogene Veach Beals has had. Her mind is constantly busy and active by reading and researching about the people, who have made the history of this magnificent sport of rodeo, as well as what is happening in the sport today. Imogene has certainly been an integral part of it. She was honored with the Tad Lucas Award, given by the Rodeo Historical Society, in 2001 for all her rodeo-related accomplishments and a lifetime dedicated to the sport of rodeo. The honor was well deserved. At the age of 92 her mind is as sharp as ever. She has a wealth of rodeo history and amazingly knows just where to find it. Imogene has certainly dared to be different!

The World Champion of Western Couture
Patricia Wolf

Patricia Wolf is known in the Western clothing world by women as one of the best couturiers of any era. She has been doing it for over a quarter of a century. But her passion for design started much earlier, although, she had a major detour in her young life which she also felt very strongly about. The twists and turns that she encountered and how she handled them all, makes her a perfect candidate for this book.

As a young girl of ten, with her mother's guidance, she made her first dress. It was a lilac cotton sundress with a scalloped bodice. After that no piece of clothing she owned was safe. She embroidered designs on anything she owned to make it unique. She always de-constructed her jeans, adding holes that didn't exist so she could put interesting fabric to peek through the holes. Often she added braiding and all kinds of fun additions. She even beaded the moccasins she wore.

But this fascinating woman had a most interesting journey from childhood to reach this plateau. She lived in the eastern part of the United States where 'western décor and clothing' were generally unavailable and seldom seen, except on a movie screen. Her life holds a series of developments, each unique to the next, before she entered the world of Western couture. She truly dared to be different.

Her Story

Patricia Wolf was born Patricia Ott in Philadelphia, Pennsylvania, to John and Bernice Ott, on April 1, 1942, 15 minutes before midnight. Her father was a tool and die man who belonged to the machinist union. The family, of Irish and German descent, was Democrat, through and through. No arguments. No discussions. The family always voted a straight Democrat ticket! Her father was asked by his company to take a promotion and hold a supervisory position. This meant he could no longer belong to the machinist union. He refused. He was very dedicated to his union.

Patricia's mother was a stay-at-home mom, and had her hands full raising seven children. After first born, Patricia then came along Joan, a year and a half later. Next, Christine was born, then Bill, Denise, Amy, and Matthew. After Patricia left home mother Bernice became a school crossing guard. In Philadelphia, at that time, school crossing guards were trained by the police department. They were required to wear uniforms and got the same benefits policemen received.

Patricia wears her favorite outfit, a green canvas cowgirl skirt and vest with plastic trim.
Photo courtesy of Patricia Wolf.

Her Cowgirl Outfit

As a youngster, around five, Patricia had developed a fascination with Texas. She had posters on the wall in her room of Texas (which now she thinks were probably photos of Arizona). She, no doubt, had seen these scenes in western movies of that era. She made up her mind she wanted to live in Texas. She loved the cowgirl look. Her folks bought her a green canvas cowgirl skirt and vest, trimmed in brown plastic fringe. She wore it constantly. It finally got so dirty her mother had to wash it. When she dried the outfit the plastic fringe rolled up, but Patricia continued to wear it, as it was still her favorite outfit.

A Tragedy

Patricia was first born, but 18 months later along came Joan. They were very close and played together most all day every day. At age five and a half Joan got an illness in those days they called brain fever. Her fever was very high. Unaware little Joan was allergic to penicillin, the medicine of choice in those days; this was given to her, hoping to lower her high temperature. Instead her fever soared even higher, and she died.

Patricia in her communion dress with her little sister, Joan. *Photo courtesy of Patricia Wolf.*

Little Joan had always looked up to big sister Patricia. When Patricia took her first Holy Communion she wore a beautiful white dress. Joan loved the dress and was looking forward to inheriting it for her first Holy Communion. Instead she was buried in the beautiful white dress.

Patricia, at age seven, had never been exposed to death before, and it had taken her baby sister! When someone lifted her to see her sister-playmate in the coffin Patricia thought Joan looked as if she was sleeping. She reached down to give her little sister a kiss. When her lips touched Joan's cheek if felt hard and cold as marble; a chill went down Patricia's spine and she began to scream fearfully. Someone hurried her up the stairs at the funeral home where the funeral director's family lived. Once she quit crying she realized there were other children there. For a time, Patricia sat and watched a children's program on a tiny television with the director's children until she was calm.

Following that horrible experience Patricia began to have nightmares about the funeral experience. She would wake up and think she could see Joan at the foot of her bed. She had night sweats and cold chills. She began going to her new baby sister Christine's crib and climbing in it where her parents would find her sleeping in the crib. They finally decided the best thing to do was take Patricia and baby sister, Christine, to a relative's house at the beach. Hoping the change in place would stop the nightmares. Patricia remembers the beach seemed like a very calm place to her, and eventually the trauma of Joan's death disappeared. To this day Patricia still enjoys the beach and its calming influence.

The Ott family was Catholic. All seven youngsters went to Catholic school. In her parent's generation, it was a Catholic family tradition, the oldest boy and girl in the family, should consider either the priesthood or becoming a nun. When Patricia was in the sixth grade she knew she wanted to become a nun, but she never talked about it and she never told a soul.

When Patricia was in the eighth grade two nuns visited her class at Saint Matthew Parish School. One of the nuns asked how many in the class were considering joining a religious order, which meant becoming a priest or nun. Patricia remembers everyone in the class raised their hands – but her. She thought to herself, "This is a bunch of stupid people! I'm the only one who is really going to go, and it's none of their business." She never raised her hand. Today she admits she always had a bit of a 'rebel attitude.'

Patricia's family was a typical middle class family. Her parents never encouraged further education after high school. Patricia was committed to the Church. She went to mass every morning, and took communion. The Catholic rule was to fast from midnight until you have communion. Every morning she grabbed something she could eat, on the way to school, after communion. She was very dedicated.

When she turned 14 she was old enough to work and was hired at the Catholic Nazareth Hospital. She desperately wanted to earn her own money. Her first job was taking care of bedpans and such, but shortly, she was assigned to work in the doctor's kitchen. She helped the nuns prepare meals for the doctors. Since she was under-age, the law did not allow her to work after 10 p.m. Today, she remembers that she would often clock out at 10 p.m., and return to work even though she didn't get paid for the extra time. On Christmas Eve she worked until midnight.

Everyone in the kitchen was required to wear a scarf over their hair. One day she forgot her scarf and found a 'babushka,' that one of the Polish immigrant women that worked in the kitchen, had forgotten to take home. These immigrant women were known for not being too clean. Patricia wore the 'babushka' on her head during working hours.

A day or so later she discovered she had lice!! Everyone at that time called them 'COOTIES' and she was mortified! When it was discovered she had lice her mother was stunned. It was common knowledge only dirty people got lice! How did her daughter end up with these 'cooties'? Patricia finally admitted she had used one of the Polish ladies' 'babushkas.'

Patricia had long, thick, black hair and it was extremely difficult for her mother to meticulously use a special comb to rid her oldest daughter of the dreaded bugs. Her mother was also concerned her other children would get them from their sister. They were extremely cautious and her mother was forever laundering the bedclothes. Fortunately, Patricia was the only one in the family that caught the 'cooties'.

Patricia felt she was an 'ugly duckling' as a youngster. In junior high she was skinny and taller than most of the boys in her class. At ten years old she began to wear braces. She remembered she and some of her friends were playing a kissing game and no one wanted to kiss her. She went home and cried and cried. Her mother and dad felt terrible that their daughter had to endure such rejection. They didn't know what to say.

A few days later she was reading the Sunday funnies and the sun was shining in through the window on her face. She heard her dad say to her mom, "Look at her, she's so beautiful! How could any boy not want to be with her?"

He walked over to where Patricia sat reading, put his arm around her shoulders and said, "You're going to be a late bloomer, and you'll keep getting more and more beautiful all your life."

By the time she entered Saint Hubert High School her father's prediction had become a reality. Her teeth were straightened; she had filled out and was quite shapely. She never wanted for boyfriends. But she never waivered from her decision as a 6th grader to become a nun. When she began dating a classmate she said, "I just laid it out to them. I was going to become a nun when I graduated. That didn't seem to bother any of the boys. I still had lots of boyfriends. Most were Catholic, and I even dated one Jewish boy." She was socially active in school. She joined the drama, Latin and French clubs and was also active in student government.

When she was 16 she got the dreaded chicken pox from her younger siblings. She had an extremely hard case of it. She swelled up like a balloon, and itched inside and out. Still wearing braces her mouth was so swollen the inside of her mouth was bleeding. When her mother called Patricia's orthodontist, he sent his wife to the Ott house to remove some of Patricia's braces, just to give her some relief.

As a youth Patricia attended a summer camp called the Red Feather Lighthouse Camp. It was a typical summer camp in Chester Springs, Pennsylvania. It was lots of fun, swimming, hiking and just being a kid. At first she was a camper, then a junior counselor and finally a full-fledged Coun-

Graduation photo of Patricia from Saint Hubert High School. *Photo courtesy of Patricia Wolf.*

selor.

As a counselor she met some Quaker people there and joined them on weekends packing lunches and helping to weatherize the homes of elderly poor people. Sometimes they had only a sheet, instead of glass, in their windows. Everyone had a partner with whom to work in this project and Patricia's partner was a Merchant Marine about 15 years older than her. It was rewarding work and she enjoyed the association she had with all ages of people and from different walks of life.

Patricia told one of the nuns at school about her weekend work. The nun called her aside and told her she could no longer work with that organization because it was not through her Catholic affiliation. The nun said Catholics had similar programs and she could work with them. Her 'rebel feelings' popped up again and she resented being told she should not be working with these people that did so much good for people that needed help.

But, like a good Catholic girl, she followed the nun's admonition. She began working with a Catholic club sponsored by the Sisters, but it did not have the direct association with the poor. Patricia spent her time writing speeches to encourage people to be inspired to do work for the indigent. She truly missed the 'hands on' experience she had previously enjoyed with her Quaker friends.

The ruling in the Catholic Church did not allow a student to actually apply to be a nun until they were a senior in high school. Patricia admired and thought a great deal of her art teacher, Sister Mary Magdalene. The first day of her senior school year, she went to Sister Mary Magdalene and asked her to be her sponsor. She also asked her aunt, Sister Eleanor, to be a sponsor.

Patricia Announces Her Decision

At the dinner table in the Ott home each evening the family discussed a variety of different things. Sometimes the subject was sex, other times murders, gory details were even described. No subject was too shocking to be discussed among the family. Patricia felt the dinner hour was the proper time to announce to her family her decision to become a nun.

When she announced it she said, "Mother, will you go with me to an appointment I have with Mother Superior? I want to become a nun."

Everyone at the table was shocked and sat looking at her in stunned silence. Finally the silence was broken when her little brother, Bill, burst in to tears.

When the uproar and crying stopped, her parents asked what Order she was considering. She mentioned she was considering the Carmelite Cloister. This is an Order where, those who were accepted, spent their life in prayer, meditation and work, and never see or speak to their family again. Patricia went on to tell them if she didn't join the Carmelites she would join an Order that went on medical missions to Africa, where they blended their religious teachings with medical work. When Patricia finished telling them of the Orders she had chosen her mother burst in to tears, saying she would never see her daughter again.

When the time came Patricia finally chose to join the Sisters of Saint Joseph. This group of nuns was allowed to go to college and train to be teachers. The Convent was located in Chestnut Hills, a section of Philadelphia. Part of the acceptance process was to be given a physical. Next she was given some questions to answer to determine if, by her answers, she was a likely candidate. In the word association portion of the questionnaire she was to define or describe the word listed. When she got the word 'dating' her rebelliousness popped up again, as it did in eighth grade when she wouldn't let anyone know she planned on being a nun. She answered the word by writing: "Dating papers is very important for organization."

She passed the physical and the tests. Next she was to bring a 'dowry' of $500, and a steamer trunk with the specific clothing she was required to wear once she was received. All the items had to be bought at a specific store, which included a corset, chemise, a certain type underwear, and a specific type of brassiere.

To earn money for the dowry that summer she worked in downtown

Philadelphia at Rumsey Electric Company. Her job was in their filing room. She remembers that her supervisor fell in love with her. They attended a tent revival in Feasterville which was most interesting to Patricia. She had never been to a revival as the Catholic faith had nothing like it.

The night before she was to enter the convent hurricane-like winds blew down trees and did a tremendous amount of damage to the area where she lived and in the direction of the Convent of the Sisters of Saint Joseph, in Chestnut Hills. It was almost impossible to get there the next morning as the city hadn't had time to clean up the debris.

The group of girls going in to the Order for the first time is called a 'party.' Patricia remembers her 'party' included 105 girls, six others were also named Patricia. The usual amount of a party, up until then had been around 20 girls, this was an exceptionally large 'party.' They were the first of the 'Baby Boomer' generation.

Patricia had one bad habit; she had started smoking when she was 14. When she picked up the habit, as many youngsters do, she would steal her parents' cigarettes. Her Christmas present from her folks was a carton of cigarettes when she was 16. They told her from now on she was to stop 'stealing' their cigarettes and buy her own.

Of course, when she entered the convent, the cigarette smoking habit had to disappear. However, on her way to the Convent she smoked her last cigarette. Her sponsor, Sister Mary Magdalene, who was taking her, said disgustingly, "You are smoking in your black and whites!"

Before she entered the convent door she flipped her cigarette to the ground. Was Patricia's 'rebel attitude' coming out again?

As she entered the parlor where they were to meet she looked around and realized practically all the girls were crying. Patricia was shocked, "I couldn't understand why they were so sad. I thought it should be the best day of our lives."

The girls were overwhelmed with emotion as they said good bye to their family members. The realization they would no longer be living with their families had set it. She remembers some of the girls went so far as to change their minds and dropped out that very evening.

For the next six months Patricia was classified as a postulant. In the dictionary, the definition is 'a candidate for admission in to a religious order.' The postulant was required to wear black clothing, stockings and shoes. She

Sister John Matthew (Patricia) after taking her vows. *Photo courtesy of Patricia Wolf.*

still had her long black hair. The head is not shaved until after Reception Day when they became a novice. In six months time, 25 to 30 girls that had entered the convent in Patricia's 'party' had dropped out.

Reception Day is when the postulants are officially received. There is a ceremony much like a wedding ceremony. Every postulant wears a wedding dress. During this ceremony as each girl is presented it is announced, "Patricia Mary Ott no longer exists. Sister John Matthew is now married to Christ." At that moment each postulant becomes a novice. A novice is described as 'someone who has joined a religious order but has not yet taken their final vows'.

Sister John Matthew

Prior to the 'wedding ceremony' each postulant is to pick three choices of names to be called as a Sister. Their given name is not acceptable. If the postulant has no preferences she asks for 'God's will' in a name. This merely means the people of the Church will choose names for the girl. Patricia picked John, because it was her father's first name and Matthew because she attended Saint Matthew's Parish School.

Once the novices are announced by their new names they are escorted to a dressing area where they remove their wedding dress and get in to their habit. Then as a group they return to the church. They are not supposed to look at anyone in the audience. Patricia, with head bowed, knew she heard her mother burst into tears when she saw her daughter in her habit for the first time.

As novices, in the Order of Saint Joseph, they were allowed to go to college and learn to be a teacher. The college they attended was on the same campus as the convent. It generally takes a novice two and a half years to get a bachelor's degree because they go right through all year, with no breaks for summer. Novices do not fraternize with the other students in college and on campus. They walk to and from the 'Mother house' in which they lived. Patricia took all the required courses to become a teacher.

The steps necessary to become a full-fledged nun are numerous, and it takes approximately ten years to reach the top level. The Catholic Church hierarchy wants to be absolutely certain each person is totally committed to the requirements of the religious order.

Becoming a Teacher

The next step for Patricia—Oops, Sister John Matthew—was to take the vows of poverty, chastity and obedience, to become a junior sister. Sister John Matthew's first mission as a junior sister was at Saint Bartholomew School located on the same campus as the convent. She was sent to teach a fifth grade class. Although she had not received her teaching degree, they were still allowed to teach. However, teaching fifth grade was unusual for a junior sister. They were usually asked to teach the second and third grades, never the higher grades.

The nuns were never seen coming and going to a destination alone. They always traveled in pairs. Her mentor, Sister Saint Claire was supposed to be a help to Sister John Matthew for her first year. Unfortunately, instead of being a mentor she was more of a 'tormentor' to the young sister.

Sister Saint Claire was manipulative, and put much of the menial preparation work of teaching on Sister John Matthew. Especially the art work decorating their classrooms. Sister John Matthew always had talent as an artist.

Since she still had to complete her education, Sister John Matthew went to college on Saturday. Sister Saint Lawrence was her partner, a friendly girl, not five feet tall, from her party.

The bus route was quite lengthy and the sisters were the first on, and the last off. Sister John Matthew suffered from motion sickness. By the time they reached the college she was quite nauseated from the ride. She spent most Saturdays in the infirmary throwing up. Eventually, Sister John Matthew was given special permission for her father to drive her and her partner, Sister Saint Lawrence, to the college and return them to the convent after class.

"One day on our way back to the convent my dad took us to our house, which was forbidden by the Church," recalled Patricia. She asked the rather plump Sister Saint Lawrence who was with her, "Are you going to tell on me?"

The chubby Sister answered, "Not if your mom has food."

When Sister John Matthew knocked on the door her mother answered and about fainted she was so surprised to see her daughter. After her mother recovered from the shock she ran and told all their close neighbors the news. One by one they came to see their neighborhood novice, Patricia – oops, Sister John Matthew. Everyone was thrilled to see her.

Patricia remembers when she got to her childhood home she had been gone quite a while. She had been in the Convent, the Church and large school buildings for so long. She said the house looked very small. It was difficult for her to realize her family had lived in such tight quarters. One bathroom took care of nine people.

"It seemed surreal. I then realized why that was one of the reasons the Church forbade young sisters from going home," she said.

Another year passed, and it was time for the sisters to take their vows of poverty, chastity and obedience again. Sister John Matthew was teaching eighth grade. She spent her time out of class saying all her prayers and preparing for her class.

One day in class the subject was about adultery and divorce. She told the class that the Church didn't condone adultery or divorce. In her eighth grade class was a mentally challenged student, Richie, who suddenly began to cry as they discussed the Church's views on adultery and divorce. Sister John Matthew discovered while talking with Richie that his mother had been abused by his father, and was in a wheelchair because of the injuries she sustained. Richie's mother had divorced his father.

Richie and his mother now lived alone. Richie was worried about his mother being considered a bad person by the Church because she divorced his father. Sister John Matthew consoled Richie and told him his mother was a good woman and that what she had said about the Church's view did not include his mother. He finally stopped crying.

A few days later Mother Superior called Sister John Matthew to her office. When she arrived she found that Richie's mother had called to commend Sister John Matthew for the way she had handled Richie in class.

Richie's mother told Mother Superior since she divorced his father Richie had been worried about how the Church felt about his mother being divorced. Richie had tossed and turned night after night and had a very hard time sleeping. Richie's mother had told the Mother Superior after Sister John Matthew told him his mother was a good person and the Church did not include his mother in their position on divorce. Richie had finally been relieved. For the first time, since the divorce, Richie had slept through the night.

Instead of commending Sister John Matthew for how she handled the situation Mother Superior said to her, "Who told you to rewrite church doctrine?"

Sister John Matthew was given penance for her actions. She was required to help cleanup after a fundraising jubilee that had been held on the church grounds. During the clean-up Patricia found a bottle, half full of green liquid. It happened to be one of the liquors that had been served during the Jubilee. It was crème de menthe.

"I slugged it down and later that night I was howling at the moon," laughed Patricia, as she recalled the incident.

"When Mother Superior called me in I told her I didn't know it was liquor. It just tasted sweet, so I drank it," chuckled Patricia.

Mother Superior gave Sister John Matthew another penance.

Sometimes for penance the sister had to kneel at the door of the refectory (dining hall) and kiss the sisters' feet as they passed by. Another penance was to go to the sisters in the refectory on your knees and beg for food.

"One time all the sisters gave me nothing but mashed potatoes," she laughed. It seems although they were dedicated to the church they still had their sense of humor.

The nuns put on plays. *The Sound of Music* was chosen. The sisters had rewritten the words of the songs in the musical, to include words describing the life of a nun in the Convent.

"We are 16 going on 17" was changed to say "We are postulants going on novices, innocent as a rose". When they performed for the audience, people enjoyed it so much, Mother Marie Estelle, the mistress of novices, and director of the musical decided to 'take it on the road.'

Actually, 'taking it on the road' meant from time to time, Mother Marie Estelle would call the performing and singing sisters together and announce she had invited nuns from another convent to come and see it for the first time. They performed it again and again.

The End of an Era

Another year went by and it was time to take their vows again. During the year Sister John Matthew had been experiencing some health problems. She wasn't sleeping well; she had stomach aches, and had been losing weight. One day at the school where she taught she had a fainting spell during recess. As she was lying on the steps before she recovered she heard a student saying, "Don't touch her, she's a nun, get the snow shovel." Sister John Matthew could never understand what the young man meant by his reference to 'get the snow shovel.'

When taking their vows the sisters were required to kneel down, put their praying hands in Mother Superior's lap and she would say, "Are you ready to take your vows?"

This year when it was Sister John Matthew's turn and she knelt in front of Mother Superior and was asked the question, "Are you ready to take your vows?"

Sister John Matthew yelled, "No!"

Even Sister John Matthew was surprised at her own answer. But what was done, was done! Mother Superior or someone in her staff took Sister John Matthew to doctors, priests, and even a psychologist. Their conclusion was that Sister John Matthew was on the verge of a nervous breakdown.

"I just couldn't do it," admitted Patricia. She tried her best but it just wasn't God's will that she become a nun.

After all the meetings with doctors, priests, and psychologists and her evaluation was completed, she was told to come to the parlor of the Convent. When Sister John Matthew arrived Mother Superior was standing there next to a suitcase.

Sister John Matthew stood in front of Mother Superior who said, "We are going to send you home today. Your mother has brought you some clothes to wear. Go put them on and come back in here. Your mother will be waiting for you."

Patricia went back to her cell (each sister's room is called a cell and no one else is allowed in another sister's cell). She took off her habit and dressed in the clothes her mother had brought. When her mother received the call to come get her daughter, she hurriedly brought her own clothes even though she was larger than her daughter.

When Patricia put on the clothes from the suitcase they were several sizes too large. The clothes just hung on her. When she went back to the parlor she was a sad sight for her mother to see. Her mother burst in to tears at the sight of her. Patricia's mother was very emotional and cried often. Patricia admits she inherited that same trait from her mother.

Mother Superior said to Patricia, "Don't ever be ashamed,—you tried." Then after a long pause, she added, "Just don't bring your babies back to visit us."

She handed Patricia her $500 dowry and said, "Go buy yourself some new clothes."

Patricia and her mother walked out of the Convent silently. Her uncle, a taxi driver, was waiting for them. When they got in the taxi he handed Patricia a cigarette and a beer and said, "It will all be better soon, Patricia."

It had been a long time since she had been called Patricia.

A New Life

She hardly remembers what happened when she first went home. She spent three years in the Convent. She was in shock. She continued to do the same thing she did at the convent—pray, fast, go to mass, and take communion every day. It took awhile before she could adjust to the life she knew before she made her commitment to become a nun.

Her girlfriends were thrilled to have Patricia back. They came to see her as soon as they heard the news. In time she was part of the group just as she had been three years before. One day her girlfriends announced they were going to take Patricia to the beach with them for the summer. They said they would all get jobs at the beach, in the various hotels and tourist attractions.

Patricia got a job at a place called Wildwood Manor in New Jersey. It was one of the oldest nightclubs and hotels in the area. They had a supper club and many of the big-time entertainers of the day were performing there, such as Phyllis Diller and Tony Bennett. Patricia was required to wear a little short outfit and serve the customers of the supper club.

After the summer at the beach Patricia came home refreshed and was ready to take the next step in her life. She immediately went to teaching school. It wasn't as fulfilling as she expected. She decided she would look for another type of job.

Her early training to be a seamstress came back and she designed a 'Ralph Lauren'-styled suit, in navy blue. She could sew and make anything she wanted. Her hair had grown out by then and she put it up in a bun, and went to the Bell Telephone Company to apply for a job. She looked very professional.

The person that interviewed her said, "You look just like Holly Golightly!" Patricia was thrilled as that was quite a compliment. Holly Golightly was a character in a very popular movie, *Breakfast at Tiffany's*, and was played by movie star Audrey Hepburn. Patricia got the job as a service representative.

She had also applied for an airline hostess position with Trans World Airlines. In the initial interview she dropped her purse and her lipstick rolled under the interviewer's desk. When she got down on her hands and knees to retrieve the lipstick she knew she had blown her chances of getting that job. Had she been hired, her tendency to get motion sickness was bound to cause her to 'wash out' when flying. Things happen for a reason.

She began dating again soon after leaving the convent. In the fall, she became engaged to Tom Sweeney, a teacher at Saint Josephs, a private preparatory school for boys. The engagement was short-lived as they eventually broke up.

Patricia had stopped going to mass, communion and confession. Her father confronted her about not going to church and gave her an ultimatum. Either abide by his rules and go to mass, communion and confession or leave the house.

Patricia knew it was time to leave home. She packed her bags and moved to Hermosa Beach, California. Her grandparents had moved there just a few years earlier. She went to work at Sears, and bought herself a small motorcycle for transportation to get to and from her job. It wasn't long before Patricia met some other girls and moved out of her grandparents' home and in to an apartment with the girls.

The 1960s

This was the Age of Aquarius, the 1960s, Flower Power and Free Love! As *Abba*, the famous Swedish pop group sang "It was the age of free love and the age of no regrets."

Many people, especially the young adults of this era, slipped easily in to a new life-style. They were called Hippies. The Baby Boomers had become adults and were seeking something different. Peace and love, man! Patricia was no exception.

One day while walking leisurely on the beach, her favorite place in the world, Patricia noticed two people walking toward her. As they got close enough she recognized the woman as her friend Lynn, who called, "Patricia, please meet my baby brother!"

She looked at the young man with Lynn, who she said certainly did not look like someone's baby brother to her. He looked like a 'sun god.' His name was Bill Wolf. After talking for awhile she learned he was going to college in Colorado on a football scholarship, but was also very interested in art. He was visiting his sister, Lynn and her husband, but had to leave shortly to get back to college.

A year later, Patricia, and her roommates, were preparing for the upcoming Thanksgiving. They decided to invite some of their friends for Thanksgiving dinner. Patricia thought of Lynn and her husband, and went to their place to extend the invitation. When she arrived 'baby brother' Bill was there. Lynn and her husband had gone to visit his family for the holiday. Bill had a college friend with him so Patricia invited them to come for Thanksgiving dinner.

The fellows accepted the invitation, as did other friends. After their lavish dinner Bill headed to the kitchen and washed all the dishes. Patricia says, "In fact, he never left — I knew he was a 'keeper.'"

After a year of being together Bill began to be concerned that he had not completed his college education. He and Patricia talked it over and they decided he had no choice; he must go back and get his college degree. When he left Patricia felt her heart was broken. She feared she might never see him again. She knew he was her soul mate but knew she could not stand in his way. He had to go back to school or he would forever wish he had.

Life went on for Patricia. But after a couple of semesters away from each other Bill returned. He missed Patricia as much as she missed him. They both knew they were very much in love and if they were together they knew they could do anything they wanted to do.

Bill had been into skydiving previously, but sold his parachute and bought a car to get back to California and Patricia. She had a panel truck, in which they lived for a time. She was designing and making dresses and blouses out of used lace tablecloths she would buy at the Saint Vincent de Paul thrift store. On the weekends they would browse the local boutiques and sell her designs.

Bill sold his car and bought a treadle sewing machine. He also decided to change his name to Sam. He just felt more like a Sam, than Bill, and Patricia liked the name Sam. Lots of changes were taking place in their lives. It didn't take long before they decided the panel truck was too small for them to continue living in. They put it up for sale and sold it in no time.

They used the money from selling the panel truck to buy a used 1951 school bus from Gillig Manufacturing. The bus had previously been a Mount Shasta school bus and still had Mount Shasta written on the side of the bus and on all the seats. Their plan was to convert the school bus to a living space where they could work and sleep. It was 1970 and they bought it with the intent the bus would be their new home.

The Grateful Dead Connection

The bus license plate was 150 AHH. Unknown to Sam and Patricia the band, the *Grateful Dead*, who became so popular and stayed on the top of the music charts for years, came to the Gillig Manufacturing plant the same day, and bought the second Mount Shasta bus.

The *Grateful Dead* was an American rock band that formed in 1965 in Palo Alto, California. Their music was so unique; they would blend music types such as country, bluegrass, psychelic, etc., and get result other bands of the era had not found. The *Grateful Dead* license plate was 151 AHH, just one number different than Patricia and Sam's bus.

Patricia laughingly said every time they would go to a *Grateful Dead* concert they never had to pay. People directing traffic at the concerts, would look at their license plate, and assume they were 'family' since their license was only one digit different than the band. They always had an up-close parking spot for the music.

The school bus in time took on a very different look than that of a school bus. Sam used an old airplane canopy as a skylight, which let in a lot more light. It also allowed anyone over 5'7", like Sam, to stand up straight in the bus. They quickly put the interior decor in place, to be liveable and made a work area.

They spent their time making denim and lace jackets, sheepskin coats, leather caps, leather sandals, baby moccasins and even gourds with bamboo and dried flowers. They had two treadle sewing machines and at times both were busy being used. Sam also made jewelry using silver and gemstones. They traveled up and down the west coast from one art festival to the next. Having everything they needed under one roof allowed them to set up at art shows easily and at the same time keep an eye on their growing family. They all ready had one son, Indio, and were expecting another.

Another Baby

When it was time to have their second child they decided they would handle the birth themselves. Sam's mother was a nurse and had given them the birthing instruments they would need. They read all the books on birthing and just knew they were prepared. They would have their newborn at home, in the bus.

Their young son, Indio, was thrilled with the upcoming birth and wanted to be there, too. When Patricia went in to labor they were ready. "We can do this," they both said.

The Wolf family dressed at Christmas in their *Age of Aquarius* garb. *Photo courtesy of Patricia Wolf.*

However, things got difficult. When Indio saw blood he was immediately sent to stay with a neighbor. Sam and Patricia proceeded. The birth was long and difficult. After the birth, a boy they named Zachary, Patricia did go to a hospital for repairs she had incurred. Today she says of their birthing experience, "Don't try birthing at home without the proper help!"

Once Patricia had recovered all was well with their world again. Their home, the bus, was their safe haven. The family was happy and content. The boys grew and became their pride and joy. Meanwhile they continued to create and work on their art.

Patricia has always considered leather as her main medium. Her Western designs always sold well. In those days there was very little Western clothing to choose from and purchase except blue jeans, square dance dresses and polyester shirts. She added embellishments to her unusual leather clothing like antler and silver buttons, twisted fringe and beading. She was a front-runner in using these unique items. Other designers had rarely considered using these ornamental extras in those days.

In between art shows, they would find a secluded park, or federal land, and stay for there for awhile. They would use kerosene lanterns at night and the park's shower and/or bathroom facilities. The boys, Indio and Zachery, could play in the out-of-doors to their hearts' content. They had their big German Shepherd dog, *Blue* as their protector and nanny, with Sam and Patricia within earshot, just a stones throw away. Meanwhile Sam and Patricia would work and create their designs preparing for the next show.

Sam and Patricia called their bus the *Prairie Schooner*. When not working on products to sell they continued to make improvements to the bus. With both, their creativity and artistic efforts, it became more efficient, and handsome. When first arriving at a place, knowing they would be there for awhile, they would open a bank account in a local bank, and register for general delivery mail service at the post fffice. That way they could cash the checks they received when selling their products, and could order leather, and other supplies used in their designs, to be sent to them.

The Bus Becomes a Home on Wheels

A couple of years after they bought the bus, Sam decided they needed to raise the entire roof of the bus to gain much needed space. He found an old barn where he could work on it regardless of the weather. He sawed the roof off the bus and it was raised in sections.

A friend, who was a professional welder, began welding one inch steel box tubing to join the sections together. As Sam watched the process, in time, he learned to do much of the work himself. When the structural work was complete the sides were covered with sheet metal. The windows and doors were framed in wood.

Finishing this major overhaul and completing these improvements took him eight months. The results were worth the wait. Wood floors, colorful ceramic tile and built in cabinets finished the job. Now they had a bedroom loft for the boys over the hood, and a master bedroom loft for Patricia and Sam at the rear. It was beautifully crafted, very unique and attracted lots of attention wherever they went.

Their means of transportation caused lots of attention and in time they began meeting others who had concocted and designed a variety of these 'housebuses' and 'housetrucks.' Many of these people were artisans, as were

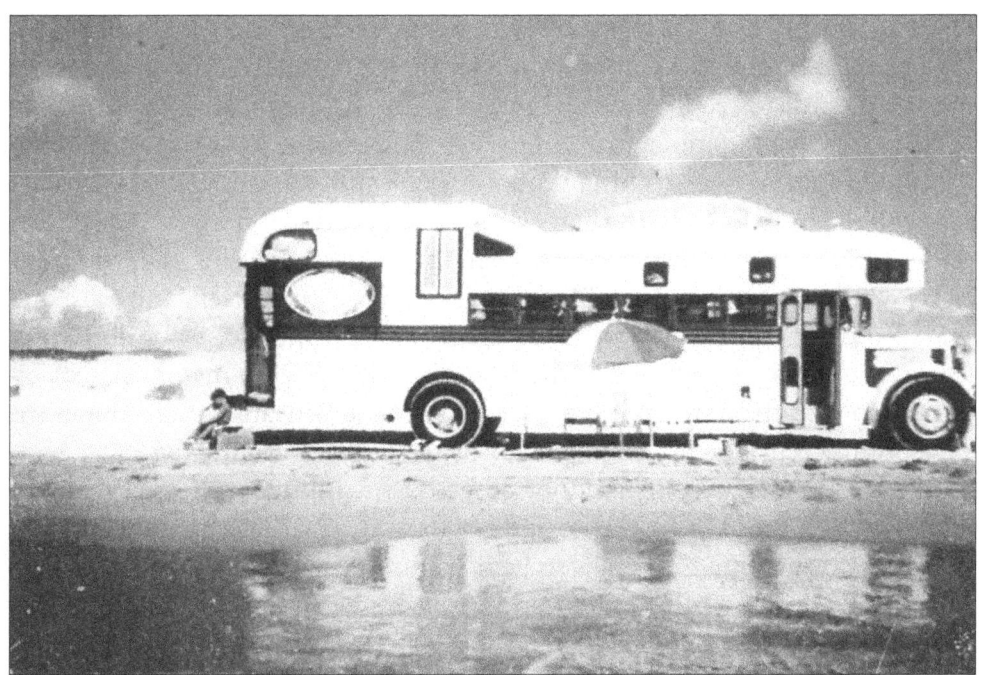

The "Prairie Schooner," created from an old school bus by Sam and Patricia. They lived in it, with their boys, for seven years. *Photo courtesy of Patricia Wolf.*

the Wolfs. Soon they found themselves traveling by a caravan of these land yachts.

Although each person they met had their own unusual personality and style they found themselves bonding in ways others who have never experienced this gypsy-nomadic life can only wonder about. Their children have had a childhood many of us who spent our youth in one place can't even imagine. (A great picture book entitled, *Some Turtles Have Nice Shells* by Roger D. Beck documents these hand-built housetrucks and housebuses, including Sam and Patricia's *Prairie Schooner*).

The raising of the entire roof of the bus was going to be expensive. It would also take a great deal of time. It was necessary Patricia and Sam work harder than ever. Figuring the cost, even though Sam would do much of the work, made them realize they had to finish many more designed denim and leather pieces before going to the next show, which happened to be an art show in Sausalito, just over the Golden Gate Bridge and across the bay from San Francisco.

The show was going exceptionally well. Patricia and Sam were selling their designs 'like hotcakes.' The 'powers that be' of Levi Strauss, major denim manufacturers headquartered in San Francisco, showed up at the show. They had come to see what was being designed that might be appropriate for their company to manufacture and sell to the public.

When they looked over the Wolf's designs and artwork they immediately recognized the quality of their work. The additional bone and silver ornamental accessories they were using on their products was the 'icing on the cake.' Representatives of Levi Strauss sat down with Patricia and Sam and ended the conversation by offering them both positions as staff designers. This was quite a compliment to them, and was definitely a major opportunity for most craftsmen. However, the two nomad artisans turned down the Levi Strauss representatives as quickly as the words were spoken.

"We can't give up our freedom," they both admitted. The couple loved their way of life and knew they could not exist within the corporate confines of any major manufacturer—even Levi Strauss. They thanked the representatives for their impressive offer and never gave it another thought. They knew what they wanted to do.

For six years they moved from place to place in their *Prairie Schooner*. They enjoyed their ability to pick and choose where they went and what they designed. They also decided when to stop and 'smell the roses.' After all, they had two children to raise. In addition to home-schooling Indio and Zack they wanted the boys to enjoy their childhood.

At one of their best shows, in Park City, Utah, another leather maker, who was on the board of the show, got the board to 'blackball' Patricia and Sam. Some art shows are 'juried' which means artists have to submit their work to a designated board chosen to represent the show. The board in turn makes the decision as to which artists are approved and those that are not. The Wolfs were told they could not participate in the show. Their products were not accepted for the show. They were shocked. They had never been turned down before. Eventually, they learned the leather-maker on the board didn't want Patricia and Sam's products as competition. After getting over the shock they were quite annoyed to hear they had been turned down.

Refusing to back off Patricia and Sam showed their work on a piece of private property, adjacent to the show. They were harassed, asked to leave and eventually admitted it just wasn't worth it. Fortunately, George Cullen, a 'mover and shaker' of the Renaissance Faire held between Magnolia and Plantersville, Texas, had visited with them previously. He had invited them to come and be a vendor at his show in Texas. He had told them the Renaissance Faire had only been happening for two years, and yet they had tremendous crowds. As he left them his business card he told them he felt it would be an excellent place for them to sell their products.

The hassle at the last show made their decision easy. It was a good time to move on. They contacted Cullen and said "We'll be there," and headed to Texas. It was 1976.

Moving On

On their way to the Faire they decided to stop in Smithville, Texas. The town was small and the main street had only two or three blocks of retail businesses. The town streets were full of big old oak trees and beautiful older homes. They found everyone they talked to friendly and easy-going. They liked the size of the town and the people. In fact they asked for a place to park their bus for the night and were told about a piece of property two miles south of town. When talking to the owners of the property they were told they could rent it if they wanted to stay longer. Patricia and Sam said they'd like to think about it.

They spent the night and after a few days of relaxation headed on to the Renaissance Faire. Their welcome on arriving at the Faire was also warm and friendly. Their leather caps, weskits, and sandals were a huge success. In fact, they worked into the night to keep from selling out.

Everyone they met had a smile on their face. It was such a comfortable and welcoming feeling, and everyone who came to the Faire was so relaxed and complimentary of their goods. When they finished at night, and could talk in the privacy of their bus, they began to realize this part of the country might be a place they would like to consider and maybe even to stay permanently. They had traveled in their wonderful *Prairie Schooner*, with their two great boys, for six years. It was time to settle down.

After the Faire they returned to Smithville. They did some more looking around and went back to the owners of the property they had first seen. They made a deal to lease the property. But first they had commitments on the east coast and told the owners they would return after the Christmas holidays.

They headed east. Their first stop was a Christmas show in New York, then another in New Jersey where they sold their wares. Afterwards they drove to Philadelphia to visit with Patricia's family.

In addition to the family, everyone that still lived in her old neighborhood came to visit. They came to see Patricia, meet Sam and the boys, and see their bus. The *Prairie Schooner* was such a novelty everyone wanted a tour. They were amazed to think these two artists and their boys had lived and worked in this bus for six years. The children were home-schooled by Patricia, who had all the credentials of a teacher. All their artistic designs were created and made right there in this uniquely converted school bus. The neighbors were astounded at the results of their creativity and the life they had led.

The Wolf family returned to Smithville in the *Prairie Schooner* and never left. A hundred year old farmhouse sat on the property and they decided to move in to it, and give themselves more room. It was a wonderful novelty to actually have indoor plumbing for a change. The property was 280 acres which allowed the boys plenty of room to explore and ride their newly acquired ponies. Their new 'home' was situated next to a cemetery and Patricia loves to say that "people are dying to be their neighbors."

At first they took a sabbatical from their artistic talents. Indio was in the sixth grade. Zack, who was ready for the first grade announced he wanted to go to a real school. Enough said, the boys began going to 'real' school. Patricia became a substitute teacher. When she wasn't teaching she worked with a community action program that helped poor families improve their living quarters. This was similar to the program she was involved in during her high school years with her Quaker friends and she knew she loved helping and improving the lives of those in need.

Sam meanwhile bought an 18-wheeler. He chose to drive the big diesel truck and primarily hauled produce. Sam was one of the first to provide Whole Foods, a highly success grocery chain today, with produce during their early years. In fact, when Sam started hauling produce Whole Foods was located in a converted house on Lamar Boulevard in Austin. In time, the store moved to bigger quarters. Today they are a nationally known successful grocery chain that promotes organic produce and grass-fed meats. It is on the NASDAQ Stock Exchange and has become extremely successful.

It was just a matter of time before Patricia and Sam got back in to the clothing business. Their first work area was the dining room of the old farm house they lived in. They began to hire a few local people. Patricia taught them how to do the various jobs necessary to put these unique designs together. The employees learned the art of sewing leather, and other fabrics, painting horses, bison and Indian designs on leather, fringing, braiding and many more things.

In time, they moved from the dining room to the bunkhouse situated behind their house. A few years later they had so many employees and needed more space. They moved to the 'skyscraper' in Smithville, a three story building downtown and filled all three floors with employees and products.

By the early 1980s Patricia moved into wholesale designing. She got a showroom in the contemporary area of the Dallas Fashion Market in 1982. At that time she was designing women's clothing primarily in suede. Some pieces were designed with hand painted Egyptian drawings. Many of her major retail buyers recommended she move her showroom to the Western clothing section of the market which was on another floor.

In 1986, Patricia took their advice and rented a temporary space on the fifth floor where the Western wear was situated. It was called The Territory. The temporary area was designed to look like rodeo bucking chutes. She presented her first Western wear collection. She had a Black and White Collection. Patricia had designed jackets, skirts, tops, and even boots with black and white hair-on hide decorating unborn calfskin boots. Lines of people wrapped around the chutes to get in to see her collection. Her designs were so innovative and included things never done before in the retail market.

Eventually she moved into her own Patricia Wolf Corporate room in The Territory. Patricia was now designing western wear using rhinestones. She was always a front-runner and always adding something new and fresh to her products. No one else was doing what she did. She designed an Indian wedding dress of all white leather that was outstanding. She was also dressing Miss Rodeo Texas, and many other rodeo queens, in her one-of-a-kind strikingly creative signature lambskin, 'blinged' out, pageant gowns.

By this time Patricia had become a highly successful Western couture designer. She had been encouraged to also add the Denver Market. It was the largest Western market in the United States. In the1980s she shared a showroom at the Denver Market, with Australian Outback, a company that sells clothing such as coats, jackets and such using oiled canvas. Patricia's designs in gold deerskin were skirts, jackets and tops, with hand-painted designs. The designs were such a hit, people were stacked outside, noses pressed to the windows, before they even opened for business.

Patricia's Following

Patricia has a loyal following of customers, both wholesale and retail. Some of her accounts, such as the Hide Out in Jackson Hole, Wyoming, have been ordering for 20 to 25 years. Ask any of her fans, her work is original yet classic, never goes out of style, and is passed on from mothers to daughters.

When Patricia started, she was a pioneer in the business. She still stands strong in the business, in spite of those that have tried to copy her and produce goods in China at a lower price. Her line continues to expand. Home furnishing is now a major part of her collection. She is proud to say her products are 'Made in Texas.'

Back home in Smithville, Patricia needed to change locations. Years before she actually made a move she had asked the owner of a downtown grocery store how much he wanted for his store. He gave her a price, but told her he was not ready to sell. In 1996 she again asked the grocery store owner if he was ready to sell. He was and sold the building to her for the same amount he had quoted her years before. Her present location sits on the edge of downtown Smithville in the former grocery store, with her neighbors and friends as her employees.

Patricia and Sam are helping raise five beautiful grandchildren, and two step-grandchildren. They work at least six days a week, eight to ten hours a day. They build their own booths and represent themselves at trade shows such as the Cowboy Christmas at the Wrangler National Finals Rodeo in Las Vegas; the Houston Stock Show and Rodeo trade show; in addition to the numerous wholesale clothing markets throughout the year. They just stopped doing the Renaissance Faire that brought them to Texas last year. They have designed costumes for the film industry. Many of their products appear in catalogs under different names.

Whenever they can get away for a long weekend they head for their beach house on the Texas coast. It was designed by them, of course, and they love working on it. Patricia loves the beach and enjoys building intricate sand castles. Her house of worship is Mount Pilgrim Church in Smithville. When she is asked about retiring she says she will spend her time visiting the sick and elderly. At 72, Patricia is still going strong with little thought to retirement.

Their oldest son, Indio, is retired with 20 years in the military, and saw action in the first Gulf War. When being discharged he became a visiting drug counselor at junior high schools in and around Texas. Now he is retired from doing that and is a teacher in Smithville. Their youngest son, Zachery, designs and makes furniture, belts and leather jewelry for the Patricia Wolf Company.

Patricia Wolf has been honored with awards galore, some of which have included;

Best of Show, Dallas Market

Best Western Designer, *True West Magazine*

Best Natural Fiber Designer, State of Texas,
Department of Agriculture

Fine Arts Fashion Award in Textile and Costume Institute,
by the Museum Of Fine Arts, in Houston

and too many more to mention in detail.

Patricia Wolf has filled her life, from the Convent to the Age of Aquarius and Flower Power, to finding her soul-mate and traveling with their family in a housebus as she evolved in to the Western Designer of the Ages. She has truly dared to be different.

During my interview with Patricia and Sam, I had the opportunity to see their housebus, which sits behind their 100+ year old home. The *Prairie*

Pat and Sam at the beach.
Photo courtesy of Patricia Wolf.

Schooner has weathered, inside and out, and yet it has spent its static years in Smithville as the playground for their children's children and other youngsters from the area.

The intricate blue tile work that decorated the bathroom and the edges of the kitchen cabinets, are still in place. The boxes where Patricia grew sprouts, when fruit was unavailable, to keep her family from getting scurvy, is still above the kitchen sink. The overhead bedroom for the boys can be seen as well as their own private sleeping quarters. Notes by the grandchildren are found on the kitchen table as they fantasized in their special 'Magic Bus' that meant so much to the generations before them. It has seen the wear, and is beyond repair, but it still sits as a magnificent monument to the Wolf family and a life of living well.

Eastern Legacy, Western Attitude
Claire Belcher Thompson

Most girls, born on ranches, were put atop a horse when they were still in diapers. Probably by a loving dad, a grandpa, or a cowgirl mom who spent more hours horseback than on the ground. Some youngsters stayed on a horse for the rest of their lives and were fortunate enough to be brought up knowing the true meaning of a cowgirl. But not all cowgirls began that way. Some young-uns cut their teeth on silver spoons, or in the middle of a major city, never knowing a thing about a horse, like how soft his upper lip is when it nuzzles up against your arm, or how the trusty steed will stand there when you fall off and wait for you to scramble to get back up.

It's not their fault, those city girls, who didn't start out with 'country smarts.' But some of them learned the ways of a cowgirl, sometimes purely by accident, and even became some of the best cowgirls of their era. Back in the beginning of rodeo and wild west there were women who bulldogged steers, rode broncs, trick rode and roped, rode race horses or were Roman riders (standing with one foot on each horse's back), after starting out in a much different world. The story of Claire Belcher Thompson is that kind of a story.

Claire's Story

Claire (whose real name was Gladys Rogers Emmons) was born in Mansfield, Massachusetts, on February 4, 1902, to Florence and Henry Emmons. In 1907, her mother, Florence, divorced Emmons and moved west, to Texas. Much of her early life in the southwest is not known. What is known is that her mother brought Gladys back east to her grandparents, David and Frances Rogers Harding, and left her with them in Massachusetts. What reason Florence had for not wanting to raise little Gladys is lost to time. Some relatives had heard stories passed down through the generations that it was because she wasn't attractive enough, others had other thoughts. Grandfather David Harding was quite successful in the tool and die business, but had also invested in other things, including a ranch near Uvalde, Texas. It is presumed Florence was living on this Uvalde, Texas ranch when she returned to Massachusetts to deliver Gladys to her parents.

The following year Florence married William Harrison Furlong and moved to his ranch near Laredo, Texas; where they raised cattle and horses. Apparently, she married and divorced often and for some reason there was no room in her life for Gladys. Florence also trained horses. When her father, David Harding, died in 1909 and Florence was called to come home for the funeral she informed the family she was too busy training her horses.

Gladys (Claire) and her sister, Florence Emmons, taken in Mansfield, Massachussets, 1908. *Photo courtesy of the Harding-Barnes family, through grandson of Florence.*

The Hardings, and Gladys' aunt, Mabel Barnes, lived in Mansfield, Massachusetts. Her grandmother and her aunt raised Gladys to be a proper young woman. Aunt Mabel was an accomplished pianist. When Gladys graduated from high school she attended LaSalle Junior College and studied piano and sewing. She continued her musical studies at the New England Conservatory of Music until 1920. Her aunt also introduced her to the world of horses and riding, English-style. She rode and competed in dressage competitions in and around Mansfield. Gladys took to the equine life with ease and was an excellent horsewoman.

Gladys met a young man by the name of Sumner Barton Kirby. They fell in love and when she turned 18, they married. The following year, 1921, they had a daughter, and named her Miriam Frances. They were overjoyed with their tiny baby girl, but their joy was short-lived. Only a few days old the baby became ill with meningitis. The doctors did everything they could to save the tiny infant but the baby died ten days later. The sudden death of her daughter devastated Gladys. Her grief and disappointment were too much for either of the young couple to handle. Their marriage soon fell apart.

It was a tough time for young Gladys. In spite of the fact her grandmother and aunt did everything they could to help her overcome her grief. She tried several things; going back to school, working with the horses at the stable, but nothing made her happy.

Gladys Emmons, later known as Claire, taken in 1918. *Photo courtesy of the Harding-Barnes family.*

Claire Meets a Cowboy

No one is certain where Gladys met rodeo performer Bob Belcher but it is possible she attended a rodeo in or around Boston. His competing event in the rodeo arena was as a bulldogger. The event fascinated Gladys and the happy-go-lucky, handsome cowboy gave her a new direction. It is not surprising she found Belcher exciting. His cowboy life was so far removed from her proper upbringing, the life she had led with her grandparents, and the disappointment of losing her baby. She became enthralled with this new and different world of rodeo as well as with the handsome bulldogger.

It didn't take Belcher long to realize Gladys had an exceptional ability with horses. She rode well and handled horses with confidence and ease. She learned quickly and had the willingness to attempt new things, even when there was a measure of danger involved. In fact, it wasn't long into their relationship that she insisted he teach her how to bulldog steers. In no time she had accomplished western horsemanship talents new to her. She had no idea she could master bulldogging.

By 1925 they were working with the 101 Wild West Show, based in Oklahoma. She was listed in their program as 'Claire Belcher, Lady Bulldogger.' Why she called herself Claire is unknown, however, it was a common thing in Wild West and rodeo for women, and even some men, to use a nom de plume. Often, it was to keep their family from knowing of their rough and tumble profession. Whatever her reasons for the name change, she went by the name of Claire from that time on in the western world. At first she was listed as Claire Rogers, but quickly her last name began appearing on programs as Belcher.

She found she had multiple talents as a cowgirl and even went so far as learning to ride broncs. During that era 'lady bronc riding' was quite prominent in rodeo venues. She also rode in relay races, and mastered the art of trick riding. A Kansas City newspaper stated in 1925 that 'Claire and Bob Belcher led the Grand Entry of the 101 Wild West Show there.'

A Favorite with the Press

She won second in a trick riding contest at Kirksville, Missouri, and won first in a lady bronc riding event in Aurora, Illinois, in 1926. The following year Claire's name was often listed in the *Billboard's Corral* column. *The Billboard* was a vaudevillian newspaper that primarily reported events happening in the theatres on Broadway and across the country. But other entertainment venues were also reported.

The column titled *The Corral* was devoted to performers and competitors of rodeo and Wild West shows. Claire was mentioned as being with the Miller's 101 Wild West Show; Foghorn Clancy's ten week rodeo traveling through the midwest; the Belle Fourche, South Dakota rodeo; and that she had 'bulldogged' a steer in 18 2/5 seconds at Kiowa, Kansas.

It was also reported by the *Chicago Tribune*, August 23, 1927, page 11, that she was 'seriously injured' when thrown from her horse in a relay race at Tex Austin's Chicago rodeo. The article told of her sustaining a skull fracture, internal injuries and a broken wrist. However, at the same time, it was reported in the *New York Times* she would be appearing at the Madison Square Garden Rodeo in October.

Cowboys and cowgirls had to heal fast, because if they could not perform they didn't get paid in Wild West shows as a performer or when they competed in rodeos. At rodeos, while competing, it was always a matter of doing well enough to get 'in the money.'

A later article in the *New York Times* reported that Bob Belcher and Mike Hastings had a fist fight which ended in Mike Hastings having to pay a fine. Belcher complained in court that the jealousy of his wife, Claire, competing against Hastings' wife, Fox, had caused the two men to have an altercation. Belcher was quoted as saying Hastings "put oil of mustard on a young steer Claire was bulldogging, which caused the steer to throw her and fracture her ribs." When Belcher confronted Hastings the fight began. After hearing the background of the case the court judge changed the charge of 'assault' to that of 'disorderly conduct' and fined Hastings $5.

Claire and Fox Hastings were both talented women that were often pitted against one another in matched bulldogging events at various rodeos. Since the sport of bulldogging is primarily a sport of men, and requires a fair amount of muscle strength, plus being willing to leap from a running horse to the horns of the steer, most cowgirls did not participate in this event. Rarely did these two glamour gals have much competition in that event. If they were not at the same rodeo they were asked to perform the bulldogging feat as an exhibition. But if they were both in attendance and competing, rodeo producers knew that to promote their challenge would attract a great deal of spectator attention.

Claire seemed to be 'everywhere' in the rodeo arena by 1928. It was evident that she was a 'darling' of the media and for good reason. She was obviously quite talented in many venues from the bulldogging to relay racing to bronc riding and trick riding. She also had an outgoing personality, and being well-educated gave her the ability to be eloquent allowing her to speak

Claire on *Patches*, a 101 Wild West Show horse, featured on the front page of Mid-Week Historical, printed by the New York Times Co., July 14, 1928. *Photo courtesy of the Harding-Barnes family.*

Claire in South Dakota, date and photographer unknown. *Courtesy of the Harding-Barnes family,*

well. Many women performers in the sport did not have this training. Her ability to talk with those not familiar with rodeo made it easier for reporters to obtain a good story. It was no wonder the reporters would seek her out.

California Frank Hafley's Wild West Show and Rodeo went to Havana, Cuba, and Claire's performance there was reported in the periodicals. Later that same year she was with his show at the Toronto Fair, in Canada. She also taught horseback riding at a Tampa (Florida) Riding and Hunt Club for a time. Then at San Antonio, Texas, in March, she was in the trick riding.

Next report was at the Houston rodeo she broke her arm bulldogging a steer. The souvenir edition of the *East Oregonian* newspaper for the famous Pendleton Round-Up, that year had an article on her abilities entitled, *Give Claire Belcher a Buckin' Bronc in the Great Outdoors.* In the article it quoted her as saying, "I wouldn't trade my lot to be the wife of the Prince of Wales. When I marry it will be some man who can do the things I do—but do them better. Until I meet him I'm just satisfied to jog along as I am." The Madison Square Garden Rodeo that October reported she won fourth in the trick riding contest.

The *Monte Vista (Colorado) Tribune* had an article, as did the *Quarter Horse Journal* magazine and the program of the El Paso (TX) Ranchmen's Reunion & Rodeo reporting her special exhibitions of bulldogging steers from the fender of a Chevrolet automobile in 1929. She also rode broncs at these events as well as at the Chicago and Burwell, Nebraska rodeos. Sometime during 1929, she and Bob parted ways. By the end of that year it was announced in the *Billboard's Corral* column that she had married another top bulldogger and was now 'known as Mrs. Jack 'Red' Thompson.'

Claire Changes Names

Stelzer Jack 'Red' Thompson was born in Alma, Arkansas, November 9, 1903. He became a steer wrestler and lived in Springtown, Texas, near Fort Worth. In 1928, he won the World Series Rodeo at Madison Square Garden in New York City for dogging his steer in 17 2/5 seconds.

Claire on *Rimrock*, at the Aurora Fairgrounds. *Photo by R.R. Doubleday, courtesy of the Dickenson Research Center, National Cowboy & Western Heritage Museum, Oklahoma City.*

The Madison Square Garden rodeo was, unofficially, the predecessor to the National Finals Rodeo; the Finals as known today didn't begin until 1959. To win a first place at the Garden event was a major win for any cowboy.

In August of 1929, at the Ski-Hi Stampede in Monte Vista, Colorado (where Claire bulldogged from the fender of an automobile) Red was declared the champion bulldogger with a time of 37.4 flat on three head. At the World Championship Rodeo at the State Fair of Texas in 1929 Red came in third, with a time of 12 1/5 seconds (for one steer). This cowboy was also a trick roper who won many trick and fancy roping contests. Apparently, this was the man Claire had talked in the *East Oregonian* newspaper article that she was looking for that 'could do the things she did—but do them better.'

The two traveled the 'rodeo road' for the next few years from Fort Worth to Tucson to Cheyenne to Chicago to Madison Square Garden and London, England. Their names often appeared in the 'win' column of rodeo results from all those locations and more. They had a wonderful life and this young cowgirl, raised in the east, knowing nothing about the western way of life before had taken to it with ease and seemed to enjoy it immensely. In fact, in many interviews she would tell reporters she was born in Uvalde, Texas. It is surmised she thought by telling her true birthplace in Massachusetts would be less believable for a cowgirl of her abilities.

London, England

Tex Austin was a well known rodeo producer and held well-respected rodeos in the early days. In 1924 he had taken a group of cowboys and cowgirls to England to perform. They went to show the people of Great Britain how tough and talented the American westerners were when feted against broncs and doing what is a cowboy's job on the ranch. It was a huge success and those that went with Austin were 'wined and dined' by the elite of London and treated like major celebrities. In 1934, Austin again put together a group of 100 cowboys and cowgirls, Claire and Red included, and made his second trip to England.

Their embarkation location was Montreal, Canada, where they boarded the ship, *Aurania*. The cowboys and cowgirls were scheduled to compete at White City Stadium, in London, from June 9 to the July 6. There was much camaraderie among the cowboys and cowgirls during their time at sea. Everyone had plenty of time to visit and really get to know one another. Claire and Red were so happy and content they couldn't imagine anything happening that could mar their wonderful life.

Upon arrival in London the rodeo attendance was just as good as it had been ten years earlier. But the Humane Society wasted no time in arriving at the stadium. They were highly critical of certain rodeo events, especially the calf roping and steer wrestling. The steer wrestling event was changed to such a 'namby-pamby' event some of the contestants were disgusted and refused to compete; including Red. They thought it most humiliating. The Humane Society required that a band be put around the steer's middle and a ribbon was tied on the steer's back. The cowboy had to ride by and take the ribbon off. It was a ridiculously simple feat for the 'doggers.' Plus the prize monies were lowered because it was so simple and easy for the competitors. There was no opportunity for the cowboys who only competed in the bulldogging event to win any money.

The calf roping event was changed so the competing cowboys had to use a breakaway rope and the time was stopped when they roped the calf. The

Humane Society refused to allow the cowboys to tie the calf down. It was no wonder that the crowds dwindled. Much of rodeo's excitement, toughness and thrills, had been taken out of each performance. It was too tame and that's not rodeo as it was known.

Meanwhile, Bob Crosby, a world champion calf roper, had brought his roping horse, *Hog Eyes*, with him on the ship to London. The horse was first owned by Roy Adams who found him roaming the hills of Arizona. Adams was intent on making a roping horse out of him. The little bay seemed to like the speed and all he was trained to do, but he wouldn't stop bucking.

Once as he was being hauled to a rodeo the trailer overturned but *Hog Eyes* came out of it without a scratch. Crosby, who had come to London ten years earlier with Tex Austin, knew the wear and tear on horses during the trip overseas so he chose not to bring his best horses.

Hog Eyes had a questionable reputation and the inability of anyone to cure him of bucking didn't help. By the time *Hog Eyes* arrived in London he had many scratches, was extremely nervous and had a very bad disposition. Somehow the little bay stepped on a piece of wood and it flew up and ran a sharp point of the wood into his neck, cutting a terrible gash.

Red and Crosby saw it happen and Red helped the roper doctor the horse. The wise cowboys determined the gash needed time to heal and it would not be smart to try and compete on him. Crosby borrowed another horse for the roping competition. Meanwhile since Red only competed in bulldogging, and the animal rights people had taken the 'wind out of the sails' in the event, he made it his job to continue to doctor the horse. The severe gash became infected and in no time the horse was in bad shape. Claire and Red spent many nights in the horse barn, nursing the little brown horse. They wanted to make sure *Hog Eyes* was improving. Red became very attached to the little horse during this time. If he was not watching Claire compete, he was by *Hog Eyes*' side.

Claire, fortunately, rode broncs well in London and scored high each time she rode. By the time the rodeo ended she was declared the Champion of the Lady Bronc Riding event and won $1,000. Knowing how strongly Red cared for the horse, Claire decided to use some of that money and offered to buy *Hog Eyes*. Meanwhile, Crosby had become discouraged with the horse's injury, plus his disposition to buck, and was ready to make a deal. Red bought the horse from Crosby for $300. The Thompsons took him back to Texas. It was said the horse was worth $500 or more, if he hadn't been in-

Red Thompson, Claire's husband and a well-known steer wrestler. *Photo courtesy of the Harding-Barnes family.*

jured. Red was sure he got a bargain when he bought *Hog Eyes*.

Once they arrived back in Texas Red spent many hours working with *Hog Eyes*. He had been a calf roping horse for Crosby. Red knew he needed to educate the horse as to what was expected of him in the bulldogging event. It would be a very different routine than what he had been trained to do as a calf roping mount. Red and Hog Eyes had bonded during the little horse's injury and recovery time.

The horse took to his new responsibilities and directions from Red quickly. He and the bulldogging cowboy were a great team in the arena. Red knew he would be. Red loaned *Hog Eyes* to other competing 'doggers' and if the other contestants won money riding him, a fourth of their winnings went to Red, the owner of the horse. Red was winning his share of bulldogging events, and *Hog Eyes* was winning even more.

The first cowboy, other than Red, to ride *Hog Eyes*, in a bulldogging competition, was Hub Whiteman at New Harmony, Indiana in 1934. Hub, of Clarksville, Texas, needed a mount, and had been watching Red and *Hog Eyes*. He asked Red if he could ride him and Red agreed. When Hub got mounted *Hog Eyes* began to buck, but then settled down. When the rodeo was over Hub and *Hog Eyes* had won the bulldogging. Until Hub found a horse he wanted for his own he continued to ride Red's little pony, and they always did well. The only other time he bucked was once when Bob Crosby borrowed him to ride. Maybe *Hog Eyes* had a good memory. Crosby was known for being tough on his horses.

The 1935 rodeo season found Claire and Red here, there and everywhere competing and performing. At the Burwell, Nebraska, rodeo in 1935 Red won the steer wrestling. He had a total of 54.8 seconds in three go-rounds plus the finals. It was one of the couple's favorite rodeos and they made sure they were there every year.

The following year, as he defended his title there, he was badly gored by a steer during the final day. Red was rushed to the local hospital where the doctors discovered he had punctured his intestines and had to be operated on immediately. It was a serious operation and his recovery time was long. When he started improving he knew he was going to be all right. In fact the next year, 1937, he was at Burwell to compete again and won second with a 41.2 second total on four head.

Meanwhile Claire continued to compete and win her fair share of prize money. She won seven out of eight days at Colonel W. T. Johnson's Centennial Rodeo, held in Dallas, Texas, (June, 1936) and tied for first with competing bronc rider, Fanny Nielson.

Injury Interrupts Winning Streak

It wasn't until Claire got to Madison Square Garden in October of 1936 her winning came to an abrupt halt. She drew a good bronc belonging to Colonel Johnson, named *Firefly*, and she had an exceptional ride. When the pick-up men, Everett Bowman and John Bowman, attempted to take her from the saddle on *Firefly* to the back of Everett's pick-up horse, the disaster happened. Claire's foot got tangled in the bronc saddle. As Everett tried to move away from the bronc Claire felt a heavy pull and saw her heel come back and touch her thigh. Everett realizing she was injured carried her out of the arena and straight to the Garden's medical room.

One look at her leg by the medical staff and they sent her directly to the hospital for treatment. Her right foot was broken and many of the smaller bones in the foot were crushed. The doctors put her in a cast wired and bolted together "in accordance with the best modern surgical practice," as was quoted in a *Boston Sunday Post* article, November 1, 1936, of Claire's injury. *The Post* account was quite dramatic in description, but did honestly say the Thompson's total source of income was gone due to this injury and also mentioned Red's injury a few weeks prior in Nebraska.

Claire, in part, was quoted as saying, "Colonel Johnson does have without a doubt, the best and toughest bucking horses in the world today. I know this because I have ridden at nearly every rodeo in the world and there is no distinction at the Colonel's rodeos between the girls' horses and the men's horses, we all draw for them together. Could the little shows pay all this money for horses? No, because they don't make it. And after all, I suppose a rodeo is a business proposition for the promoters as well as a living for the lucky cowgirls and cowboys. And Colonel Johnson has been like a father to all cowgirls and cowboys in need. I have never known him to turn down a cowgirl or cowboy in need of money because of injuries."

At the same time Claire sustained her injury at the Madison Square Garden Rodeo, a large faction of cowboys were preparing to strike at Colonel Johnson's Boston Garden rodeo. It started briefly after the New York rodeo ended, giving the cowboys, cowgirls, and stock, just enough time to get to Boston on the Rodeo Train.

Although Colonel Johnson had been asked numerous times in the past, by the cowboys, to up the prize money and include the entry fees in the purse, he always refused. This time he had no choice; 61 cowboys had signed a petition and refused to compete. The manager of Boston Garden told the Colonel if he did not comply with their requests he would see that the Colonel would never have another rodeo at the Garden.

The Colonel knew the time had come for him to agree to their wishes and upped the prize money more than $5,000. The cowboys called their new organization 'The Cowboy's Turtle Association.' It was the first time the cowboys ever succeeded in being an organized unit and having any say in prize monies offered.

The "Turtles' charged dues. Red saw the benefit of the organization and joined immediately. He was given Cowboy's Turtle number "four." At first, only competing cowboys were allowed to join. Eventually the 'Turtles' changed their decision and let rodeo performers, including cowgirls, join. After all, if they were to perform at a 'Turtle' sanctioned rodeo they had to be a member of the Cowboys' Turtle Association. Claire also joined. Her Turtle number was 610. Everyone knew this was a big turning point in rodeo and rodeo was on its way to becoming bigger and better than ever.

Claire and Red continued to rodeo. But by 1938 Red began to have some physical problems. His earlier injury from being gored was the cause of his problems. Claire stayed home instead of going to rodeos and tended to Red. The 'rodeo family' is a close knit group and it was soon learned by most competitors the Thompsons were not able to compete. Claire was hired by Ma Hopkins, the publisher of the popular *Hoofs & Horns* rodeo magazine, which reported all the news from the arena about cowboys and cowgirls. Claire wrote a column called *Cowgirl's Comments*, which kept everyone apprised of where certain cowgirls and cowboys were performing and how they were doing.

She also wrote an article on good friend, Dick Griffith, a world champion bull rider and trick roper. She wrote another article on Jimmy Nesbitt, a very colorful rodeo clown. Claire enjoyed Nesbitt and thought he was one of the best in the arena at that time.

By rodeo time at Burwell, Nebraska and Sidney, Iowa, Claire was asked to perform and was hired to trick ride. Red seemed to be improving but he was not in any shape to compete so he stayed home. Claire knew she needed to make some money. Their bills were mounting and they had very little income.

Most of Claire's time was spent caring for Red, but he just didn't seem to be able to improve. In fact, it was obvious his condition was gradually deteriorating. Much to their disappointment their income dwindled even more.

Claire continued to compete in rodeos, when she could, and hoped they could live off her winnings. In time they realized it was not enough to pay all their bills, especially Red's medical bills that were getting higher weekly. Many of their rodeo friends, such as Tad Lucas, and her daughter, Mitzi Riley, helped as much as they could. Mitzi recalled both she and her mother helping Claire put on a rodeo somewhere around Fort Worth. It could have been at Richard Ackerman's Bar C Ranch, near Fort Worth, that held weekend rodeos. Claire's family knew she had assisted Ackerman during this time and the proceeds went toward Red's medical expenses.

Claire also assisted the Marine Corps. in their recruitment for World War II. The war had a bad affect on rodeos. Of course, the men were either recruited or volunteered to go to war and this left many jobs the men normally handled during peace time. Now the women had to step in and take over and complete these jobs. The women tackled these jobs with great enthusiasm and worked diligently. Meanwhile Claire juggled her responsibilities with work and taking care of Red, who continued to get weaker.

Two of the very first all-girl rodeos were held in 1942. Faye Kirkwood was the ramrod and held one in Bonham, Texas, where Claire was featured as a trick rider and rode steers. Vaughn Krieg's All Cowgirl Rodeo was held in Paris, Texas, that same year and again Claire was asked to perform.

The ranch Claire and Red had near Fort Worth finally had to be sold just to pay their bills. Previously Claire had rented their spare bedrooms to help defray costs, but in time it just wasn't covering everything they owed and they had to sell the ranch and move to smaller quarters. By this time Claire had begun caring for other invalids, in addition to Red. This was short-lived, as it required her to be away from him for too long a time. One of the women she was caring for weighed more than Claire could handle. She had lost so much weight due to worry and concern over Red that she just didn't have the strength.

It wasn't that they didn't have help. They had many friends that tried their best to help them. Claire's aunt, Mabel Barnes in Massachusetts, sent Claire $10 each month. The First Baptist Church in Fort Worth also helped financially to pay for Red's medications. This was confirmed by copies of letters written by Claire to pastor, Dr. Frank Norris.

Red is Baptized, with Hog Eyes

Dr. Norris of the First Baptist Church had a radio program in Fort Worth. Red often listened to his programs and one day he called the good doctor and asked him if he could be baptized at the church. Of course the doctor agreed and then Red asked, "Can my horse, *Hog Eyes*, be there with me when I'm baptized?" It was a strange request but Dr. Norris saw no harm in it. He knew what love Red had for that horse. He also knew this cowboy being baptized, with his horse attending, would attract much attention. The date was set for December 8, 1944. Dr. Norris decided to broadcast the baptism on his radio show.

There was a great deal of promotion before the Sunday of Red's baptism. That Sunday morning there was a huge crowd at the church ready to witness it. The choir was singing hymns when Red was carried in on a stretcher. A side door opened and a friend was holding on to Hog Eyes' halter. They slowly walked to the front of the church where Red was placed. "Come here *Hog Eyes*," Red said weakly. The horse obeyed and walked to where Red could reach out and touch his muzzle. Dr. Norris began to eulogize the horse and his close relationship to Red. Many of the people in the congregation were so touched by his words they had tears rolling down their cheeks. When Red was finally baptized and emerged from the water he grabbed the hand of Dr. Claud Bonam, one of the stretcher-bearers, and asked him to get a bucket of the water he had been baptized in and throw it on *Hog Eyes*. The water was tossed on the bay's head. *Hog Eyes* never moved a muscle until the water was thrown on him, then he shook his head spraying water on everyone who was close by. Dr. Norris was a very impressive speaker and as he described the event over the airways thousands of people from around the country were glued to their radios. The following weeks many folks contacted the doctor and told him how inspirational the event had been and how it had touched them.

Red continued to fail, and the following year lost his eye sight. Claire did everything she could to make him as comfortable as possible. It was truly a difficult time for both of these well thought of rodeo hands. Claire was always bringing *Hog Eyes* for Red to touch, and talk to, but in May of 1950 Red got so bad he had to be hospitalized. Claire knew it was near the end for Red and she could hardly bear the pain she felt in her heart, she loved him so. On one of her many visits to see Red in the hospital he told Claire he'd like to see the little horse one more time.

That night after all had settled down at the hospital, and everyone had been readied for sleep, Claire brought *Hog Eyes* to the hospital. She had made arrangements with the janitor earlier. She unloaded him from the trailer and took him to the back of the hospital. She put him on the freight elevator and quietly took the little bay up to Red's floor. When the door opened, luckily there was no one in sight, the hall was vacant. Red's room was just a few doors from the elevator.

Claire prayed she could keep *Hog Eyes* quiet. It was as if the little horse realized he needed to be quiet and his hooves barely made a sound on the shiny tile floor. Red was thrilled, but could hardly lift his weakened arm. Claire helped him and he stroked the horses face until he had no strength left. Claire and *Hog Eyes* left as quietly as they came. No one was aware of the incident but it meant so much to Red. A few days later, May 9, 1950, Red died.

Claire was at a loss. She missed him terribly. All of a sudden there was a huge void in her life; she had cared for him so long. Her friends were very concerned about her. She knew she had done what she had to do and all she could do for the man she loved. She had no regrets. It took a while, but eventually she pulled herself together and went back to what she loved best — competing.

Girls Rodeo Association

In 1948 the Girls Rodeo Association had been organized and by 1950 there were numerous rodeos being held for women, especially in Texas. Claire joined the new Girl's Rodeo Association. She rode saddle broncs and was a columnist for *Powder Puff and Spurs*, a magazine started for the G.R.A.

She opened a horseback riding school in Bandera, Texas, in 1953. Bandera, known as the 'Cowboy Capital of the World' offered lots of opportunities for students, especially during the summer. There are many dude ranches located close by and although they all offered horseback riding, many of the 'dudes' wanted some basic instructions before they could riding properly.

A few years later she and Frank Lohre were managers of Cobb Park Riding Stables in Fort Worth. She eventually married Frank and they moved to Florida, in 1959. The *St. Petersburg Times* reported in the July 26 issue that Lohre and Kittrell Horseshoeing had opened a mobile horseshoe shop with a large stock of varied shoe sizes. How long this lasted is lost to time.

Claire and Frank moved to Lake City where she taught horseback riding. Claire took *Hog Eyes* with her to Florida and kept him on the Frank Thomas ranch about 12 miles from where she lived. At least three times a week Claire and *Hog Eyes* communed,—about Red, no doubt! Information is sketchy but it is known that at one time Claire was forced to sell the old horse, but as soon as she was financially able, she bought him back.

Hog Eyes died, in 1969, on the Bascom Norris ranch, near Lake City, Florida. A service was held for him and flowers were put on his grave by all the little girls in the neighborhood who had come to love him.

Claire (Gladys Rogers Emmons) Thompson Lohre died April 11, 1971, in Lake City, Florida. Her body was sent home to Mansfield, Massachusetts, and she is buried in the Spring Brook Cemetery, next to her aunt Mabel. There was no headstone, until recently, when a family member saw that a stone was placed at her gravesite. Her life was full of joy and sadness, but like a cowgirl, she handled the situation with true western style. What a change she made from her early urban lifestyle in Massachusetts to the life of a cowgirl in Wild West shows and rodeo. She truly dared to be different.

Much credit must be given to Doreen Alfonso and Ellie Baldwin, great-nieces, to this cowgirl, who took it upon their selves to research this relative's history extensively. Doreen's father idolized his cousin Claire and told his daughter, Doreen, before he died, he wished they knew more about her life. Because of their thorough, diligent and on-going research Claire Belcher Thompson has been inducted in to the National Cowboy Hall of Fame and has been submitted to the National Cowgirl Hall of Fame for consideration.

Author's Note - Just recently a letter and uncompleted autobiography, dated 1936, written by Claire (Gladys Emmons) about her early life and how she became a cowgirl was found by her great-nieces. The papers were found in the Harvard University Houghton Library among the papers of George Brinton Beal. Beal was primarily a writer of circus lore. It is presumed he had asked Claire if he could write a book of her experiences. Claire's family surmises that the account written by Claire was 'slightly exaggerated' in order to further encourage Mr. Beal to write her story. It is not complete and does not mention her marriage to Red Thompson. It is assumed that once Red was injured and eventually was unable to compete, this proposed book became unimportant to her.

Gun Totin' 6th Grader
Violet Hnizdil Christopherson

"Put that gun down, Violet. If you shoot him you'll go to jail," whispered Vernon, her twin brother.

The 11-year-old girl had grabbed an ancient shotgun that was kept near the back door of their farmhouse. She wrestled with the heavy gun to see if it was loaded. Her little hands were shaking as she fumbled with it. But she was so angry. Their father had a temper. In an argument with their mother he had struck her knocking her to the floor. Their mother's nose began to bleed and a big purple bruise, on her cheek, was beginning to get darker.

This wasn't the first time the twins had witnessed their father abusing their precious mother. It happened too often and Violet couldn't stand it any more. She hated him. She was determined to see that he never hurt anyone again!

Violet and Vernon were on the make-shift porch where no one could see them. She lifted the rifle to her shoulder with every ounce of muscle she could muster. She prepared to enter the room where her father sat.

"Open the door," she demanded of Vernon.

"Violet, he's not worth it. If you don't kill him he'll beat us all," whispered Vernon as he held the handle of the door.

She stopped and thought about what he had said for a few seconds.

Vernon was frantic, and in a whisper he said, "You'll go to jail. Please, I would die if you were sent away."

Violet's shoulders dropped, and she lowered the gun and finally put it back in its place quietly not to arouse suspicion. She was so mad she couldn't even cry. She turned and walked out the door and headed down toward the draw south of the house. She had to get away and cool down.

Vernon followed her, not saying a word. The winter air was cold, probably about 20 degrees, on the High Plains of Colorado where the wind blew every day.

Violet was so mad she was unaware of the temperature. She felt like her blood was boiling in her chest. She walked behind a shed and leaned against the far side, where no one could see her. The air seemed to slowly go out of her body, like air leaving a balloon, relieving the hatred she felt earlier.

"I hate him, Vernon. I just hate him," the young dark haired girl said, and the tears began to trickle down her cheeks. "I know it's not right to hate someone, but I can't help it. He is so mean to mama."

"Me, too," said Vernon, "I hate him too, but you can't kill him. Then what?"

There was a long silence as Violet thought about what might happen.

The Hnizdil family. (Front Row) twins Vernon and Violet. (Back Left to Right) Paul, Adeline, and Anna Lee. *Photo courtesy of Violet Christopherson.*

Her eyes widened as she visualized a police car from Sterling, the county seat, 17 miles in the distant east, speeding down the dirt road and careening in to their driveway with sirens blaring. Two policemen jumping out of the car before it barely stopped with guns drawn. She could see herself being handcuffed and placed in the backseat. Going to jail or worse! Yes, Vernon was right. Killing her dad was not the solution.

This is Violet's Story

Violet and Vernon were the youngest children born to Frank and Blanche Hnizdil. Frank was born in Czechoslovakia and immigrated to the United States as his cousins had done before him. He was 16 and had worked as a baker in 'the old country.' Whether he had a ticket on the ship or was a stowaway is unknown. Regardless, he made his way to northeastern Colorado as he had relatives that had settled earlier in the vicinity.

At first he was hired as a cowboy-cook for a large ranch. The ranch managers sent him to Wyoming to cowboy and cook on a sheep ranch. By 1908 he had saved enough money to homestead at Willard, Colorado. He worked on his 620 acres diligently during the year, except he spent the cold harsh winters of the plains, in California. In 1914 he wed Josephine Vodda and brought her to Willard. They had two sons, Tom and Frank. Josephine died, causes unknown.

Frank then married Blanche Sevit, of Omaha, Nebraska, and had six more children. Their first child was a son they named Charles Wayne. Frank had counted on this child being a girl. He wanted a girl so bad. It was obvious he had no interest in the newborn boy.

When Blanche's sister and husband came to visit them at Willard, it was quite evident to them Frank was not happy about the baby being a boy. They offered to take him home with them and Frank did not hesitate.

Charles Wayne went to live with his maternal aunt and uncle in Omaha, Nebraska. Fortunately the next child was a girl they named Anna Lee; then came Paul, then another girl, Adeline. Violet and Vernon, the twins were born in 1936.

It was not unusual for immigrants from Europe to continue living in the United States, much the same as they had lived in the old country. Although they often came to America to free themselves from the persecutions suffered there. The very things that encouraged them to leave their homeland and come to America were the scarcity of food, crowded quarters, religious persecution, and no means of making a decent living. Although it had been a very hard life that forced them to come to a new country they often treated their children and family poorly. The same way they'd been treated in 'the old country.' After all, that is all they knew.

In the old country talk of America and the opportunities there were well known. Young people were eager to find a better life, even if it meant some hardship in the beginning. "It had to be better than what they had," many thought. And it was. Land was available and there were numerous ways of making a living. However it took time to establish one's self in the new country and to adjust to a new way of life.

Frank Hnizdil had a hard time adjusting in many ways. For one, he didn't think it necessary that his children have a social life. In the old country children worked as soon as they were old enough, Every one in the family, youngsters, too, had the responsibility of helping to make a living. He was not at all pleased that the United States laws forced parents to send their youngsters to school. As far as Frank was concerned that was enough! That is all he would allow. They didn't need to go to church, school programs or community social activities. They should stay on the farm and work.

That didn't keep his youngsters from wanting to do the things their classmates were doing. They yearned to be able to attend plays, musicals, basketball games or church. But it was useless to try and convince Frank Hnizdil. No amount of talking could sway him from his old world thinking. Going to school was enough! No discussion!

Children Find Play

There was much work to be done on the farm but in spite of their father's rules, once it was done the children found ways to entertain themselves. Violet and Vernon, and their older sisters and brother, spent many hours playing hide-and-seek. It was their favorite past time. Since they had no horses or bicycles for riding it didn't require anything but clever creativity in finding the very best hiding places. Some of the choice spots were cleverly chosen, such as climbing to the top of the windmill.

When this high and clever place to hide was picked the first time "It" never thought to look up to this elevated spot when searching for those hiding. It was dangerous to climb so high. But once this special spot was used and discovered "It" would look there immediately and a new hiding place would have to be found. Sometimes those hiding would cover themselves with hay in the hay stack. Climbing to the top of the haystack always required "It" to climb there as well to find those hiding snuggled into the stack. Sometimes a good place was just a low spot in the terrain, which couldn't be seen until "It" was almost stepping on them. The children were always challenged to be the one to find the 'best' new hiding spot.

All five of the children became a very close knit unit. They knew it was necessary for them to 'stick together.' Their father's unreasonable decisions and occasional outrages happened too often.

After the 'rifle incident' Violet lived for the day she could leave the farm, and her father's wrath. She threw herself in to her school work and looked forward, every school day, for the yellow bus that came down the gravel road to pick them up and take them away from her father. School was always fun and she had many friends but the gnawing in her stomach about the problems at home were always with her.

The Twins Go to School

When she and Vernon, her twin brother, entered the first grade there were six youngsters in their class. Their teacher, Mrs. Jones, was a wonderful teacher. But in the big brick two story schoolhouse at Willard, Colorado, there were only two rooms used for grades first through eighth. One teacher taught the first four grades in one room and the second teacher taught the fifth through the eighth grade in the other room. Teaching four grades always gave the students free time when the teacher was teaching other grades. It was always fun to listen to the older classes, and learn things early, before reaching that grade.

Willard had once been a much larger community with many more students and the school house had been built to accommodate larger numbers. When progress seemed to 'kill' the town many who homesteaded in the area sold their acreage to others or simply left it for new places. The small town of Willard, by 1942 consisted of a couple of stores, post office, train depot, two grain elevators, a Methodist Church, and an automotive garage, and a teacherage. But at one time it had bustled with activity.

Now that the area population had grown smaller the town was waning. The first year of school for the twins Willard still held high school on the second floor of the building. The following year the high school students rode the bus from Willard to Merino, a town of 400, where they attended a consolidated high school. The Willard school then had no need for the additional rooms, or more than two teachers.

Once in awhile there was a school program at night. Most times Violet and her brothers and sisters didn't attend, unless they had a part in a school play. Oh, how often they wished they could go to the social activities in the community.

There was a basketball gymnasium in the basement of the big brick schoolhouse. During recess and lunch hours, the students played basketball. There were no bleachers, just benches around the outer perimeter of the playing court. In Violet's grade were five girls and her brother, Vernon. By the time they reached the sixth grade the Willard girl's basketball team was quite good and could hold their own against teams from nearby communities. Most of the girls on the Willard team got their height early. They were a team to be reckoned with, so they thought.

Blizzard of the Century

During the Christmas holidays of 1948 a blizzard hit the area that was one of those 'once in a lifetime' storms that was talked about for years. Although the Hnizdil home was adequate it had never had to deal with the likes of this storm. On a Sunday morning in early January, 1949, a strong, cold northwest wind blew all day. In the cold grey day the chill was almost unbearable for man and beast. The cattle were all huddled at a windbreak.

Violet's two brothers decided to go to a neighbor's who had been ill and help him with his chores. They left in the morning and did not make it back until after dark. The wind never stopped blowing. It started to snow during the day and became a full-blown blizzard, with temperatures getting as low as 20 degrees below zero. The winds were at least blowing 50 miles an hour. The small unnoticeable cracks on the north side of the house would allow snow and cold in. The heater in the living area ran continually but just barely kept the house warm enough.

Violet's older sisters were ill and near pneumonia. The following day it was discovered that water was dripping from the ceiling over the girl's bed. The ceiling began to bow and everyone was afraid it was ready to collapse. Fifteen inches of snow had blown in the attic and because of the heater warmth in the house, it was melting. Vernon, Violet's twin, was the smallest boy. He had to crawl in the attic, with a coal shovel, and get the snow and dirt that had filtered in scooped in to a basin. He would then pass the basin down to his father, who would empty it, give it back to him, and Vernon would fill it again. Fortunately the ceiling didn't collapse during this storm.

After several days the blizzard ceased. When the weather cleared the boys and their dad went outside to check any damage. They also needed to find how many cows had made it through, even though they were in the barn. The snow had sifted through every building on the place because of the winds. The hogs made it; many of the chickens did not. The pheasants and rabbits froze to death whereever they had hoped they could set out the storm. School was not back in session for days. Roads were closed, trains weren't able to run, and mail was not delivered. The old-timers were all saying they'd never seen anything like this blizzard.

When the days began to warm and the snow began to melt the roads

Eighth Grade Graduation, Willard, Colorado, 1950. (Left to Right) Reverend Lyle Schossow, Vernon and Violet Hnizdil, Carol Smith, Bonnie Hayes, Lou Ann Eakin, Gail Hughbanks (author), and teacher, Kitty Holthusen. *Photo courtesy of the author.*

became quagmires of mud. It wasn't unusual for the school bus driver to ask the biggest boys on the bus to get out and help get the bus through a muddy place. Banks of snow in this prairie land where few trees were growing were seen well into the spring. The blizzard began in Canada and covered a large part of the Midwest. The people of the Willard area were very fortunate no one was killed. Many in other communities weren't as lucky. Violet shuddered to think about her brothers that had ventured out in that blizzard, having gone to help a neighbor. She knew they could have died.

When the twins graduated from the eighth grade it was truly a commencement. The high school students from their community were sent by school bus to a consolidated high school in Merino, about twenty miles away. The high school was a white frame building. It was less than half the size of the big school house at Willard. But it was teaming with students. They met new friends and school mates from other communities and it was fun being part of a larger class. Eighteen students entered Merino High

School including Violet and Vernon their freshman year.

Summer Fun

During the summer before her senior year in high school, Violet had taken a job in Estes Park, a resort town on the edge of Rocky Mountain National Park. She worked at the resort as a telephone operator and met many people. She was amazed at how many people came through the area and how many new people she met in just those few summer months. Her time there was so social and full of fun. She had never been so happy. There was no comparison to the existence at home on the farm, in the shadow of her father. It reinforced her decision that when she graduated she was definitely going to move to a city where she could meet lots of new people.

Violet Meets Phil

When Violet graduated from high school in 1954 she attended nursing school in Denver. She became an LVN and went back to Sterling to work. While still in Denver she met Phil Christopherson. Phil was older and had been married and divorced. Violet fell in love with Phil. She was always attracted to more mature men.

Phil worked for a trucking firm, and was financially stable. The two always had a good time and it wasn't long before Phil asked her to marry him. After they wed they lived in Sterling where Phil continued to work for the trucking business. It wasn't long before Violet and Phil had their first child. A boy named Phillip. In the next few years two other children were born, Gail and a second son, Kevin. They transferred to Casper, Wyoming, as Phil's job required, then they transferred back to Sterling for a time, then to Hayes, Kansas.

Phil was ambitious and a very hard worker. It was his dream to own his own trucking firm one day. In 1980 that dream came true. He started C & S Trucking Company with a partner in Casper, Wyoming. After three years the partners had a difference of opinion and Phil started PC Transport, Inc. Their firm hauled liquid fuels from oil fields to marketing areas, and liquid fuels used for other purposes, such as propane, butane, asphalt, etc.

As the business thrived so did the family. Violet was mother to three active children as well as taking on the community and social responsibilities for the family. She saw that the children got their school work done and were active in various extra curricular activities. Violet played golf at the country club and joined a bridge club. These were typical activities for women of this era that were at home caring for their families.

Phil, as many husbands of that era, did not expect Violet to be an active participant in their trucking business. She and Phil had pledged that her role in their marriage was to raise and care for the children and fulfill their community responsibilities. Meanwhile this allowed Phil to run the business. It worked well and as the company grew they bought and developed trucking centers as far away as Louisiana and Texas. Where ever oil was being discovered Phil wanted to have his trucking firm represented.

Joke's on Him

The only time Violet was ever called on to help with the business was when one of the drivers was ill or unable to drive. She was very adept at driving those big transport trucks and did so willingly. When on Interstate Highway 25, that wends it's way on the eastern side of the Rockies from New Mexico through Colorado and Wyoming to Montana she would listen to an occasional trucker talk on the CB radio. Every trucker had a CB and it was a great source of making contact with others on the road when a trucker traveled alone and tired of the silence and monotony of the road.

She overheard a lonely trucker say to another trucker, "Hey, are those whores still hanging around up there at the truck stop ahead!"

Violet could not help but interject when she heard this disgusting piece of drivel. Picking up her speaker she said, "Not since we kicked your mother out of town."

There was total silence on the CB. The trucker that made the inquisitive comment was obviously unable to utter a word. She laughingly told, "Not another word was spoken over the CB radio for miles."

The business grew to such a size and Phil was so busy traveling from one location to the next he decided to take flying lessons. He soon learned to fly his own plane in order for him to get to his distant business locations as quickly as possible. Without relying on commercial planes he didn't have as many delays in his busy schedule.

This went very well until October 27, 1989. In bad weather Phil's plane crashed near Midland, Texas. Phil was killed instantly. He was 58-years-old.

Violet Takes the Helm

Violet was in shock when she heard the news. The thought of anything happening to either one of them had never entered her mind. She was a strong woman, however, and quickly realized there was little time for grief. This high dollar business they owned was now her responsibility and hers alone. Although she had never needed to be a part of the business she had gleaned some knowledge of what happened day to day from listening to Phil talk about it. On the other hand, there was so much about the business she didn't know.

The unfortunate timing of Phil's death left Violet in charge of PC Transport, Inc., which at the time was deep into a lawsuit against them for millions of dollars. The lawsuit was due to someone being killed on the job. Also the insurance company that carried Phil's life insurance was claiming he wasn't insured.

Violet's problems were no longer limited to overseeing the family. Now she had the insurance company to deal with and their entire company was at stake. Fortunately for Violet there were various long-time employees of the company that were there to help in anyway they could. Each day Violet learned more and more from them. They explained every little detail of this complicated business to her. She had to learn fast and she did. For these fine, loyal people, Violet will ever be ever grateful.

Not only did Violet have the lawsuit to deal with she also had to take on the responsibility of meeting with all the major customers of the company. An important meeting was scheduled, in Denver, Colorado, for one of the company's most important customers just 45 days after Phil's death. Violet prepared herself carefully for this meeting.

The day Violet left Casper to drive to Denver was the tail-end of a major blizzard. The highways in that part of the country were well maintained and were always relatively clear of snow in a short period of time. Violet and son, Kevin, got in her big purple Cadillac and headed south on Interstate 25. As she neared Cheyenne she had been listening to music and was becoming more relaxed. The roads had not seemed as bad as she had expected. Suddenly the heavy car began to slide. As Violet tried to straighten the car it just kept sliding sideways. BLACK ICE!! The treacherous unseen slick ice-covered surface of the road, that is undetectable, in this part of the country. It is so very dangerous primarily because a driver can not see it and often it puts vehicles in to a dangerous slide that can't be controlled. The big heavy car plowed up the snow in the barrow pit and finally came to a standstill when hitting a large electric light pole in the field beside the highway. The crash was so violent the pole they hit was taken out.

Major Injuries

Violet was knocked unconscious and suffered severe injuries. The para-medics arrived quickly. Miraculously Kevin had been sleeping and was not injured. The car door could not be opened and they had to cut the top of the Cadillac to get her out. An ambulance rushed her to Cheyenne where she was taken to the hospital emergency room.

At first doctors weren't sure how badly she was injured. On examination her left arm was practically destroyed and required extensive surgery and more. Her left hip was broken, as was her left knee and ankle. She remained in intensive care for the next month. By the time she was well enough to be moved back to Casper by ambulance she was in a full-body cast, where she remained for another six weeks. Dr. John Barrasso did reconstructive surgery, which was followed by extensive therapy.

Meanwhile the business rocked along. Fortunately Kevin, Violet's son, had been working with his dad in the business for several years before Phil's death. He was a tremendous help to Violet and a real asset to the company. Also, the devoted employees that had been with the company for some time worked diligently to see that the firm continued to survive. The first few years, after Phil's death, and with Violet's accident and severe injuries, business was touch-and-go. Some of their customers had shifted their business to competitors.

The government began cracking down on the trucking industry. Drivers were required to have drug-testing before they could be hired. If drivers were ticketed for speeding or traveling in trucks without the right credentials, tickets were not only charged against the driver but went on the company insurance records as well. This caused company insurance rates to go sky-high. It was not an easy task to find good drivers.

Violet spent many hours in necessary rehabilitation, but her injuries finally healed. Additionally, with long hours of diligence and complete commitment to the company things began to look up. Kevin continued to be a tremendous asset to Violet in their business.

Kevin Makes World Record Flights

Once PC Transport, Inc. started to be more profitable Violet found, that although she had healed, she needed some kind of outlet to release the tensions of running a multi-million dollar business.

Son, Kevin, had been involved in hang glider competitions for years. In fact he made three world record flights in the event. To his knowledge no one has ever foot-launched a hang glider that has beaten his last record of 287.447 miles. This was from Whiskey Peak in Wyoming, August 2, 1989, to a landing on the Bob Faulk farm on the Pine Ridge Reservation in South Dakota. His total flight was 8 hours and 50 minutes with an on-course time of 6 hours and 20 minutes; giving him an average groundspeed of 45.66 mph. Kevin's average altitude for most of the flight was 15,000 feet and thermal strength averaged around 1,000 fpm.

All his records in hang gliding from a foot launch have been from Whiskey Peak, located in central Wyoming. The first record was in 1988 and he went 224 miles into Montana. His record was passed a month later in California. His second record was in June of 1989 and he went 247 miles.

In hang glider competitions the glider is generally hauled to the summit of a mountain by vehicle and placed where the pilot can run with it to launch into the sky after he studies the thermal winds. Thermals come up the side of a mountain; he chooses the 'right time' to launch. From there he works the glider to get the best thermals and flies as far as he can without touching earth. The winner is the pilot that flies his glider the farthest without touching the ground. He is only equipped with his ability to manage the thermals, a radio and a demand oxygen system. He uses the radio to instruct the person on the ground that follows him in a vehicle to pick him up when he finally does land. Sometimes this can be hundreds of miles away.

Violet often was his 'driver on the ground,' and they communicated by radio. He called her 'Supermom' and she enjoyed the competitions. Once Kevin took Violet, in tandem, on the hang glider, and at first she was enthralled. As the flight continued, however, there was a time she got queasy and became very unsure of what was happening. By the time they landed Violet climbed over into the sagebrush, threw up several times and no longer had any interest in learning any more about hang gliding. This was definitely not a sport Violet was interested in pursuing.

Violet gets her elk, taken on her ranch in the south Big Horn Mountains, October 9, 1992. *Photo courtesy of Violet Christopherson.*

Violet poses with her mountain goat, taken near Cody, Wyoming, September 25, 1993. Mountain goat licenses are very rare to draw. That year Violet was one of only seven given, with 15,000 requests made. *Photo courtesy of Violet Christopherson.*

Big Game Hunting

Kevin also was an avid big game hunter. Hunting in Wyoming for antelope, elk, and deer doesn't require traveling far away. Nor does it require leaving the ground! Violet realized this could be done not far from her home in Casper. She picked up a rifle, and tried her hand at hunting. She found she was a good shot and it wasn't long before she was spending all her spare time hunting in and around Wyoming.

She and Kevin often hunted together. Eventually she desired a larger challenge and put down the gun and took up bow hunting. She hunted with a bow until she killed a magnificent bull elk. The law does not allow a hunter to carry a gun, if they are hunting with a bow. When she watched this huge magnificent animal struggle to his death, which was not quick, she changed her mind. It was very painful for Violet to see this beautiful specimen die slowly. She has returned to hunting with a rifle.

She invested in 6,000 acres of land in the Big Horn Mountains about 80 miles west of Casper. She dedicated this land exclusively for hunting strictly by her family. She is planning to keep it in pristine shape, just the way it was hundreds of years ago. Violet spends as much of her spare time there as possible. She spent several years building a lodge on the property.

It thrills her to see her grandchildren following in the footsteps of her and Kevin by hunting. Some of her trophies, in addition to the elk, include a 185-pound male mountain lion, a mountain goat, moose, deer, antelope, wild pheasants and wild turkey. All these animals are native to the area in which she lives.

Meanwhile the business is thriving and is highly successful. She has often been approached to sell the business but it is her goal to keep it going for the outstanding employees that were there for her when Phil was suddenly killed and when she incurred her terrible accident. At this time the company has 38 to 40 trucks and hires leased trucks when necessary.

Mountain lion taken by Violet in a deep canyon near Kaycee, Wyoming, March 7, 1995. *Photo courtesy of Violet Christopherson.*

Reasonable and Prudent

The author invited Violet to go to the Calgary Stampede after she had taken over the business. We drove to Calgary by way of Kalispell, Montana, and I had several stops along the way to visit with various rodeo friends. We planned to spend four days in Calgary. I had received media passes for us when we arrived. I was there to gather historic information about the Stampede first hand.

After two days I had finished my interviews with several cowboys and Violet admitted she was ready to head home. She was very uncomfortable being away from the business for five days. Violet always took her responsibilities seriously and although she had good people handling things she needed to get home. Her level of responsibility toward the business was uppermost in her mind.

Violet takes her mule deer at her Ten Sleep Ranch, October 17, 1997
Photo courtesy of Violet Christopherson.

After driving through Montana where the speed limit was 'whatever is reasonable and prudent' and we got near the Wyoming border Violet said to me, "Gail, when you reach the state line, slow down to the speed limit. The Wyoming highway patrolmen are very strict and will give you a ticket if you are speeding." As we entered Wyoming I was vigilant to drive the speed limit.

A short time later Violet pointed out one of her big liquid transport trucks on the eastern horizon kicking up a trail of dust as it was wending it's way toward Interstate 25.

Violet said, "That looks like one of our trucks. Would you mind stopping so I can see who is driving?"

I immediately slowed down and pulled over on the shoulder. Once the truck, pulling a 'pup' (a smaller tank on wheels behind the truck), got on the Interstate it passed us like a streak!

Violet asked me if I could speed up and catch the truck. We were in a small Infiniti sedan, but it had a lot of get-up-and-go so I stepped on the gas. We got to 70 miles an hour, then 80 and more. It was definitely faster than trucks were legally allowed to drive. We were in the left lane and she asked if I could get up alongside the truck. When I did she rolled down the window, stuck her arm out and with her thumb pointing down waving her arm up and down as if motioning for him to slow down.

The driver looked at her, apparently not recognizing her as the owner of the company truck he was driving, and ignored her request. Her comment then under her breath, as she rolled up the window, was, "He'll know who I am tomorrow."

As we drove on toward Casper, Violet explained that her company has a safety department that hires drivers, and they are tested for drugs. Getting good drivers with good driving records is absolutely mandatory in a business like hers. She explained if they get a ticket for speeding or anything that is considered driver-responsible he, the driver, gets the ticket but the incident is recorded on the company's driving history, which can be extremely costly to the company as far as their insurance is concerned.

Today, years later, she is still going to the company on a daily basis. She is responsible for many of the administrative decisions for the company, as well as the final say on any company policies. Her work ethic and sense of responsibility run deep.

It is interesting to note that when Violet's father, Frank Hnizdil, died of natural causes, it was Violet that was contacted of his death. Obviously he had listed her name and contact information where he was infirmed. Although she was ready to kill her father for the abuse he had shown their mother when she was a youngster. She admits, her backtalk and lack of respect she showed him the rest of his life, probably made her his favorite child. Violet certainly dared to be different.

The 'Gem' of the Pacific
Anna Lindsey Perry-Fiske

She always called herself a cowboy because that's what her daddy called her. William Lindsey always said his daughter, Anna, was the best cowboy in the family, despite the fact she had two brothers. She always found a way to get out of the house and work with her dad, whether it was herding cattle, branding, or riding horseback over the land they owned on the island of Hawaii. Their island is the largest in the chain of Hawaiian Islands. She went to work early and stayed late, until the job was done. It was no wonder she spent her life accomplishing a multitude of challenging projects put before her.

Anna was born February 20, 1900, to William and Mary Lindsey. Brother Bill was older, and Charles was born after Anna. Her first horseback ride was when she was two-weeks-old, when her mother put her in her saddlebag, and rode back to her home at Waimea from Hilo, where Anna had been born. She was always drawn to the out-of-doors and as soon as she was old enough she had begun accompanying her father to help with ranch chores. William Lindsey was one of the best ranchers on the island. His excellent ranching skills is why he had been hired as the manager of the Parker Ranch for a time. The Parker Ranch neighbored the Lindsey ranch and was huge, requiring many paniolos (cowboys are referred to as 'paniolos' in Hawaii) to keep their vast herds of cattle. This managerial responsibility was only given to the most qualified men.

The Lindsey family lived near the town of Waimea, located in the center of the north side of the island. The setting was idyllic. The foliage was lush due to the rainfall and temperate climate. The weather at Waimea was always a little cooler than it was near the ocean, just a few miles away.

Anna's mother, Mary, was an avid horsewoman, but she was also determined to teach her only daughter the proper social graces that were expect-

Studio portrait of Anna taken in the 1920s.
Photo courtesy of Anna Ranch Heritage Center Archives.

ed of women in those days. It was always a tug-of-war between Mary and her husband to commandeer Anna's time. But William always allowed Mary to have the time to teach the young beauty the necessary social protocol. Anna took her mother's training to heart, but as soon as she accomplished the social lesson or kitchen task her mother had for her that day, she would bolt out the door and head to the barn, in hopes of finding her father.

She loved to immerse herself in ranch work. Whether she was working with the horses, cattle, or learning which fork to use at a formal dinner, she grasped it quickly. She totally concentrated on each task at hand, was a quick learner, extremely bright and quite a charmer.

The history of the island was an important part of the family history and Anna grew up knowing her family had ties to the land that were seldom awarded to those that had arrived from other countries. Father William's ancestry was part-Hawaiian. Mother Mary came from both European and Hawaiian lineage.

Historically, Lord George Vancouver, of Great Britain, visited the north area of the island with Captain Cook in 1778-79 and discovered that the upper area of Waimea had a cooler climate, plus more rainfall than the rest of the island, and provided beautiful grassland. Located at an elevation of 2,500 feet Waimea's climate was different than that of the land along the coast.

In 1794, five cows and one bull were brought to the area from Monterrey, California. Before that there were no cows on the island. The only animals indigenous to the Island were pigs, dogs and rats. Vancouver suggested to

King Kamehameha I that he put a kapu (a stop) on killing the newly acquired cows in hopes they would multiply. The King followed his advice and word was spread that it was a serious crime to kill cows.

In time the cows multiplied so well, they were everywhere. The bullocks (as they were called in those days) became a menace to people. Occasionally they attacked islanders and attempted to gore them. The cows were also destroying crops to the point the natives began to build rock fences to keep them at bay and away from the produce fields. King Kamehameha III, who ruled in 1830, realized the cattle had become a major destructive problem. He dropped the kapu and put a bounty on cow hides.

This gave the natives a new source of income. It even encouraged outsiders to come to the island to join in this new market of a cash bounty for hides. But the job was not an easy one. The capture, killing and transporting of hides was all done on foot. Although horses had been introduced to the Island in 1803 the native people did not have the skills of working cattle by horseback. In fact, it wasn't until three vaqueros from Mexico were brought to the island, by the King, to teach the local people cowboy arts, including how to manage and collect cattle by horseback.

The vaqueros referred to themselves as espanols and from that word came the newly developed Hawaiian word paniolo which means Hawaiian cowboy. In the beginning the cattle were strictly gathered and killed for their hides, and nothing else. There was a good market for hides. At first the carcass was left to rot where it was killed. In time, however, they realized that the meat of the cow was tasty and they began saving the beef instead of letting it rot. The Hawaiian dinner fare expanded greatly to include beef, not just pork, fowl and fish.

Anna's Heritage

Anna's ancestors were from diverse backgrounds including British, European, and Australian and Hawaiian ali'i. Ali'i means from chiefly heritage. Jim Fay, Anna's great-great-grandfather, was an Australian colonist who came to Hawaii as a cow-hide bounty hunter. In short time he found that he loved this new found location and started the first successful saw mill in the area. He married a Hawaiian ali'i named Ka'ipukai, and they had one child, Mary Fay, who was not only beautiful, but very popular. Mary Fay met a handsome British naval officer, Thomas Weston Lindsey, and fell in love.

When the lovers realized her parents thought she was too young to marry, they eloped. He 'bought himself out of the navy,' which was possible in those days. They returned to Waimea to live. Shortly after their son was born Thomas became ill with consumption. Thinking he would receive better care if he returned to England he left his wife and child on the Island. Unfortunately, he died while in England. Before he died he begged his brother, George Kingston Lindsey, to go to Hawaii and look after his wife and child. George kept his promise, fell madly in love with his brother's widow, Mary Fay Lindsey, and they eventually married. He adopted his brother's son and together they had 11 more children. Anna's grandfather, Thomas Lindsey, was one of their sons.

Grandpa Tom had a tendency, in his later life, to imbibe in the spirits too much. He made a deal with young Anna that whenever she saw him getting tipsy, she was to warn him, and he would reward her in gold coins. As time went on Anna gathered quite a stash of gold coins from her grandfather's enjoyment of liquor. She kept the gold in a talcum tin for safe keeping.

When the time came for Anna to go to school she first went to a small school in Waimea. It didn't take long before her parents realized how very smart she was and such a quick learner. They decided to give her the best education they could. They sent her to Kohala Girls School as a boarding student. Although the school was not more than 20 miles from the ranch Anna missed her family. She often would call home crying and begging them to come and get her she was so homesick. Of course, she missed her family, but she also missed the horses and cattle and the out-of-doors she loved so much. When Anna was nine her parents decided she needed to go to school further from home. Hoping this would eliminate her evening call begging her parents to let her come home. Anna was sent to Sacred Heart Academy, a boarding school run by Catholic Sisters in Honolulu on the island of Oahu.

It was necessary in those days to take an inter-steamer from the harbor at Kawaihae, a two hour surrey ride from the Lindsey home. Anna's mother accompanied her to Honolulu. It was a 24 hour trip to the island of Oahu, with stops on the island of Maui. Nine-year-old Anna was thrilled with the new city that bustled with traffic, tall buildings, and much activity. It was nothing like the small sleepy village of Waimea. Anna liked the school and, after a brief period of the recurring homesickness, she dove right in to the activities at school. She learned to love the nuns who taught there.

More Land Added

During this time Anna's father, a very forward-thinking man, wanted to buy a 300-acre piece of property in the Keawewai district belonging to George Washington Lincoln. The area in which he was interested held an abundance of water, even in times of drought, and had lush rolling pastures. The price was $10,000.

William discussed this purchase with his father, Tom, who decided to give the money needed for the purchase as a gift to his son. Coincidentally, when the purchase was made, Anna was home from school. She rode her horse, in front of her parents, also on horseback, and carried the $10,000 in gold, tied in gunny sacks behind her saddle. It was eight miles to the new site, where the $10,000 was handed over for the land.

As she grew up this newly purchased property became Anna's very favorite place. She loved hearing the sounds of the waterfall outside the Lincoln house. Throughout her life it became a haven of peace. She could come to this land alone and work through any difficulties she might be facing. Each time she went there with a problem, by the time she returned to the family ranch, she would have worked through her concerns and knew what action she needed to take. Seldom did this solitude at Keawewai ever fail to give her the answers she needed.

Back at Sacred Heart, youngster Anna enjoyed her time there. However, her realistic way of looking at life sometimes caused her to get in to trouble with the nuns. The required dress at school was a full length high-collared, long-sleeved Mother Hubbard garment.

At first, Anna accepted the dress code, but the nuns required the girls to bathe while wearing the dress. In time, Anna decided there was no way a person could really cleanse themselves while wearing the cumbersome clothing that ballooned around her when getting in the tub. She decided she would ignore the rule and bathe without wearing the dress. When Sister Ladislaw walked in and saw Anna naked in the tub she yelled and covered her eyes. Anna was punished for her decision to bathe naked. She was not allowed to leave the convent for her actions.

But Anna made the best of it. She got out her talcum tin, where she kept the gold coins she had gotten from her grandfather Tom. She had a classmate go across the street to a Chinese store and buy the necessities for a picnic. It was Anna's first experience as a hostess as she held court with her classmates on the spacious lawn of the school. Her mother's training to be a hostess had paid off.

While at school Anna made a close friendship with another student, Lucy Searle, from the island of Maui. Through Lucy, Anna had met Queen Liliuokalani, a former Hawaiian monarch. The queen had been deposed in a coup in 1893. On many Saturday mornings the girls would visit the Queen's home. Occasionally they would spend the weekend. The Queen loved music and was the composer of numerous Hawaiian songs. Waikiki Beach was very quiet in those days and the Queen had a long pier built out into the ocean. A bedroom for the Queen was built on the pier and often the girls and the Queen spent many hours relaxing there.

The Queen died in 1917 at the age of 79. Anna joined the throngs that attended the funeral of this beloved former monarch. She sang in the choir during the funeral; tears streamed down her face for the loss of her dear friend.

Anna's life was grand. She loved school, her friends, the visits home, returning to school, and the nuns who taught there. One day at school her mother arrived and announced they were moving her to a new school. Anna was shocked! She had no idea why her parents insisted on this change of schools. Her grades were excellent, she like the school. Why would her parents decide on a change of schools?

Much later in her life Anna decided that possibly her young enthusiasm and a random statement to her mother, that she might like to become a nun, had made Mary Lindsey overly concerned. The transfer sent Anna to St. Andrews Priory, a private girl's boarding school run by the Episcopalian Anglicans.

Throughout her life Anna did everything with total focus. She gave each task all her effort and might. Whether it was surfing, piano lessons, or studying millinery in school, she was quick to catch on and learn. She gathered many talents she could draw on. She was also very popular with her classmates, and especially the boys. When she went home on holidays to visit her family, she always had numerous invitations and parties to attend.

Meanwhile, her father was busy with a multitude of projects. He was determined to make money so that he could send all three of his children to good schools. In addition to running their ranch, he worked as assistant to the manager of the Parker Ranch. His responsibilities for the Parker Ranch were varied. He caught wild goats to sell to the Filipino plantation laborers as they considered goat meat a delicacy. He sold polo ponies and race horses to people on Maui. It always inspired Anna, when she was home, to help her father in one or more of his endeavors. She always gained new knowledge from each experience.

At the same time, the Lindsey home was always filled with friends and neighbors. Anna's mother always put out quite a fare of delicious foods, and entertained with ease. No matter how busy her father was he was always social and hospitable to visitors. It was idyllic for Anna and she loved every minute of every day.

Marriage

At the young age of 19 Anna replied, "Yes," to the marriage proposal from Henry Lai Hipp. He had been proposing to her for more than three years. Their parents were good friends. Henry had completed his college and was a law school graduate. Since members of the legal field were few and far between on the island he had become a District Court Practitioner, a special judgeship in the Hilo area. The handsome young judge, of Hawaiian, Irish and Chinese descent, had an athletic build and with Anna's natural beauty they made a very handsome couple.

Judge Hipp and his bride moved to Hilo after their honeymoon. Surprisingly, they were seldom included, as a couple, in the social life of Hilo. It was a shock to Anna as she was very busy with invitations to teas and other activities with women, during the day. Hipp moved in the highest professional circles during the day, but when the evening social life invitations failed to arrive Anna was totally confused.

She grew up in a community that adored her, and she adored everyone there. But for the first time in her life Anna discovered discrimination. Henry's Chinese heritage was not accepted in Hilo society. Being Caucasian or part-Hawaiian was acceptable, but nothing else. Once Anna realized this was a major obstacle in their social life, as a couple, she merely created her own social activities. The marvelous training from her mother, as she grew up, to be a perfect hostess served her well. Knowing proper etiquette and how to entertain 'properly with flair' made Anna's parties a total success and they became the 'talk of the town.' Everyone in Hilo wanted to be invited to the Hipps soirees.

Anna's bliss in Hilo was about to change. It soon became apparent to her that something was amiss in their marriage. Henry swore he loved only her, but, unfortunately, he couldn't resist the numerous other women who were attracted to him. Anna was very disappointed in the fact her union with Henry had not produced children, but it might have been a blessing.

She did not discuss her uneasy feelings with anyone. No one was the wiser. When her brother, Charles, was diagnosed with Hansen's disease, her personal feelings were set aside. It was such a horrific illness, and so little was known about leprosy. The people of Hawaii that were diagnosed with the dreaded disease were sent away to a colony on the Island of Molokai where they were to live out the rest of their lives away from their families. They suffered such severe physical changes. The law allowed a spouse to get an automatic divorce because there was no cure for the illness, and they would eventually die. The spouse was considered to be given a 'new lease on life'.

Anna took Charles' wife, and two children, Richard and Florence, into her home. When the children weren't in Waimea with Anna's parents, who were appointed their legal guardians, they were with Anna at her home in Hilo. She loved their presence and always had a close relationship with the children, especially Richard.

Often Anna would go for long horseback rides around Hilo and found the time reflective and soothing to her troubled marriage situation. Her father sensed that something was wrong. He thought one of the main things Anna missed in Hilo was her time spent horseback in the hills of Waimea. He sent her some horses from the ranch. In no time Anna had secured some land and developed a riding stable. She told the county that if they would let her build stables on the land when she finished with the improved land it would belong to the county. With the assist from her father the stables were built in no time. She spent much of her time there teaching horseback riding to others around Hilo.

Years earlier Eben Low, a businessman from Honolulu, and former ranch owner on the island of Hawaii, had asked Anna to be a pa'u rider for parades and various Hawaiian events held throughout the year. It was an honor for anyone from Hawaii to be asked to be a pa'u rider. Of course, Anna was proud to have been asked and always accepted. Her beauty and grace represented Hawaii well.

A Pa'u Rider

Historically, in the early days of Hawaiian society it was necessary for everyone to travel to and from an event by horseback. The women would wear their finery, but to protect their elegant clothing from the elements they would cover themselves with a large swath of cloth. In time, the cloth continued to be used, but more as a tradition. The fabrics and design of this outer wear became less a protection and more colorful tasteful fabrics were used, such as velvets.

A pa'u rider rode horseback with the cloth almost reaching the ground, and completely covering the rider's clothing underneath. Beautiful leis also adorned the rider, and the horse. It is a most impressive and colorful tradition that is still being carried on. Anna was known as 'the Queen of pa'u riders,' and always led the group.

Eben Low visited Cheyenne Frontier Days in the early 1900s and found the rodeo competition exciting. He went back to Hawaii and with an invite from the Cheyenne 'powers of the day' he chose three paniolos to accompany him back to Cheyenne Frontier Days in 1908. Ikua Purdy won first in the steer roping event in the Wyoming capitol and another paniolo won third. The Hawaiians were quite thrilled to come to the mainland by invitation and out-rope the best cowboys in the country for these top honors.

Through her stables Anna became quite familiar with the horse world in the Hilo area. This wasn't her first experience with horses. Her father had been training and selling horses to the other islands for years. She had grown up acting as jockey to some of her father's best race horses, but only for practice. In Hilo she discovered horse racing was quite popular and it wasn't long until she became a jockey at the Hilo track. She also trained other jockeys. Those in the race world were always trying to find the fastest race horse. Anna was a multi-tasker. It was easy for Anna to do a multitude of various projects simultaneously. She had learned from her father who also had been a multi-tasker. Her days were full.

On a trip to a racetrack on the island of Maui she discovered a horse that intrigued her. When she saw him work on the track, and timed him, she knew she had found a winner. He was a thoroughbred called *Maui Parrot*. She contacted her father and told him about the horse. Her father made a deal with the owner, to exchange several good horses for *Maui Parrot*, and he was purchased. They quietly transported him to Hilo. Changed his name to *Kaala*, and worked him on the track before daylight.

They worked him early because they didn't want anyone to be aware of his extreme speed. Unfortunately, after he won his first race in Hilo the management of the Hilo Jockey Club banned him from racing at Hilo again since he was a registered thoroughbred. Anna pleaded with them to upgrade their racing program and expand it to include thoroughbreds. Her requests were dashed. So much for her racing days, Anna moved on.

Husband Henry decided to get more involved in Hawaiian politics by 1935. He ran for a seat in the Territorial Legislature. Like a good wife, Anna campaigned for him diligently putting her usual daily routines aside. After the votes were counted it was common knowledge that he won the seat due to Anna's popularity.

Anna was also very active as a Commissioner of Parks and worked with the Outdoor Circle of the Hilo Women's Club. Their objective was directed toward the beautification of the parks around the city. Much of their efforts went toward planting and nurturing a variety of trees and plants in the area. This included torch ginger, jacaranda, banyan trees and hibiscus hedges. These projects and the care of her nephew Richard, and, occasionally, her niece, kept her busy. She tried to keep from thinking about the undependable, philandering Henry and his shallow, unfulfilled promises. When they had married Anna joined the Catholic Church and the vows she took were important to her, she tried her best to be a good wife.

When Anna was notified her father had fallen from his horse and broken his leg she immediately rushed home to his side. It was necessary that she help her mother care for him. Having never been unhealthy or have a need for doctors William refused to go to the hospital or have a doctor come to the house to set his leg. He insisted on the ancient Hawaiian method of lomi lomi to cure his leg. Lomi lomi is a method of massage, which didn't do a thing to improve his leg. He continued to be bedridden. Day by day he became weaker and sicker. Anna and her mother were by his side continually, but nothing helped. It wasn't long before he died.

Divorce

With her father gone Anna knew she could no long put off the inevitable task of divorcing Henry. Her mother needed her at Waimea. When she consulted with the Catholic priests they were already aware of her marital

Anna sorts cattle. A typical day in the saddle for this 'cowboy', 1970s.
Photo courtesy of Anna Ranch Heritage Center Archives

situation. She received permission, as a divorcee, to continue in the church and receive communion. It was common knowledge she had been an exemplary wife and probably should have left Henry years before. She closed all her activities and businesses in Hilo and returned to Waimea to live and care for her mother.

Shortly after the funeral of her father, her brother Bill, a police officer, came to the ranch insisting that he should be the one to handle his father's estate. It was well-known by both Anna, and her mother, that Bill had no interest in the ranch, and never had. It was suspected that Bill thought the estate was quite a financial empire, and he wanted to make sure he got as much of it as he could.

When his mother told him that she would not allow him to handle the estate Bill immediately hired a lawyer and sued his mother. Anna's mother was greatly saddened to think her son would stoop to such a low point. In the past, the family had to bail Bill out of several financial messes. He seemed to be good at getting into financial difficulty. By this time he had married and had children. The judge ruled in Anna's favor to run the ranch. It was a well-known fact around Waimea, William Lindsey considered Anna his 'best cowboy.' He had taught her as much as he could about cattle, ranching and handling finances. This angered Bill to the point he never spoke to his mother again.

Financial Problems

It didn't take long for Anna to realize that the ranch was not the financial empire Bill had thought it to be. In fact, it was in horrible financial trouble. During her father's illness he had turned the running of his businesses over to a loyal friend, who the entire family thought was trustworthy and could handle the situation and the finances. They misjudged his ability and the ranch was on the verge of total collapse and bankruptcy. Taxes had not been paid, bank accounts were depleted, the cattle had been sold off and the monies from the sale of them had been taken by the 'trusted' friend who had been in charge.

Anna realized she had people to feed and bills to pay and absolutely no money. She refused to tell anyone in her family of the dilemma. Her mother's health was not good and she was still in mourning over her husband's death. Anna knew she would have to handle this matter without a word to anyone.

She quietly went to the manager of the Parker Ranch, A. W. Carter, and told him of her situation. The Parker Ranch was the largest ranch on the island. He offered to loan her the money provided she would put the Lindsey ranch up as collateral. It was a generous offer. Anna was aware that Carter was in hopes she would not be able to pay off the loan. In turn he could then include the Lindsey ranch to the Parker holdings. Anna accepted the loan and was determined to make those monthly payments to the Parker Ranch. She also knew she had to sell some of the family property to ward off other creditors that were threatening to put liens on the holdings if the debts were not paid.

She went to a good friend, Judge Osorio, in Hilo and with his guidance as an astute financier; he aided her in how to auction property. When she was ready to sell she put up signs, sold properties at auction, and even acted as her own auctioneer. Anna's quick learning abilities enabled her mission to be completed and she left with signed checks in hand. When the debts were taken care of Anna made the remark, "When you're poor, you can do the impossible. You have to!"

Returning to the ranch with money to feed and take care of her family Anna was determined to run the ranch in such a way that she could make it profitable. Her first chore was to fire the untrustworthy man that her father had counted on. She knew she had to handle the ranch herself. It was also her policy to never discuss with anyone any financial difficulty. After the chores and work was done each day, she would dress up and be seen at various events around Waimea, as if she didn't have a care in the world.

When it became necessary to borrow $4,000 at the bank, she had no problems. She bought steers and fattened them on their best grassland. By the time the note was due she had sold enough to make the payment on the note and pay regular amounts on the Parker Ranch note, too. She was advised by her father's banker to continue paying the Parker note on time, but use the extra money to make money. His advice worked. Each time she had extra money she invested in more cattle. She found a market for her beef in Hilo. In the meantime, she also saved enough money to buy out her brother's portion of the ranch.

Anna and her mother became closer than ever after Anna took over the ranch. They not only shared the ranch house, but shared their feelings. Her mother Mary always told Anna she did not want to be a burden, but she began to suffer with heart trouble. "I want to go quickly when I go," her mother said. Anna paid little attention to what her mother said because she just knew her mother would live a long life.

One day while working on horseback she saw her helper rushing toward her in the family car. He jumped out and told Anna to hurry home. Her mother was very ill. She jumped in the car, handed the reins of her horse to her helper and rushed to the ranch house. When Anna arrived and rushed in to the house her mother was already gone. Anna was amazed. She knew her mother had willed herself to go quickly.

Anna's mother dying created a huge void in her life. Not only her mother's death caused Anna's life to change drastically, but she lost her niece, too. Her brother Charles' ex-wife took the niece away to live with her. That left just nephew, Richard, and Anna on the ranch. As Richard neared college Anna was aware that her childhood friend, Thelma Parker Smart, had put in her will that the children of Parker Ranch employees be given scholarships to help with their education. Since Richard's father, Charles, had worked as a cowboy at the Parker Ranch during summers before he was sent away, she felt his son should be eligible.

The monies were approved and Anna sent Richard to a boarding school for his high school education. This decision left Anna completely alone on the ranch, but she knew it was the right thing to do, and she was determined to see the ranch become successful.

Anna studied cattle. She read everything she could find on all aspects of cattle raising. Much new information was found in cattle magazines from the mainland. New techniques were continually being developed. The more she studied and learned the more she appreciated the land her father had bought and realized that she not only owned some of the best grazing lands on the island but some of the very best sources of water, too. Having enough water was always a concern when raising cattle. In time, no one in the area knew more about raising cattle and using the newly recognized ways to improve a herd than Anna.

The manager of Parker Ranch called her and asked if she would come to his office. Anna was puzzled by the request. She knew she had been paying the loan on time. She couldn't imagine why he wanted to see her. When she arrived he said, "Why is a pretty little thing like you working so hard on the ranch? You should sell it."

Anna was even more determined than ever to make it a success. He told her he knew several buyers that would give her what it was worth. Anna informed him it was worth much more to her than money and that she had no intention of ever selling the ranch.

The anger she felt when she walked out of his office spurred her on. She bought the portion of the ranch her niece and nephew had inherited and became the sole owner. She designed a sign and placed it on the road at the front entrance which read, "Anna Ranch." The print looked like it was written with a lasso and to this day it still stands at the entrance to the ranch.

Anna worked six days a week on the ranch. She called herself a cowboy because she did exactly the same work a cowboy would have done. Since her father's death in 1939, Anna has ridden the pastures, checked and moved cattle, fixed fence, branded, bought and sold cattle and even did the work in the slaughterhouse. When it was absolutely necessary she would hire a few day-working paniolos for a few hours.

But regardless of her cowboy days she enjoyed dressing up at night, no matter how tired and spent she might feel. Once she would arrive at a party or social engagement her exhaustion seemed to slip away. Anna was very popular in the community and it was just not a party without her. A party invigorated her and the way she danced or enjoyed it no one would have thought she had a problem in the world.

She still scrimped to make things work, but she had learned so much about ranching she made up her mind she was going to make a major change in the ranch. She was going to the mainland and buy the best bulls she could afford in order to improve her herd. Her goal would be to buy steers that produced more and better flavored beef. Before she could act on this decision, however, a world crisis changed her plan and that of everyone else. World War II was announced.

Anna had ridden her horse to her beloved Keawewai, completely unaware anything was about to happen. This was the part of the ranch that had the best grazing land and the most water. It was remote and there was no communication in or out of this part of the property. That was actually one of the reasons why she loved it so. It was her 'get away.' When she was there she was at peace. The following morning, December 7, 1941, when she arrived back at the main ranch she found a Parker Ranch cowboy waiting for her. He said, "Miss Anna, Mr. Carter said the Japanese attacked Pearl Harbor this morning and it looks bad. He said to tell you to turn your radio on and stay by it"

It was in no time before the hills around Waimea were teaming with military forces. A base opened shortly and 30,000 soldiers were soon stationed in and around the area. It was necessary to keep the entire island safe from harm and under surveillance. Business thrived for the farmers of the area after the new base was up and running. There was a built-in market for all the beef Anna and her neighboring ranchers could supply to the G.I.s. But the problem was the prices were controlled by the military and it was hard for the local ranchers to make a profit once they had the carcasses cut up by butchers. The butchers charged such a high amount for their services it took almost the entire profit from the government-controlled pricing.

Anna decided her only choice was to learn to butcher her own steers. It was difficult to receive the proper credentials from the Board of Health, but Anna learned, and was the first woman to receive a butcher's license. She sold her beef to markets as far away as Honolulu but her main customer was the Hilo Meat Company. Anna always stayed loyal to those who had been good to her. When she nearly lost the ranch the Hilo Meat Company was part of the group that supported Anna.

Since the nights required a complete blackout during wartime the social life around the island had to change. Socializing continued but had to be done with afternoon teas, dances and such. The military was appreciated by the local people and the G.I.s soon became acquainted with many of the local people who volunteered and worked at these events involving the soldiers.

Anna was active in all these endeavors but was especially committed to the Red Cross. She tried to keep from letting any of the military personnel know she was single and living alone on the ranch. She had many young soldiers asking her for dates. An older Colonel told her if she was seen with him, he knew the younger men would cease to bother her. She followed his advice and it worked beautifully. The Colonel, no doubt, enjoyed her company, too.

Although Anna was very willing to serve as a volunteer she was most committed to making the ranch as profitable as possible. She personally bought steers with her loans. Other local ranchers watched what she bought and it wasn't long before other ranchers realized she knew exactly what she was doing in the cattle business. In a short while, she was able to pay off the rest of the Parker Ranch loan of $19,000.

A. W. Carter was no longer at the ranch, but in Honolulu, and Anna was determined to show him she had succeeded in paying off the loan. There was no way the Parker Ranch could lay any claim to her ranch. She made a trip to Honolulu just to see him. She dressed to the nines, walked in his office and placed the receipt of payment in front of him. It was evident by the expression on his face he was shocked. "How did you do it," he asked? She answered by saying, "Hard work, determination and faith!"

Anna was blessed with many suitors. Several officers stationed near Waimea became really good friends; some often rode horseback with Anna on the ranch when they were not on duty at the base.

A New Interest

No one seemed to interest Anna more than Lyman Perry-Fiske. He had been born in the North Kohala area of the island. His family had established the Awini Land and Coffee Company. His father was English and his mother was Hawaiian. Lyman left the area as a young man of 20. His education was gained by his own efforts. He began working very early in his life. His jobs interfered with his normal schooling, but since he had such ambition, untiring energy, and willingness, he always was placed in charge of other workers.

Although his work hours were long, he would study the books at night. These books qualified him to become a civil engineer. He passed the exam and began his civil engineering career which took him all over the world, including China and Tibet. He was quite taken with Buddhism while in Tibet and studied in a monastery under a lama. He was called home from Tibet when he was notified his father was dying. On his return to Hawaii, he began working as an engineer with the City and County of Honolulu.

One of his long-time friends was Anna's cousin, Edwin Lindsey, who brought him to the ranch to meet Anna and her mother, who was still living at that time. He was charming and both Anna and her mother enjoyed his company.

Although he often proposed to Anna she was determined to stay single. At least until she had the ranch in a profitable position. Lyman came to visit from time to time, and they often rode horses and talked for hours. It was evident they had a strong affection for one another but Anna held tight to her conviction to stay single. The ranch was producing a profit but Anna continued to work as hard as ever.

Eventually her health began being affected. The doctor told Anna in 1943 she had to get away from the ranch. "Take a vacation and I recommend you take at least a month away," he insisted.

When Lyman heard the news, he offered to come and oversee the ranch while she was gone. Anna knew he could be trusted and he knew enough about running the ranch that she didn't have to worry while away. It just so happened that just previous to the doctor advising Anna to get away, she had given in and became engaged to Lyman. When the month was over and Anna was ready to return after regaining her strength and enthusiasm she informed Lyman she was coming home and he could leave. He informed her he wasn't leaving the ranch.

When she arrived on the Island she stopped in Hilo and stayed with her long-time friend, Kate Koehnen. She mentioned to Kate Lyman's reluctance to leave the ranch. Kate laughed and told Anna that was his way of forcing Anna to marry him. At first Anna was shocked, as it had never entered her mind that might be his reason. Once she thought about it she realized she, too, was ready to marry. Anna and Lyman were married in Kate's home later that year.

Anna and Lyman's days at the ranch were happy and full. Anna always prepared the meals, which included using the best china and silver. The table was always elaborately set. Once a meal was over they left the house and spent the days out-of-doors. They moved cattle, mended fences, checked the feed, or whatever was needed to be done at the time.

Anna and husband, Lyman Perry-Fiske dancing at Waikiki, 1940s. *Photo courtesy of Anna Ranch Heritage Center Archives.*

Their social life was full. Lyman was accepted into the community by everyone and not an event was held that they didn't receive an invitation. Nights, when they were home, Anna worked on the ranch books and Lyman read incessantly. In time, they admitted their lives were perfect—except for one problem. Neither had ever had children. It was a void in their lives. They knew they wanted to do something about it. In Hawaii the custom of 'hanai' is to adopt a child. Anna and Lyman were ready; however, it took a few years before this would happen.

After the war, Anna threw herself in to further improving the ranch. She needed to go to the mainland and buy an exceptional bull that would raise the quality of her herd. She knew from studying that she did not have the resources necessary to buy the kind of bull she needed.

Yutaka Kimura was probably the most knowledgeable cattleman on the

Island. Anna talked with him about her plan. He agreed with her and knew Anna was exactly right. He had studied cattle since a child and was hired by Carter for the Parker Ranch to aid them in upgrading their herd. At one time, under his direction they had the largest herd of purebred Hereford cattle in the world. Yutaka was Anna's biggest fan.

She decided that she would 'hire out' to dairymen in the area. She offered to go to the mainland for them and buy good quality milk cows. She met with them and told them what she could do for them. When they consulted with Yukata he informed them of Anna's credentials and his confidence in her ability. They were very willing to have her represent them. She made three trips to Seattle and bought the best milk cows available. By then she had earned enough money to buy her chosen bull. She always took two paniolos from the area with her to accompany the cattle back by ship. The freighters they were shipped on had no facilities for passengers, but the paniolos were allowed to accompany the cattle. Meanwhile, Anna sailed back on a luxury liner and enjoyed the voyage at sea. The dairymen were extremely pleased with her purchases for them and this garnered her quite the reputation as a top-rate cattle buyer.

On a third trip, she bought her carefully selected fine Holstein-Friesian bull. He traveled from Seattle to Honolulu to Kawaihae. She trucked him to the ranch and put him in a separate area where he could adjust to his new surroundings. He was sired by an All-American show bull named *Carnation Governor Imperial*.

The change from the Seattle damp cool climate to the tropical Hawaiian air would require that he become used to the change slowly. Three weeks after arriving Anna found him lying in the pasture—dead. It was such a shock. No apparent reason for the death could be found. It was a major disappointment but Anna kept her composure. no one was aware of her deep regret. "Don't cry about it, just have the faith and strength to go on," was her philosophy.

Anna's goals did not change. She was to get top prices for her beef. She decided cross-breeding was the answer and she began to experiment. Her research continued as she studied the bulls of various breeds on the mainland.

Vivian, the daughter of Anna's brother Bill, was one of Anna's favorite young people and she often accompanied Anna on her trips to Honolulu.

Vivian had married a police officer in Kona and they had a son. One day Vivian came to visit Anna, which she did occasionally. She left to pick up her husband, John Silva. On the way Vivian lost control of the vehicle and was severely injured. Her husband had minor injuries. When Anna got the news of the crash she hurried to the hospital. Vivian asked her, if she didn't make it, would Anna take care of her son, Weston. Of course, Anna agreed thinking her niece would be all right in time. Unfortunately Vivian died. Her injuries were much more serious than anyone suspected.

When Anna told John Silva and her family of Vivian's request, and her desire to care for Weston, they all agreed to honor her wishes. Silva knew Anna could give Weston far more than he ever could. Meanwhile, the maternal grandmother who had been caring for Weston combined with her grief over losing her daughter, was not willing to give up her grandson for adoption, in spite of his father's willingness.

When Weston was five-years old Anna and Lyman went to court to adopt the boy. His grandmother still continued to care for him. Although he didn't come to live with Anna and Lyman in Waimea they supported him as their own. When Weston was 11-years-old Anna insisted he come and live with them.

When Weston came to live on Anna Ranch it was discovered that he had a spot on his lung and was on the verge of having tuberculosis. Anna nursed him back to being a healthy boy as quickly as possible. He was exceptionally bright but it was discovered that the heavy load at Hawaii Preparatory Academy was almost too much for him.

Anna observed his daily routine and watched him labor over his homework far in to the night. She finally recommended that he get up early, with her at 4 a.m., and do his homework when he was rested. It was no time before he was excelling and receiving the highest grades.

He graduated at the young age of 16. He enrolled in the University of Hawaii and easily made the dean's list. Anna encouraged Weston to come home to Waimea for various special parties and events she hosted. At one such party, the theme was to wear costumes. He showed up dressed as a woman. Much later in his life it would occur to Anna that her adopted son might have been trying to tell them of his sexual preference by dressing as a woman.

Politics Again?

During this time Anna was approached by a Republican territorial legislator who had decided not to run for re-election. "Anna, why don't you run for my office, since I'm not going to run again," he suggested.

Anna had helped her first husband, Henry, campaign. Many people told her he won his elections because of her reputation and campaign efforts. The more she thought about it and as others continued to encourage her, she decided to run. She campaigned hard and invested much of her money in the endeavor. Lyman sat quietly by, not encouraging and yet not discouraging her decision. At the very last minute the legislator who talked her in to running changed his mind and entered the race.

Election day Anna knew the Republican votes were going to be divided between her and the incumbent. The Democratic candidate, Akoni Pule, won the election. After the loss Anna re-evaluated her thoughts on politics and what she had learned. During the campaign quite a few people had approached her, expecting her to give them favors, for their votes. They even suggested she give them sides of beef, for their votes. She realized how many compromises a politician was forced to make when in office and knew she didn't want to live that way. Her loss in the election was considered a relief as she learned much about her own beliefs and values. She would never consider a political position again.

Which Breed?

Meanwhile Anna went back to her in-depth research on which breed of bull she needed to improve her herd. She knew she wanted a large bull with plenty of meat and one that could tolerate the weather in Waimea. The Brahma seemed to have both qualifications. She decided that crossing a Brahma bull with her Hereford cows was the best decision.

She picked the Fisher Ranch in California to visit as they had produced champion Brahmas. When she met Mr. and Mrs. Fisher they were shocked at her appearance. They had expected their 'Hawaiian cattle rancher' to look differently than the way Anna presented herself. She was wearing a very stylish black suit and hat designed for her by a San Francisco hat-maker. They laughed and told her they thought she looked more like a socialite than a rancher. Anna immediately became friends with the Fishers and they shared many views on how to raise cattle successfully and profitably. She picked their best bull and the sale was made.

The new 'chosen' bull arrived at the ranch and as soon as he adjusted Anna put him in a pasture with her heifers. He got right to work. When the calves were born Anna hosted a 'baby luau' to introduce her new calves to her friends, of which some were cattle raisers. When they dressed out at 120 pounds heavier than the average beef carcass she was delighted. She bought three more bulls from the Fishers. The Anna Ranch grew and the profits followed.

Anna began to host elaborate events for the Heart Association. Since her mother succumbed to heart trouble this organization was important to Anna. Her parties were always a huge success and much money was raised for the cause. She also enjoyed the Easter Seal party that was held annually at the Royal Hawaiian Hotel in Honolulu. The best Easter hats were picked and auctioned off. Anna truly loved her fashionable hats that were elaborately designed for her. In spite of her love for them she always allowed one to be auctioned off. Nearly every year her selection would bring one of the highest prices sold. One of her Easter hats brought $1,100.00 at one luncheon. Another year, her creation brought $800 for the fund.

Her friend, Pudding Lassiter said of Anna, "She always made a grand entrance at any event. She would always out-dress everyone else that attended. She invited my mom, my sister, my daughters and me to ride in the Hawaii on Horseback programs. She loved parties and to socialize."

Anna continued to have great luck with her crossbreeding of Brahma and Hereford cattle. The consensus was there was not a better tasting beef. However, Anna was called in by one of her customers, the owner of Supersave Supermarkets, in 1961. The butcher cut off a steak, which was huge, and placed it on a normal-sized plate. Because of the enormous size of the steak it hung off the sides of the plate. Anna never realized the steak's huge size. In spite of the good taste, its size made it look downright unappetizing on the plate. Her roasts were a different story, but she didn't have as many customers requesting roasts. Hotels and restaurants wanted good steaks.

She continued to research and decided she wanted to try the Charolais breed. Again she went to California and bought three bulls from the most renowned breeder of the Charolais. She also bought some heifers as well. Years later when the announcement of the arrival of the Charolais breed to Hawaii was promoted a few people remembered Anna had been using them

Representing Hawaii at a Centennial Celebration of the Royal Canadian Mounted Police, in Lethbridge, Canada. Anna wears one of her Pa-u' outfits. *Photo courtesy of the Anna Ranch Heritage Center Archives.*

for years.

"People have short memories," was Anna's only comment. By that time she had proven that the two breeds, Charolais and Hereford provided not only very tasty meat with excellent texture, but sold very well. The ranch continued to be extremely profitable. In time, the Cattleman's Horse and Bull sale was held in Waimea annually. She no longer had to travel to the mainland to buy top stock.

Numerous other innovative ideas were tried by Anna when other ranchers refused to change what they had done for years. There were several plants in the area that often choked out the good grasses and were extremely difficult to get rid of. This included lantana, emax and guava scrub. One night at a dinner party Anna was placed next to Richard Frazier who had been working on an aerial spraying process that would control the weeds.

During their conversation he lamented to Anna that he couldn't get any of the ranchers to allow him to use airplanes and helicopters to spray it on the crops.

Anna told him she would be willing to try it, but she also did not want to use airplanes or helicopters as they might upset her cattle. Instead, she asked why they couldn't apply it from a truck. He agreed and set it up to be applied from a truck. In short order, her fields and pastures were full of grass with no weeds. Again Anna was a trendsetter.

A community-spirited individual, Anna was often asked by various dignitaries to ride horseback representing Hawaii and the equestrian history of the Islands. The pa'u rider was unique to Hawaii. When a person rode horseback in the early days on the islands, to and from an important social event, it was important to protect their fancy clothing. They wore a cloth-coverlet. The coverlet was originally to protect their 'best' clothes from dust, mud or moisture. But eventually the coverlet, when being worn historically, was made of a beautiful fabric and almost touched the ground. Worn with it was an elaborate headdress, as well as beautiful leis worn by the rider and placed around the neck of the horse. Anna had been representing the history of Hawaii since she was a young woman. In 1961, she was chosen as Queen of Hilo's Kamehameha Day parade. Her pa'u costume was red velvet. Red was the color that represented the big island of Hawaii. It was outstandingly elegant.

Old Hawaii on Horseback

Anna was the chairman for the American Heart Association. She was searching for a unique and different fund-raising idea for the annual event. She came up with the idea to use the phrase "Old Hawaii on Horseback". It would be a historic pageant and could be staged on the great expanse of lawn in front of her ranch house. She wrote a script and asked the best riders on the island to participate. She directed rehearsals, designed costumes and produced it. She was also a participant. It wasn't long before thousands of spectators were coming to see this production. The donations to the Heart Fund were pouring in and breaking all kinds of fund-raising numbers. For some time she held it annually with a new script and costumes each year. Because it was so time consuming for Anna, eventually she made it a bi-annual affair.

Anna was asked to be a 'marshal' of one section of the Rose Bowl Parade,

Photo taken from the garden of the Anna Ranch, Waimea, Hawaii.
Photo courtesy of the Anna Ranch Heritage Center Archives

on New Years Day, 1972, and ride as a pa'u rider. In one newspaper article, it said, "Mrs. Perry-Fiske, a grande dame of Hawaii will travel to Pasadena with a dresser, a lei-maker and thousands of island flowers". She wore a royal blue velvet pa'u, with 50 strands of jasmine around her neck, and a crown of jasmine adorned her head. Her mount also wore a white crown flower lei.

Another invitation followed and she was invited to the Calgary Stampede and the Lethbridge, Alberta, Canada Centennial Celebration of the Royal Mounted Police in 1974. These trips were always paid for by Anna, as she always considered it an honor to be asked to represent the State of Hawaii.

As Anna grew older she slowed her pace of activities, but not by standards set by most people her age. She kept busy and her most important project was to make Anna Ranch a place people could visit that would represent a woman rancher of her era. Before her death she saw the ranch listed on the Hawaii State Register of Historic Places. Anna passed away in 1995. Her entire life she dared to be different.

Who Says A Woman Can't Be President?
Lois Herbst

Some women just can't sit still, or keep quiet. But few women use their energy and voice the way Lois Herbst has in the last twenty-plus years. When it comes to the land, and how we, as stewards of the land should protect it and guard how it is used, Lois has the common sense and has done the research that is needed to make sound judgments regarding its use. She is proud to be an activist for ranchers and farmers. She lives on a ranch near Shoshoni, Wyoming, but her interests reach far beyond the borders of her State. She recognizes what is good for the country, and is not shy about saying so.

Childhood

Lois Herbst was born to Edward F. Brown and Pauline Anastacia Scherer of Ironton, Ohio, on July 11, 1933. She was the seventh of eight children. She remembers her early childhood by playing with the twin boys that had been born before her. To hear her brothers tell it, they remember that Lois always wanted to be involved when they were doing something 'naughty.' and that was fine with the boys. But often, Lois would tell on them, which got all of them in trouble. Once they placed a dead snake on the kitchen stairs to scare their dad . . . and it did.

Grandfather Scherer was a successful businessman. He had an insurance business and an interest in a local coal mine. Scherer liked Edward F. Brown because he was a hard worker. He even purchased the Kellog farm, where Lois was raised. Scherer gave it to Lois' mother so her father could work for him and his brother, Albert Scherer, on their neighboring dairy farm. Brown helped Scherers with the milking twice a day and also helped with the farming. He was paid $40 a month. Brown was raised in the hills of Kentucky.

Lois's dad farmed his own land, in addition to working on the dairy. He had a huge barn for his teams of horses, which he worked putting in fields of grain and hay. The barn was also used for some of the dairy cows. He raised pigs, milk cows, and chickens and had a big garden. This provided just about everything that was needed for his growing family. Lois remembers that he planted a fruit tree when each child was born.

One of her first recollections outside the house was when she was around two-years-old and her father carried her out toward the barn and stopped by 'her' peach tree which he planted in July, 1933. He picked a ripe peach and gave it to her.

She also remembers as a tot being told to go upstairs to nap. The wood frame house had been built before the Civil War by William Kellog and it would creak and moan. Lois imagined all kinds of scary boogie men which often interfered with her nap. The house had a fireplace in each of the rooms. The upstairs fireplaces in the bedrooms were not used and the children would race downstairs on a winter morning to stand in front of the warm fire to dress.

As she grew older she was teased unmercifully by her brothers. They chased her with snakes and worse. Across the railroad tracks was stand of trees that always seemed so mysterious. It had thick underbrush and was swampy in some areas. The children were always lured to go there, especially during blackberry season. The blackberry bushes were full of the best berries imaginable. Lois always preferred playing with her brothers, even though she was their target for pranks at times. She believes that playing with her brothers, instead of her sisters, saved her from a childhood of dolls and 'girly' play.

After church on Sunday Grandfather Scherer would have Grandmother prepare a meal for the family and friends. Lois' mother helped her mother with the cooking for these meals and became an excellent cook. Her grandfather's success was shown by the Sunday meal which always had at least three different meats. In Grandfather Scherer's later years, Lois' mother was his chauffeur, driving him to and from Ironton.

Family Serves Their Country

Lois' brother, Jake, tried enlisting in the army when he was 16 but did not weigh enough and was turned away. He began to drink *Ovaltine*, which was known to improved one's appetite. When Jake returned to the enlistment office the second time to try again he had gained enough weight to be accepted in the U. S. Army. He was stationed at Schofield Barracks in

Hawaii when the Japanese attacked Pearl Harbor. When the family heard of the attack at Pearl Harbor they immediately began trying to get or hear some word of Jake. It took some time before the family was notified that he was alive and safe.

Lois' oldest sister, Mary, was accepted in nurses training in Washington, D. C., and another sister, Rosemary, worked for a family in Ashland, Kentucky, for a time, but later joined the navy as a Wave and brother Charlie also joined the navy. Another brother Harold joined the air force.

When Pearl Harbor was attacked by the Japanese the entire country took notice. Mr. Brown went with some of the neighbors to Lorain, Ohio, and went to work at National Tube Company. He moved his family to Lorain. Mr. Brown's job was to remove chips from the tubes, by using a jackhammer. His strong work ethic made him ignore the work schedules put out by the company as to when he was to report to work. He got up early and went to work long before his shift began, and stayed late after his shift left.

Once the rest of the family was settled Mrs. Brown also felt she needed to find work. When she told Mr. Brown she planned to work he said, "What are you going to do? You can't do anything!"

In spite of his remarks Mrs. Brown did indeed go to work. She was hired at National Tube Company, too. Her position there was running the controls that flipped hot steel from different tables, as it was conveyed through the various processes on the way to becoming tubes. She received a higher wage than the job her husband held.

When the war was over Mrs. Brown was forced to give up her job at National Tube Company. The policy allowed veterans, coming home from serving their country, to have first choice of jobs. She left her job so a veteran could be hired.

The family then moved back to the farm near Ironton. However, Mr. Brown's work ethic caused his supervisor at National Tube Company to send someone to Ironton to get Brown to return to work. It seems they found they couldn't do without him. The workers knew he'd do his job and theirs, too.

During this time, after 26 years of marriage, and eight children, the Browns divorced. Although Mrs. Brown had been raised in the Catholic Church and knew the Church frowned on divorce they did get divorced.

Lois and her remaining siblings went to Green Township High School after returning to the farm in 1948. She had a good music teacher named Mrs. Zipperlen, and the school had a good band and glee club. Mrs. Zipperlen gave Lois a coronet to learn to play but she had trouble learning rhythm and had to give it up. The teacher did praise Lois on her good wind. Although she couldn't get the rhythm right when they had programs Lois often got to be the announcer because she could be heard by everyone. She did have good wind.

Lois completed her education in the small high school and most of her education, she admits, came from reading library books. A traveling bookmobile provided many of the books she chose to read. She graduated Salutatorian in her class of 21 students, and received a scholarship to Capital University in Columbus, Ohio. Her mother told her they could not afford to send her to college, and encouraged her to enlist in the military. This was long before grants were available to help students attend college. Lois joined the Air Force.

Joining the Air Force

A train trip to Lackland Air Force Base in San Antonio, Texas, began Lois' military service career. She enjoyed marching and singing. Tests showed she would be qualified to be a control tower operator but she asked to be a secretary instead. She was sent to Arizona State University for a six month secretarial course. When she completed the course she was sent to Hill Air Force Base in Ogden, Utah. Her final military assignment was at Wright Patterson Air Force Base in Dayton, Ohio.

Lois returned home after her military career. She went to work as a secretary with Good Year Atomic Corporation in Chillicothe, Ohio. She commuted daily from Haverhill with friends that worked there. In time she moved to Chillicothe. She also attended night school at the Portsmouth branch of Ohio University for two years. She was working toward a degree in secondary education, social studies and history. When required courses weren't available she moved to Denver, Colorado. Her sister, Rosemary, lived there at the time. Lois went to work for Carpenter-Trent Drilling Company as an executive secretary for the superintendent of plant maintenance. She continued attending school at night at Denver University.

Meeting Her Future Husband

On a trip to visit her sister, Mary Fender, a nurse, who was living at Shoshoni, Wyoming, she was introduced to Bill Herbst, a local rancher and neighbor. It was 1957. That evening at a dance at the Wagon Wheel Bar a married man took a liking to Lois even though his wife sat there observing his foolishness toward her.

Bill Herbst asked Lois to dance and when she told him of the other man's embarrassing actions he offered to sit with her the rest of the evening. Before they said goodnight Bill asked Lois if she would like to go break ice and open water holes, for the cattle, and then go to breakfast the following morning. She accepted his offer.

When they arrived home Lois asked her sister, Mary, about Bill. Mary gave her blessings and felt Bill, who was a neighbor, was a good man. She set the alarm for the time Lois needed to be up and ready for Bill's arrival. Mary knew how early Bill liked to get his work done.

Lois & Bill Herbst on their wedding day at the Trinity Lutheran Church in Riverton, Wyoming. *Photo courtesy orf Lois Herbst.*

The next morning Lois and Bill drove up the Wind River where they saw herds of antelope. Lois was not accustomed to seeing the graceful animals at such a close range. Bill was more interested in getting the ice broken in the Wind River so his cattle could get a drink.

Lois remembers their first date and how she watched Bill while he worked. After the chores were done they went to the Lakeside Café for breakfast. Before Bill took her home he asked Lois if he could see her again that evening. She accepted and they drove up Wind River Canyon north of

Shoshoni.

Lois made a trip back to Shoshoni, to spend Christmas with her sister. She saw Bill again and it allowed her more time to get to know him. By March, Bill told Lois she needed to move to Wyoming so they could continue to get better acquainted. On his suggestion she found a secretarial job with a legal firm in Riverton, 22 miles from Shoshoni. Bill lived in Shoshoni. His family bought the house when he was a child in school because they couldn't commute to the river ranch.

By the time Lois met Bill, the family ranch home had been destroyed, as the family land was condemned for the Boysen Reservoir that was to be built there. The move to Riverton certainly did allow the young couple to get better acquainted. On May 29, 1958 Lois and Bill were married.

Bill was a second generation rancher. His dad, Frank, from Gottschee, Austria, had homesteaded on a piece of property in the Shoshoni area in 1906. The original homestead was condemned by the Bureau of Reclamation, in 1948 for the Boysen Dam project and reservoir. This was a common practice in the Midwest during this time as so much of this land was dry. The government built dams to collect water for farmers and ranchers that owned land that suffered from little to no rainfall. Frank died that same year, and son Bill bought new land on which they could continue ranching.

Lois and Bill Marry

When Lois married and joined Bill on the ranch she was eager to learn all there was to know about the ranch. That is a mighty big chore when learning from someone who has lived their entire life on a ranch. Many things Bill did he didn't have to give it a thought. He just did them as he had done all his life. Lois asked Bill many questions and went with Bill as much as she could to learn, and to be with her new husband. She went with Bill to check cattle, irrigate, vaccinate, and whatever else needed to be done. Bill was delighted she had such an interest in their ranch.

She studied the cattle and kept records of the cattle and where they were located. They built a quality herd of Herefords. Bill had an 'eye' for picking good bulls. They were always Herefords, but in 1971 he began purchasing some black bulls for cross-breeding. The herd gradually turned to Black Angus.

Twins Arrive

When Lois became pregnant Bill bet many of his friends a bottle of whiskey that he would have a boy. The due date was a few weeks off when Lois thought she was having gas pains. Just to be safe Lois called her doctor. Since it was still winter and the temperature was looming around minus 50 degrees he advised her to come to the hospital. Although they were living in Shoshoni, since the homestead had been condemned, the doctor didn't want any delays in her getting there with such severe cold weather happening.

Lois' sister, Mary, a nurse, also arrived at the hospital and was the first to announce, "Sissy, you are having twins! Here's a little butt and here's another little butt," as she examined her.

That was news to everyone including the doctor. In fact he refused to believe it. He thought the baby was crosswise. Lois said, "When Mary bet him a coke I was having twins he wouldn't even take the bet." The duty nurses wouldn't even get a second bassinet. The two girls were delivered eight minutes apart around 8 p.m. that evening. Mother and daughters, Linda

Bill walking the twins, Linda and Karen, to Yellowstone Drug Store for ice cream cones.
Photo courtesy of Lois Herbst.

and Karen, were resting nicely.

Father Bill was thrilled with his newborns. Once he knew everyone was doing well he headed to the local bar, The Derby, to announce the birth of his twin daughters. One of his cronies called the hospital to verify that Bill was telling the truth. Once all the congratulations were over his friends reminded him of all the bets he had made that he was going to have a son. Bill made good on the bets he had made but it took a case of whiskey to pay off everyone.

Bill finally got his son, Frank, in 1962. Although he was born breach and Lois recalls the birth as horrific, she remembered he came out sucking his thumb and was a beautiful baby. Several weeks later Lois noticed that his lips were turning purple. She took him to the clinic in Riverton to have him examined. The doctor pinched the baby and diagnosed him as fine; however he hospitalized the baby because Lois was so upset. After several days of observing baby Frank in the hospital one of the older nurses recommended Lois get him to Children's Hospital in Denver.

Lois and Bill didn't hesitate. When they arrived the doctors had a hard time determining the cause of the baby's illness. Through a process of elimination, he was finally diagnosed with having a viral infection in the lining of his heart caused by an allergy to milk. Doctors advised the Herbsts leave him in their care and go home and take care of their twin daughters. They were hesitant to leave baby Frank, but knew they had no choice. Lois remembers the doctor called her on a daily basis giving her a full report on her baby son. In two weeks he was much better and they were able to bring him home.

The year Frank was born Bill and Lois bought a second place which today is the ranch headquarters. They operated the ranch from this location. The children were a part of the ranching as soon as they were old enough. Everyone would wake up at 3 a.m. and Lois would fix breakfast for the sleepy-eyed kids. Then they were off to the corral where Bill would be saddling the horses. Lois remembered Bill always mumbling he'd be glad when they were old enough to saddle their own horses. Then they trucked the saddle horses 15 miles to where the cattle were held in a pasture, after two earlier days of trailing them. The children rode their horses on a steep, rocky trail, and always came home tired but happy, full of vitality and starving.

The Children Learn to Work

By the time Frank was ten-years-old Bill had him on a tractor baling hay. The children learned to irrigate as soon as they were old enough to hold a shovel. The girls worked right alongside the men. They rode horses, worked cattle, trucked cattle, irrigated and Karen even learned to run the haystacker. Bill preferred to have the kids as part of the help because he felt they were better hands than those he had hired in the past.

The Herbst children knew when they got home from school there would be chores to do. Lois said their brood was always a joy, and it was such a pleasure to work together as a family. Although Linda and Karen were twins, they were always put in separate classes and had separate interests. Linda was interested in sports medicine and enjoyed managing some of the school sports teams. Karen found she enjoyed working on the year book and was active in Future Farmers of America. In fact, Karen became the first girl to be President of the Shoshoni FFA Chapter.

When the twins graduated from high school Linda was valedictorian of their class and Karen was salutatorian. Both girls wanted to attend college and Linda had a full scholarship. They attended the University of Wyoming located in Laramie. Each month the girls would receive a paycheck from the ranch for the work they had done growing up. That is how they paid for their college education.

Tragedy Strikes

Linda was on her way home from college for Christmas vacation, and had caught a ride with a neighbor girl, Mary Jo, in her little Chevrolet car. It was December, 1979. The roads were snowy but not bad, but when a truck jackknifed in front of them, Mary Jo did not have time to stop. The little car plowed in to the diesel tank of the truck. At the impact Linda's head slammed in to the glove compartment so hard it made a hole in the compartment the size of someone's knee. When Linda was cut out of her seatbelt she was unconscious. Those attending thought she was dead, and laid her body on a snow bank until she could be transported to a Casper hospital.

When the driver's parents were notified, they in turn notified the Herbsts. They immediately hurried to the Casper hospital. It was a Christmas holiday weekend in 1979 and the hospital staff was just a skeleton crew. Linda was seen by a neurologist immediately but the CT scan machine was not working. They were unaware until the CT scan machine was repaired that her brain was bleeding in three areas. She lay there unconscious for over a week. When she did regain consciousness she was not alert. Finally, when she was diagnosed they said it was brain damage. The neurologist at Casper released her to go home. Later it was discovered she was still bleeding in three areas of her brain.

Linda had to stay home and heal the best she could. She was not ready to go back to school at the University of Wyoming until the 1980 fall semester. Eventually she got her degree in agriculture economics. She worked for the United States Department of Agriculture in various locales in Colorado, Nebraska and Wyoming. Much of her work involved examining CRP contracts and determining if the farmers were following the required guidelines. She held this position with the USDA for ten years. Presently she lives in Cheyenne. Linda assists Karen with her ranch chores, including care of the horses. She gives unending care to Karen's rescued cats and dogs.

Karen Becomes a Landman

Karen graduated with a degree in business, majoring in accounting. Before Karen's graduation Lois was dealing with several oil men who were interested in leasing their property for the oil rights. She told them of her daughter and inquired as to how Karen should go about getting in to the oil business when she graduated. It was recommended that she apply in the land department of several oil companies located in Casper.

When Karen came home Lois and Bill showed her on maps how sections of land were marked. She also talked with a classmate who was studying petroleum studies. She began her work as a Landman in the oil industry for Gulf Oil Company. In time she became a partner in the firm of Providence Minerals LLC located in Dallas, Texas.

The winter of 1977-78 was a bad one, and feeding the cattle in their winter pastures caused the Herbsts to change from their normal procedures. It was not unusual to have to feed more in the winter but this treacherous season just seemed to have no end. The cattle were removed from their pastures and put in facilities with farmers who could provide a better maintenance program. The better nutrition allowed a better health program which in turn improved the herd. Surprisingly the need to move the cattle for better maintenance caused the Herbst's calves had a 19% gain in weaning weights.

Not Just a Housewife — A Rancher as Well

Lois was always an active part of the ranching activities from the time she married Bill. In addition to the housework and child-care she enjoyed working outside with Bill. She always took the night shift to check the heifers during calving season. She would go to bed, get up after several hours, get dressed, and go out in the pasture on foot with a flashlight to make sure no heifer was in need of help birthing a calf. Heifers occasionally have problems berthing their first calf.

In the case of a problem a heifer had Lois always called Bill to help with the delivery. The success of a 100% calf crop, with no losses, is a goal strived for in a yearly calving season but seldom attained. Lois was a cautious person and realized she could encounter a problem during this nightly check. She would set the alarm for Bill in case she didn't return in a reasonable amount of time. Fortunately, in 33 years the alarm never caused Bill to awaken and go look for Lois.

Bill seldom left the ranch, by choice. He had plenty of work on the ranch and Lois always handled the business that required traveling off the ranch, much to Bill's delight. During the 1990 calving season Lois and son, Frank, returned to the headquarters after taking care of business in town to find Bill sitting on the step, white as a sheet. They discovered he had driven quite a distance from home when his pickup quit and he had to walk. The distance was almost too much for him. Lois immediately became concerned. She knew that normally the distance would not have been a problem. She insisted he get to the doctor immediately. The diagnosis was grim. The doctor discovered he was suffering from leukemia.

They flew him to Denver in March and Lois went with him. He didn't get to return home until July, at which time the family was told he was in remission. However, he soon had a relapse and they rushed him back to Denver.

On his return home he was prescribed to go to Riverton and have blood transfusions. His body and the illness had killed his ability to produce blood. One day the blood bank refused to give him any more blood transfusions. When Lois inquired they said the paperwork they received indicated he was beyond help.

When the Herbsts notified their doctor of the refusal he called the blood bank and said, "He's out in the pasture checking his cattle. He's not dead!

Send the blood!" The blood was sent and he continued to get transfusions. But unfortunately it didn't help. He passed away in October, 1990.

Lois didn't have much time to grieve or think about what would happen without Bill. After his death she had 300 head of cattle that had to be trucked to Torrington to be sold. She also bought 19,000 acres of grazing land. They had leased the 19,000 acres for four years and she knew others were going to purchase it if she didn't. Additionally, she began studying harder the genetics and the gain and production of their herd.

Even before Bill's illness Lois began going to local meetings regarding the irrigation situation for their area. These meetings were so important to their ranching but sitting in these long-drawn out meetings was too tedious for Bill. Lois would report back to Bill what she heard. On occasion she would even video-tape a session for him. They knew how important this organization and their need for irrigation water was to the success of their business. Water is a precious commodity in that part of the country which has an average rainfall of six to seven inches a year.

Lois had evaluated her situation, the ranch, the family, and what she felt was the best way to proceed. The twins had both left the ranch and had started their professional careers. They were both holding good jobs. Frank was still helping her on the ranch. She had observed he was one of the best ranch hands and workers she had ever seen. He was always well organized when they were branding or doctoring the herd. He was also a good farmer. Bill had taught Frank all he could about the business and had made him a partner. Lois knew she could count on Frank in all phases of their ranching operation. She decided to form a new partnership with him as her partner.

Lois and Son Frank Join Forces

The Herbst Lazy TY Cattle Company, LLC, was formed by Lois and Frank in 1991. The only part of the business they had a concern about was Bill had always been the one to pick the bulls they purchased. It would now be their responsibility to decide and pick the 'right' bulls. This is a crucial part of raising a quality herd. They pulled all the information and records about the previous bulls Bill had bought.

Their breeding records could help them assess the bulls they would consider buying in the future. Lois also used the Angus Sire Directory and chose bulls based on expected progeny development. This tells about expected birth weights, milk production, size of pelvis, etc. Frank left the choices up to his mother. Lois based her decision to buy bulls from herds that had a history of good mothering, calving ease and bulls with good dispositions.

Their choices were sound as their herd continued to improve genetically and with good management. In fact, in 1994 the Herbst Lazy TY Cattle Company was submitted by the members of the Wyoming Beef Cattle Improvement Association (WBCIA) as their choice as Commercial Producer of the Year. Lois did attend the national Beef Improvement Federation convention held in Birmingham, Alabama but they did not place there.

Although Lois and Frank worked well together on a daily basis, there were those rare occasions when they disagreed. Lois remembers she had gone to a cattle meeting and the speaker talked about the most efficient and effective way to give cattle shots without injury to the animal. When Lois came back to the ranch from this meeting she attempted to explain the procedure to Frank. She was explaining that the expert had said to lift the skin and slide the needle into the lifted area under the skin so there would be no injury to the muscle. Frank blurted out, "Just do the damn thing yourself!" After the shock of his retort, Lois began to laugh, and Frank did too. He accepted the new procedure willingly.

Frank married his sweetheart, Jean Randall, in 1993. They had two children, Emma Ruth and William. Lois always found it such a joy to see the grandchildren out working with their father feeding the cattle or some other chore on the ranch. It was so reminiscent of the way she and Bill had raised their children. They always had their children with them as a working part of the ranch. In fact, during the twins' college they got a monthly paycheck from the ranch which paid for their college education. They weren't working the ranch during college, but you might say this was 'back pay' for those years growing up when they did ranch work. It has been and still is the ultimate goal of the Herbst family to make the ranch ready for the next generation.

Lois Works on Behalf of Farmers and Ranchers

Lois applied to be a member of the Wyoming Beef Council in 1996. Governor Jim Geringer accepted her application to the Council. She is quick to point out that during her time spent on the Council was the only time she has ever had her expenses paid when working or traveling for the many causes that are important to her.

She was also elected by the Bureau of Land Management permittees to the Lander District of Wyoming State Grazing Board that same year. Lois was the first woman ever elected to this board. The primary purpose of the organization is when ranchers pay fees for grazing allotments the government returns part of the money to be used for certain improvements requested by the permittees such as fencing, water and other necessary help. This board makes those decisions within the area of the State they represent. In Lois' case is was the Lander District.

Lois and Bill Herbst had been dues-paying members of the Wyoming Stock Growers Association (WSGA) as long as she can remember. However, they never attended meetings. They kept aware of the issues the group was concerned with through the association's *Cow Country* magazine. Lois attended her first WSGA meeting in 1991.

Lois heard the National Cattlemen's Beef Association was to hold a leadership meeting in Denver. She decided to attend. Unknown to her these men were recently elected state officers of the association within their states. Cattlemen attended from states across the country. One of the representatives had to leave the meeting early and asked Lois if she would speak for him to the group about the importance of cattle grazing to the communities. She accepted the task willingly. After her presentation, which was videoed, one of the board members of the Wyoming Stock Growers Association, John Erye, asked her to chair a Private Lands Committee in 1992.

The organization found that Lois Herbst did her research thoroughly and studied the problems faced by stock growers and ranchers. She talked with other ranchers and farmers in her area to get their opinions on the subject. She was extremely capable of being able to speak up in favor of what she felt was best for stock growers. In 1998 she was elected by the Wyoming Stock Growers Association as a second vice president.

Wyoming Stock Growers Association History

The Wyoming Stock Growers Association (WSGA) was organized in 1872 to protect cattle from being stolen on the open range. A stock grower could apply to a brand system started by the organization to legitimately run cattle on the open range. In time four districts in Wyoming were formed with roundups. Representatives from various ranches came to be present at these district events. Please note; this organization was formed eighteen years before Wyoming became a state in 1890. The WSGA was made up of people who owned cattle. The purpose of the organization in today's world is primarily; grazing issues including monitoring grazing allotments and grazing permit security programs. Most Wyoming ranchers use private, state and federal lands for grazing. They are involved in developing new Bureau of Land Management regulations to restore some of the benefits Secretary of the Interior, Bruce Babbitt's range reform messed with regarding how the land was used.

Members are also concerned with the issue of improvement of the Endangered Species Act and how other species can co-exist with livestock production. Predator control is a problem since the input of grizzly bear and wolf management plans were put in place. All of these concerns required members to attend as many meetings regarding these issues as possible.

The officers of the agricultural organizations within the state were asked to be part of Governor Sullivan's Round Table to write a grazing program for Wyoming. The executive committee of WSGA became concerned about the proposed legislation being positive for Wyoming ranchers. WSGA President Flitner asked Lois to be a one-person information committee and she was allowed to attend committee chairman meetings in this capacity.

Water is always a major concern and WSGA supports upstream water storage and the management of water by the State for the benefit of Wyoming; and many, many more issues, as well.

The year after Lois was elected second vice president, 1999, she was named the Agriculture Woman of the Year by the Riverton Chamber of Commerce. She was also inducted in to the Wyoming Agriculture Hall of Fame. Her credentials also included being president of the Cowbelles and working with the county as a cattlewoman. She served as County Farm Bureau President and has worked with the National Public Lands Council and the National Cattlemen's Beef Association.

Sudden Death

Frank, Lois' only son, died of a heart attack in May, 2000. He was only 37 years old. The day he died he had been putting out irrigation pipe and had two men helping him. He had left his young son, William, with Grandma Lois. Lois recalled, "At noon Frank stopped working, came in the house and said he wanted to take William home with him. It was unusual for him to do that, but Frank said, 'I want him with me.'" Lois was told later Frank

Western Women Who Dared to Be Different

Frank, Lois' son, with wife, Jean and children, William and Emma. *Photo courtesy of Lois Herbst.*

ate lunch, went in the living room to the couch to rest, made one gasping sound and died of a massive heart attack.

Lois vividly remembers, "His wife, Jean, came by to let me know what had happened after his body had been taken to the hospital. I went to the hospital and closed his beautiful eyes; he had a smile on his face. I kissed him good-bye and went to the waiting room to assure his children they would be all right."

Lois' twins were called, and immediately came home. Other members of Lois' family also came to Shoshoni. Everyone stayed busy cleaning house, cleaning and mowing the yards and finding daily chores that needed to be done. This was a great comfort to Lois, who knows it is best to stay busy when facing a crisis.

Frank was very well liked by their community and beyond. His funeral was huge. He left his wife and two young children. In time his wife bought a place near her parents and moved off the ranch. Lois knew she could not replace Frank on the ranch. He always took such good care of the cattle and kept them healthy. He was a hard worker. She didn't even try to hire someone, she merely began doing all the irrigating, checking the water and cattle herself. She only hired cowboys or help when needed. She traveled to pastures in three different counties plus raised alfalfa and corn on 316 acres. In the fall of 2008 she sold the cattle and equipment and stopped farming. She has leased the farms and grazing land to three different families.

More Honors and Awards

In 2003 Lois received the Farm Bureau Leadership Award. Another honor and important position however was her election by the Wyoming

Stock Growers Association as president-elect. Two years later, 2005, she was elected to the office of president of the Wyoming Stock Growers Association. This was quite an honor to this determined ranch woman as she was the very first woman president for the WSGA that had existed for 133 years.

When she was installed as president, in June, at a meeting in Cheyenne, the outgoing president, Phillip Ellis, presented Lois with a unique gavel made from a cedar post found on his ranch and a shovel handle. She cherished the gift.

The first thing she did as president of this organization was to get totally involved in the protection of property rights of ranchers and make sure the federal government did not over-regulate the lands and the cattle business. Lois also wanted to make sure that the history of WSGA was preserved in total. She knows all too well unless the history is preserved as we go along it can get lost a long the way. She spent two years in this office. During that time she made sure the ranchers in Wyoming were informed of anything pertinent to raising cattle and improving the herd and its conditions. The computer age has made communication much more sophisticated and more readily available to anyone interested. The *Cow Country* magazine is still a favorite means of communication for members. Many trips to Washington, D. C. during her years in office were made to attend important meetings. She also made trips to many other parts of the country for meetings of importance to ranchers.

Lois admits, "Issues do not change too much through the years. They center on protecting our property and the constitutional right to use our property as free of government regulation as possible."

The grizzly bears, put on the Endangered Species Act to enhance their presence in the Yellowstone ecosystem are now to be 'delisted' from the threatened list. Some environmental groups have threatened to file lawsuits to prevent delisting. Wolves were also brought in to this area. These animals are one of the biggest problems the ranching industry has now and will in the future until government makes some changes. There are many issues that need to be faced with animals, both domesticated and wild, and Wyoming is doing an excellent job in this respect. Thanks to people like Lois and members of the WSGA and other concerned groups.

Necrotizing Fasciitis

Lois attended a WSGA meeting at Casper in December, 2005. Her hotel room was not heating properly. Temperatures outside were minus 30 degrees. She had stood outside for more than 30 minutes for a memorial candlelight service. She was chilled to the bone and she just couldn't get warm. She had also gotten her flu shot just before she left home. She was told later the flu shot lowers the immune system for a time.

The following day she accidentally hit her hand on a plastic box in her garage. It barely broke the skin. The next day she had a red lump where she had bumped her left hand. She felt extremely nauseated. Lois called her doctor's office and was told they were too busy and unable to see her.

Trying to ignore how she felt she went to her coffee club in Riverton but began to chill. A friend drove her to the doctor's office and when her doctor saw her he sent her directly to the hospital. The doctor called the infections physician in Casper, explained her symptoms and reactions, and he told them what he thought it was – necrotizing fasciitis. This is very rare and can be deadly. The bacteria gets into the body, quickly reproduces and gives off toxins and enzymes that destroy the soft tissue and fascia, or sheath of tissue covering muscles. It also causes the body's organs to go into systemic shock. Lois' doctors stayed in consult with the infections doctor who advised them what antibiotics she should receive. This type of infection was not a 'staph' infection, but a type that people can get from someone suffering with strep throat. Where and how it happened to Lois remains a mystery.

Only one of the doctors in Riverton had ever seen this condition previously. Every system in the body can fail as a result of the severe infection and toxicity in one's system. Lois was very close to death. Two surgeries were required to remove the dead fat tissue. Fortunately, they caught it before the muscles and tendons were affected. A skin graft was done with skin from her thigh to cover the back of her hand. Since the local doctors had not treated this type of illness before there was a steady stream of medical people in and out of Lois' room. One doctor told her, "You are sure a 'tough old root.'"

Lois' daughter, Karen, wanted to come home, but Lois told her it was not necessary. The doctor called Karen and said to come home as soon as possible. Lois' blood pressure had dropped very low before surgery. Once Karen arrived she sat in Lois' hospital room and made sure she was not disturbed

Lois and some 'cowboys' pose with Vice President Dick Cheney (middle).
Photo courtesy of Lois Herbst.

any more than necessary. When Lois was well enough to go home, Karen stayed until she knew her mother could take care of herself. Fortunately, the hand healed with no impairment.

After Lois' reign as president was over she hasn't had an idle moment. She sees many issues that need her support. In the spring of 2012 she challenged the incumbent for the Republican nomination in the Wyoming House District 34. The primary issues she represents were education and federal government management of public lands. She was quoted in *The Ranger*, the daily newspaper for Fremont County, as saying, "There is only 13% of the land in our county that is private ownership. So how public land is managed really impacts us severely." Unfortunately, Lois was defeated by an incumbent.

Lois had run for the office of state representative in 1992. This was shortly after she had become active and was not elected. Later, a senator in her district died in office. She put her name up for his seat. Sixteen others did, too. However, she was one of three chosen by the senate district voters to be considered by the county commissioners who chose a replacement. Lois considered it an honor to be one of the three, although she was not the cho-

Lois at the Wyoming Republican Convention in 2012. *Photo courtesy of Lois Herbst.*

sen. Today she says, "I do not plan on seeking elected office again, but I will sure help others to be elected."

Lois is multi-faceted and not only represents the rural faction of our country she is very involved with her family. She took time to go to Florida to take care of a brother that was extremely ill and needed help for an extended length of time. She continues to spend time with her two grandchildren, in hopes they might be future ranchers on the home place. Her daughter, Karen, in addition to her position as landman in her company, has a string of highly trained roping horses that are ridden by some of the top competing tie down ropers in the Professional Rodeo Cowboys Association. Often Lois will join her daughter as they support these ropers at various rodeos. They always get together the last of July each year when the historic Cheyenne Frontier Days is on.

Lois was supporting Liz Cheney, daughter of former Vice President Dick Cheney, until she dropped out of the race for the office of United States Senate against a three term incumbent. In fact Ms. Cheney had asked Lois to be on her list of advisors.

Liz Cheney said, "Lois Herbst is a trailblazer, a fighter and has such energy and vigor. She has a very rare combination of the courage of her convictions and does the research to support it. Whether it is in the stock growers field or the political arena Lois is so important. I admire her so much."

Lois has been active in the Republican party for over 20 years. She has attended two national Republican conventions, (one as a delegate), and two presidential inaugurations for George W. Bush and Vice President Cheney. It is obvious she will do what it takes to do her part and represent rural America.

Outstanding Spokesperson for Ranchers and Farmers

People like Lois Herbst that are willing to devote so much of their time to community and country issues are few and far between. People from ranches and farms that truly know what it takes to be successful in these endeavors and what is necessary and fair for the protection and improvement of the rural faction of our country are seldom addressed in federal government. Often our politicians make decisions that negatively affect rural communities. They are convinced by lobbyists and representatives of organizations that are not concerned with problems of farmers or ranchers. It has been Lois' objective, since becoming a widow and totally responsible for the well-being of her ranch and farm, that she research and identify any issues that have a detrimental affect on rural America. She does whatever she can to keep these programs and issues from being put into effect that can hurt ranching and farming. She has an ability to vocalize her concerns, explain why and be understood by people in power that have not had the opportunity to live in or understand rural life.

Lois explains her commitment jokingly by saying, "I've been told I can't keep my mouth shut about issues I find unhealthy for ranching and farming".

Thomas J. Ryder, assistant chief of Wyoming Game and Fish Department, said of Lois, "I know her personally, and although we haven't always been on the same side in an issue, Lois Herbst is absolutely fearless as an advocate for her industry."

Lois has been a tremendous advocate for many issues and God Bless her for it. Our United States of America began with 85% rural and 15% urban citizens and in some three hundred years those numbers have been reversed. Trying to make 80% of the U. S. population understand or care what happens to our land is a major undertaking. Lois does it willingly. The time and effort she devotes toward this end she can never recover, nor would she try. Her efforts are not just helping her State of Wyoming. Her actions are positive for every rural community in America. Lois Herbst definitely dares to be different.

GRIT & GUMPTION
The Story of Adeline Long

This story is told in first person. This is my great-grandmother and I heard so many stories about her by her oldest daughter, my paternal grandmother, Winnie. I believe this is how she would have told her life story.

The Author.

I grew up in Iowa. My family owned a farm and country life there in the 1870s was grand. We often met with other families in the community, much like our family, and had dinners together. Sometimes we would eat under a big old cottonwood tree on the bank of a little creek near our place. Women would bring lots of fried chicken, potato salad, beans, and desserts galore. The young people would play ball or some other game while the men shared information about their crops, how much rain they'd had, new-fangled machinery and chores. Meanwhile, the women sat and fanned themselves and caught up on the local happenings, like new babies and the like. Often dinners were held after church and included musical programs. I always looked forward to these gatherings and enjoyed the socials and being with my family and friends.

My name is Suzana Adeline Powell Long and I was born January 5, 1861, in our farm house near Albia, Iowa. My folks, James and Mary Jane (Hornaday) Powell had moved to Iowa from Indiana before I was born. I don't know why, but I was always called Adeline. I had seven brothers and sisters. I was the sixth child.

Our folks were very loving, and I always felt safe and secure with much support from my family. Our parents assigned each child chores early in our lives. I had three older sisters and I can remember watching them do chores and trying to do my assigned works as well as they did. I think that is why we all learned to work hard and thought nothing of it. Our parents taught us to be proud of our work and what we accomplished. I don't remember any of us complaining about work, no matter how hard the task. Even if sometimes we thought it was more than we thought we could do.

All our neighbors worked hard, too. We were farm folks. We weren't rich, but we always had enough food and clothes. The folks always kept a roof over our heads. We had a lot of fun. We never spent time thinking about what we didn't have. Having so many brothers and sisters meant I was seldom alone. After our chores were done we usually played until we fell in to bed exhausted. Life was good.

I fell in love with William Clay Long the minute I saw him. Oh, he was so handsome and his smile was enough to give me the shivers. He had dark hair and was tall and lean. In our group of friends it didn't take William and me long to single one another out. He felt the same way about me, or so he always told me. We enjoyed being together and always had such a good time. We joked and laughed a lot. Soon we were dreaming and planning our future together. He was twenty-three and I was nineteen when we married in 1880. We were so much in love.

William Long as a young man.
Photo courtesy of the author.

My family raised me and all my brothers and sisters to have a strong work ethic. I had been raised to do my share, and William Long had the same work ethic. When you come from a big family everyone has a job to do. He had eleven brothers and sisters and I had seven. He worked with his family and for other farmers in the community when we married.

I had been working for neighbor women who needed help canning, cleaning or working their gardens since I was eleven or twelve years old. Sometimes I helped care for the children when a mother became too ill to care for her family. There were lots of children born in our area so I often went and stayed with a new mother until she could get on her feet and take care of her newborn and family without help. I loved tiny babies and always have. Helping mothers to give them and their newborn a good start never seemed like work to me. Regardless of the chore, William and I worked as hard as we could and hopefully we always did a good job. Although we had both been raised in families who believed in doing good work, we were pleased when we knew we'd done a job exceptionally well.

My mother would always say, "The proof is in the pudding." Since William and I had more than enough offers to work I considered our work 'pudding-proof.' We didn't make a lot of money, but always had enough. It's amazing when you are so much in love you really aren't aware of much beyond each other. William and I had our special dream and we talked about it often. We wanted to have our own home, with some farm land. We knew we wanted to raise our family on a farm, just like we'd been raised.

The land around us in Iowa was all owned and everyone had large families. When a farmer retired, or died, his oldest sons took over the land. The younger sons were left to fare for themselves. Often the younger sons would head west to the frontier in hopes of finding and claiming land of their own. Although William was the oldest in his family we wanted to find our own place. There was just something about waiting for his father to retire, or worse yet, die, that we couldn't abide by. What a morbid thought!

William was strong and could do many things. Often he would have a cough that would linger and it seemed he was susceptible to colds. Sometimes, especially in the winter, when he'd come home from work he would be so tired and exhausted. He might rest for a half hour or so, but then he'd be up and going again. I, on the other hand, was healthy as a horse and never ran out of steam.

I was so much in love I really didn't think much about William's health at first. We were young and young people don't expect to be ill and have very little concern about such things. I loved bringing him a hot cup of coffee, or some warm milk to soothe his throat. He always told me how much he appreciated it and that it always helped him feel better. When you are young and married to your best friend you never worry much about anything.

Before we married we often talked of striking out and going west to find a place of our own. We were told about a former neighbor who moved west to Colorado. He had a cough, much like William had. Word came back that the change of climate seemed to rid him of his ailment. We began dreaming about moving to Colorado to see if the change in climate would improve William's health. Oh, the more we dreamed and talked about Colorado and going there it seemed we heard more and more about how beautiful the mountains were.

Finally we just decided we must go and see for ourselves. It wasn't long after we married we just couldn't stand waiting any longer. We loaded our wagon with supplies and were ready to head west. It was early June and we needed to get there before the winter weather set in.

Off to Colorado

Our families gave us a farewell get-together and bid us well. All our families and friends were there to say good-bye. Some of my life-long friends cried, but I was so excited about our new adventure I just couldn't shed a tear. I knew I would miss everyone, but the lure of the unknown new and exciting times, with my handsome husband, was uppermost in my mind.

Mother gave us plenty of jars of food, she had canned, so we wouldn't starve on our way. She also gave us several extra quilts she had made and stored for 'a rainy day.' They were beautiful. Each one had a white background, and the pieces were made from my cotton baby dresses. Some were made from my sisters and my brothers baby clothes, too. The stitches were tiny and equal distance from each other. It was obvious she had given meticulous care in making these beautiful quilts.

I was so touched that she had given them to us. These pieces of cloth were such precious pieces of my past. I would recognize that print and could remember certain childhood incidents that happened when I wore that dress. William always enjoyed hearing me tell stories about my childhood with my family. I cherished those quilts and used them daily until they were in tatters.

The trip was a grand experience. We sang, talked about our future, and wondered what we would discover when we arrived in Colorado. It was the first time in our young lives we had no one from our family to advise us. We had never been so far away from our family and to us it was exciting. There was no one to guide us and share their wisdom. We made all our decisions. We knew we were practical people that could work out any problem we might encounter. Whether our decisions were right or wrong we were willing to take the chance. Oh, how excited we were to experience such a grand adventure!

We followed a route a neighbor had taken earlier. I won't say it was easy, but we certainly didn't encounter any problems we couldn't handle. Our team of horses was well broke, and we stopped from time to time so they could rest. As we left Iowa we crossed the Missouri River. I had never seen so much water. As we made our way through Nebraska we had fairly good trails to follow, as long as we headed directly west.

We crossed several smaller rivers called the Nemaha and Big and Small Blue Rivers. We then were told by some travelers, coming from Colorado going east, to head southwest along the Republican River in what was western Kansas.

We were so eager and nothing seemed impossible. We kept on the trail long hours and we watched the terrain change every day. We would get up early, harness the horses, and wonder what new sights we would see that day. What challenges would we encounter? At night we would camp and cook over an open fire, then fall asleep in the bed of the wagon, under mama's quilts.

Only one day did William feel poorly, and asked if I could drive the team. I was so proud to prove I could manage those horses. The rest of our trip he felt fine and we were fortunate the weather held.

The farther west we went the trees seemed to disappear. The grasses were shorter. We learned it was buffalo grass, which doesn't grow tall, but is very hardy. We knew we had arrived in the area they called the High Plains. The humidity we were accustomed to in Iowa had faded drastically. The farther west we went the humidity seemed to disappear. Dry air took its place and we were always thirsty and ready for a drink of water. We soon realized we needed to fill more jars of water at the rivers we crossed; we were always so ready for a drink.

As we rode through the grasses we had great fun spotting the wild critters along the way. Prairie dogs were visible here and there, sitting on mounds that led to their underground towns. We could hear them 'bark' as they saw us coming. It was their way of telling their neighbors danger might be near. Often when we camped, if we stopped early, we would watch the little pudgy varmints. They were so funny. They would stand on their hind legs, stretching as tall as they could, looking for a coyote or hawk that might bring danger. Then they would scurry from hole to hole, then duck underground. One little critter we watched would stand very tall, on his mound of dirt, searching the sky for some dangerous intruder. Then he would get down on all fours, waddle ten feet or so from his mound, break off a blade of grass which was obviously hampering his surveillance of the horizon, scurry back to stand up and survey his work. We couldn't help but snicker quietly at his precise efforts toward removing any thing that would obstruct his view of the area. We enjoyed watching them from afar.

An occasional coyote would cross our path, glaring at us as if trying to tell us we didn't belong there. I loved to hear the coyotes howl in the distance during the night. Some people thought it was a sad sound, but I found joy in the fact the wary 'wild dogs' were communicating in their special way. It was exciting to sleep under the stars and hear them first to the west, then to the north. In the stillness of the night we would finally fall asleep until daylight. During the day the meadowlarks had a glorious song as they would sit on some bush nearby as we passed in the quiet prairie with only the creak, creak, creak, of our wagon wheels. We spotted deer and antelope, too, but they never stayed very long. The minute they saw us they would high-tail it over a hill. When the antelope turned away from us you could see their white patch on their backside, and away they would go. A hawk would soar over us from time to time, or a magpie would light on a small bush and flex his black and white wings as we went by. On rare occasions we would site an owl and sometimes an eagle. What a magnificent creation. God must have been very joyous when he created the bird.

When we crossed over in to Colorado we had camped with some other travelers and they told us we needed to head straight west if we were going to Denver. We left the Republican River and crossed the Arickaree River going west. After many long days on the trail we finally sighted the mountains. At first they were barely visible on the far horizon. Just little grey bumps to the west. As we got closer we could see just how large they really were. They seemed so majestic in their splendor.

Oh my, what a sight when we approached Denver. Colorado had just become a state less than four years before we arrived and we were excited to be in a state that was so new to the Union. Denver, the capitol, was a bustling place, and there were so many people, everywhere. We came from such a small town we knew we would only stay long enough to ask where there was work and where we could find employment. We had always heard about the gold and silver mining in the mountains so that is where we were headed. When we inquired as to available jobs we were told new silver had just been discovered in the mountains southwest of Denver. The men with whom William and I talked told us about several mines, near Alma, and they were hiring. We hurriedly bought some needed supplies and went on our way.

Destination — Alma

Alma was 75 miles, as the crow flies, southwest of the capitol. The gold mining we had heard about, back in Iowa had played out by the time we arrived. Silver was now the new 'rush'. We were told there was no straight route to Alma, and were advised to head straight south to Colorado Springs, then west to South Park, a valley, surrounded by mountains. We rode through Fairplay, a village, nestled in the valley at the foot of the mountains. Alma was just six miles beyond. When we stopped for a spell in Fairplay we learned that two recent silver mines had been discovered near Alma. One mine was on Mount Bross and the other on Mount Lincoln.

The scenery was breathtaking. I could hardly utter a sound I was so awed as we got in to the hills, and then the mountains. It was so exciting to me. After living in an area with few hills of any size, I was enthralled with the Rocky Mountains. The closer we got the more magnificent they became. What beauty they held. I had never seen any place quite so thrilling. The air was clear and dry. The weather was so different from Iowa. Once we reached Colorado I had never seen a sky so blue. The sky was a shade of blue I'd never seen before. The clouds looked whiter and puffy. The tall pines were everywhere and so different than the trees back home. In Iowa most of our trees lost their leaves in the winter, but these trees had needles and never changed.

William had gotten used to my exclamations of awe about the scenery. He was probably just as taken with it as I because there were long silences as we looked at every view in amazement. As we approached Alma we saw a huge number of tents to the east of the road that led in to town.

We were so excited and anxious to begin our lives in this new place. We loved it the moment we got there. Nothing could daunt our excitement. William's cough had disappeared and he often commented on how good he felt. No doubt, the drier weather and lack of humidity helped his breathing. The high altitude at Alma, 10,570 feet, did not seem to bother his breathing. We learned that altitude does affect some people with respiratory problems. We were so ready to start our new life in this wondrous setting it would have taken a major catastrophe to daunt our enthusiasm and thrill in being there.

William was immediately hired to work at one of the local smelter plants. The smelter plant refined the ore found in the mountains. The plant melted the silver there and separated it by a chemical process.

We lived in the 'tent village' we saw when we entered town. Alma was a small village, which grew so rapidly there were no houses or even rooms to be found. It was six miles northwest of Fairplay, on the junction of Beaver Creek and the Middle Fork of the South Platte River. The main street, when we arrived in 1880, had three hotels, a mercantile store, two saloons, a weekly newspaper called *The Park County Bulletin*, and three churches – Catholic, Methodist and Presbyterian. The biggest businesses in town were two smelter plants which made Alma the refining center of the area.

Many people were living in tents, to the east of the main street and that is what we decided was best for the time being. We pitched our tiny little tent which we had carried with us from Iowa. It was to be our refuge during our trip west, if we had bad weather. It had seen little use until now. Some of the tents were huge, and housed numerous families, but others were just like ours.

William worked close by, thank goodness. It prevented him from having to ascend the mountain an additional 3,500 feet above Alma, to most of the mines on Mt. Bross. We also learned that the additional altitude made the air a great deal colder at the mines than it was in town.

I was hired to help at a rooming house that prepared meals for the miners that lived there. The couple, Mr. and Mrs. Watson, that owned the rooming house allowed William and I to eat there as part of my wages. This helped us a great deal. When I wasn't helping with the meals I helped Mrs. Watson with other chores around the house. William and I were making decent wages and were in hopes of finding a house, or a room, instead of the tent. We kept inquiring about a room that might become available. But everyone was eager to stay at the new mines and we continued to live in the tent. There were absolutely no vacancies in town.

Alma had been established just seven years before we arrived. In that short time it had grown in population from 150 people in 1874 to 700 by 1877. The year before we arrived a mass exodus took place as people left Alma and moved to Leadville, because of a new mining find. Leadville was a mining area north of Alma. People would rush to a new mine, then it would play out, then new finds would happen elsewhere. The census in 1880 showed Leadville having a population of 30,000. However we were told by the end of 1879 many of the mining people, and some new people, too, had returned from Leadville to Alma. The census in 1880 counted 99 men working in the mines near Alma.

Just before the snow flurries began to appear we realized we needed to replace our tiny little tent. We finally came to the realization we weren't going to find any better living quarters. We bought a larger tent which was tall enough that we could stand up in it. The couple we bought it from had an infant that had become ill. They were leaving the mountains and returning to their family back east, in hopes the baby wound improve. Doctors were scarce in Alma. We immediately sold our small tent to a young man that just arrived with no equipment and very little money. He had been hired by the same company where William worked. He promised to pay us for the tent with his first paycheck. He did pay us, eventually, but it took several paychecks.

Tent living was quite an experience. We had a small stove that kept the temperature livable. We rarely spent much time there, except to sleep. We had kindling and some coal next to the stove in a bucket, a few pots mostly for heating water, a lantern, a broom and our bedding. We really didn't need much else and had no place to keep anything valuable, except on our bodies.

After an overnight snow, our first chore, once we crawled out from under the pile of warm quilts my mother had sent with us, would be to don our coats and sweep the snow off the tent with the broom. If we didn't, the snowmelt would seep through the tent and get our bedding wet. That was not a pleasant find when coming to the tent exhausted and tired after working all day.

The Watsons, who owned the rooming house, were very kind and as winter approached they encouraged us to spend long evenings in their large living room. We gladly did, especially nights the temperature got below freezing. The living room was generally filled with 'roomers' playing cards, while others read, and some occasionally gathered around the piano and sang. A few notes on the upright piano were sorely out of tune, but no one cared. By bedtime we would bundle up and run the distance to our tent and jump in to bed under the quilts, as quickly as possible. We would laugh and talk quietly, not to disturb or awaken our tented neighbors nearby. We would hold each other until we fell asleep. As soon as we got warm it didn't take long for sleep to come, as we were generally bone-tired and ready to doze off.

I prayed William would stay healthy, but winter was harsh. On November 17, 1880, the temperature at 6 a.m., in Alma, was minus thirty-five degrees! As hard as he tried, just as the New Year began, his cough returned. He tried everything to shake it but it became more persistent. He wore his muffler over his mouth when he was out in the bitter cold. He missed a few days of work, but was insisting on going to work no matter how he felt. "Lying in a cold tent was no good. I'd rather be working," he said.

Morning Sickness?

Fortunately I was seldom sick. But I could tell something strange was happening to me. If I stood up too fast I got dizzy. I thought it might be the altitude, but we had been in the area for months and it had never affected me before. A couple of times I had to drag myself out of bed when the alarm clock sounded at 4 a.m. to go to work. One day I had barely served the miners their breakfast when I had to hurry out the door to throw up. Mrs. Watson laughed when I returned and apologized for my quick disappearance.

She said, "Well, I'm not surprised. Adeline, you know you are pregnant, don't you?"

I looked at her in shock. Pregnant! I had no idea! How did she know? By the shocked look on my face she realized I was completely unaware of my situation.

"I know you are, my dear," she said softly, "I've had it myself and seen it too many times."

I said nothing. I wasn't convinced. But she was right. In no time my dresses became tight around the waist. I could sew fairly well and in the evening by the light of the lantern I altered my dresses to fit my expanding waist; at least for awhile.

Once we got over the shock, William and I were so thrilled about having the baby. Fortunately, I never had another sick day after that one episode, with my pregnancy. I was healthy, felt good and never missed a day of work. As I grew larger we realized we could not continue our life in Alma living in a tent, once the baby came. The climate change and the mountainous conditions had helped William's health for a short while when we first arrived. But the conditions we lived in, with the severe cold weather of winter, had taken its toll on him. Although we were constantly looking for a house nothing came about that we could afford.

We had been there less than a year when we decided we should head back to Iowa. Mrs. Watson and I calculated that our baby would be born around mid-August. William and I realized we couldn't wait too long to make the trip back with me heavy with child. It was decided we would leave when the winter weather passed and spring was fully in bloom, that way we would probably not have many weather problems. Leaving our new found friends was sad but we needed to be on our way before I got too big to be of help on the trip. Early May found us leaving the mountains I had learned to love. I always loved the smell of pine trees.

Back to Iowa

Returning to our families in Iowa, we found a small house in Monroe County, near the Bluff Creek Post Office. Our first born was a son, born August 21st, and we named him Lloyd. He was a beautiful baby. Two years later Winnie was added to our fold. Two years after that we had Frank. I thought they were the most handsome children I had ever seen. William and I were so happy. Although I had my 'brood' I also had time to plant a garden, and even sold some produce to neighbors and folks in town.

I canned lots of vegetables and when we butchered a beef I canned the meat. William worked for neighboring farmers and he was always in demand because he was such a good worker. He never had to be told what to do. Although we certainly had no extra money we made do. We had so much fun with our growing family and it seemed they always played so well together; at least, most of the time.

One March day when buying a few groceries at the store I noticed a flyer on the bulletin board. It was about the upcoming land rush in to Indian Territory. The government had allotted land for the Indians in this area considering it unfit for white folks. It was an area where many tribes were to relocate when they were forced to leave their native lands when the white settlement was taking place. But some important men had been pushing the government to open up some of this land for the white man and they had finally gotten Congress to approve their request. On March 3, President Benjamin Harrison announced that at the stroke of noon, on April 22, 1.9 million acres of land would be opened for settlement. No one was supposed to 'jump the gun.' They were offering town lots or quarter sections of farm plots.

It was 1889 and there was still no land in our county or surrounding counties in Iowa to be bought. Even if someone did move on and sell their acreage we had little money to buy it. The land rush was the answer for us. When I went home and told William, later that evening, he got as excited as I was. The same thrill we felt when we went to Colorado was back. It took us no time to make our decision. We decided we were going to Indian Territory and claim land!

Indian Territory

Our family and neighbors said, "Aren't you scared, with those Indians so close?"

Having our own place was more important to us, with our growing family, than the threat of Indians harming us. Besides, when we lived in Alma there were many rumors about Indian raids. In fact, shortly after the Meeker Massacre in 1879, which was on the western slope of the Rockies, it was rumored the Utes were coming to Alma. Many of the local residents hurried to Fairplay to fort up in the courthouse. Later it was discovered a drunken miner had started the rumor and there was nothing to it.

Both of our families tried to discourage us from going. They pointed out William's poor health, and our three small children, but we were not to be discouraged. We had not had any problems of consequence on our adventure to Colorado and we were not afraid to venture away from Iowa again. We were determined to find land to own and Indian Territory sounded grand. We loaded our necessities on the wagon, packed up the children as quickly as we could, and headed to Oklahoma.

The wagon trip, with three small children ages seven and a half, five and two and a half, was difficult, but fun. We all had chores at each stop, except Frank the youngest. It was a great adventure for the children. The trip William and I made to Colorado taught us how to spot creatures native to the area we traveled through. We found it to be a wonderful past time for all of us.

In time Lloyd and Winnie were spotting the animals faster than William and I. It became a game to see who could spot the creatures first. Lloyd saw most of them first, but Winnie was surprisingly good at spotting them, too, especially the birds. They would get so excited when they saw varmints, especially the variety they had never seen before.

"I spy a fox," Lloyd would whisper. The other two would scan the area until they would scream, "I see him. I see him!" Winnie would always add, "Oh isn't he beautiful?" By this time the piercing screams would have scared him and he would scurry away. It didn't take long before the young ones realized they had to be quiet, or the animals would disappear before they could enjoy watching them.

Nights camping under the stars were glorious and the children thought we were on a thrilling pursuit. We did not arrive in time for the first "rush" in to the allotted territory, which was April 22, 1889. We arrived several months later and most of the land had been claimed. We were fortunate to find a piece of land in Cleveland County, just fourteen miles southeast of Oklahoma City. We were told of the land by neighbors of the family that had originally claimed the land.

The husband had become very ill just a month or so after they arrived and claimed the land. Unfortunately, he died and the wife and young son were forced to head back to her family in Kansas. William offered her what we had saved, which wasn't much, and she was grateful for it. She told us she was willing to give it to us for nothing, but we insisted she take what we could give her. We learned in time that often many of the original homesteaders had to give up their new homesteads and leave because they ran out of money, had no means of employment, suffered illness and all sorts of legitimate reasons. These homesteads once claimed, and abandoned or traded, were called 'relinquishments.' Our acreage wasn't the best farm land around. It was an area with many hills and would take some hard work to farm it. To us, though, it was a beautiful piece of land and it would be ours if we 'proved up' in five years.

William and I immediately got busy preparing the land for a crop. The former owners had begun to construct a small make-shift house, before the man had become ill. We finished the house, the best we could. William spent most all day turning the sod to make a small field, but in the evenings we worked on the house. It was a little cramped for our 'brood', but we managed. It was built in the side of a hill and the back wall was the hill dirt. The two sides and front were boards and was just one room. We hung a quilt up to give the sleeping area for the children some privacy. No one complained. We were thrilled to have our own place. All of us felt as though we were on a big adventure and everyone took it in stride.

William went and filed the proper forms to register our 'relinquishment'.

Every day the children would discover something new they had never encountered before and be amazed by it. What a joy it was to watch them learn, develop and grow. We kept so busy. William worked the land and I prepared our little home to be cozy and comfortable.

The widow who headed back to Kansas had a cow she called *Old Bossy*. She knew the cow couldn't keep up with them as they traveled because she was soon to have a calf. William paid her two dollars for the cow and she was thrilled. Just a few days later William found *Old Bossy* with her calf. The tiny, wobbly-legged calf was still wet from birth. He took the children down to meet the new little heifer. *Old Bossy* obviously knew the children would not harm her baby and stood quietly by while they met the little brown calf. The children loved her from the first time they saw her and named her *Molly*. They also changed *Old Bossy's* name to a more loving name, and she became *Bessie*. *Molly* became so gentle the children could walk right up to her and *Bessie* continued to trust the children with her new calf. I loved to hear them giggle as the calf nuzzled their necks. *Molly* would follow the children when they went off across the land. If she went too far *Bessie* would moo loudly, and she'd scurry back. I laughingly told William that *Molly* minded her mother better than our 'little ruffians' minded me.

We brought a crate of chickens with us from Iowa and it wasn't long before we had fresh eggs. The children took turns checking the nests for eggs, and it thrilled them when they would find one. It made me laugh to hear them call each chicken by name. I did not encourage the children to name them because occasionally we had chicken for dinner.

The children loved to play and wander the country-side. Sometimes their antics got a little out of hand. One day they had been extremely quiet for too long. When I looked out the door I could see that they were over by the shed we called the barn. I relaxed and went about my work. Unknown to me, Lloyd, age eight, had told Winnie, age five that she could fly from the roof of the barn, provided she would wear my corset and use an umbrella. Little brother, Frank, almost three, was there, too. I doubt if he had much to do with the plan.

Apparently someone came in and smuggled my good corset outside. Winnie managed to get the corset on, with Lloyd helping to lace her in it. When Lloyd and Winnie climbed on the roof, using a make-shift ladder, they left Frank on the ground. He was instructed to stay there to watch the landing. Lloyd opened the umbrella for Winnie, and she grabbed it and jumped. She could have been pushed, we'll never know. I really never heard all the details. I heard the screams from the barn and when I looked out the door the boys were coming toward the house, with Winnie in between them. Her nose was bleeding badly, and she was wailing loudly. She was shuffling along with the corset dragging along the ground. I swear that corset was right up under her arms. How she got up that ladder wearing that corset, I'll never know. Little Frank was wailing along with Winnie. For sympathy, I suppose. Oh, what a sight they were. Unfortunately, Lloyd's theory of flight had failed and Winnie careened in to the ground, nose first.

We discovered she had broken her nose, and she sported two very black eyes for a couple of weeks. No other broken bones were found. She had a few scrapes on her elbows and one knee, but they would heal shortly. My umbrella was beyond repair. The corset made it without damage, except for a few bloody smudges that took several washings to clean. Winnie was very mistrusting of her older brother's suggestions for several weeks after that. Once I was sure Winnie had no serious injuries William and I had to laugh, privately, when I told him what a sight they were. Of course, the children never knew of our chuckles for fear they might try something worse.

Life was idyllic for sometime and the weather was much warmer and required less heat in the fall than back in Iowa. Lloyd attended school and had met neighbor children he could walk to school with as it was over a mile to the schoolhouse. We had also become friends with our neighbors and occasionally had Sunday dinners together after church. The children would play games and the men would talk about their crops and such, while the women would share recipes and get to know one another. We were so happy and William never had a problem during that first winter but a slight cold, but his cough lasted for a month. I was sure we had found the place he could live without the respiratory problems he had in the past.

Typhoid and Malaria

It was in the fall of 1890 when our plans to stay quickly changed. Word came to us that typhoid fever had been diagnosed not far from our area. At first I didn't think much about the disease, but right on the heels of that announcement we were told a case of malaria had been diagnosed down the road from our place. I knew with William's weakened lungs he would not survive if he were to contact either disease. One neighbor we had gotten to know had been diagnosed with typhoid. When others close to us began contracting those illnesses I realized we needed to leave – immediately! The children were sad and disappointed when we loaded everything in the wagon and headed north. They had learned to love our new place, and the friends they had made. We were all disappointed. Although we loved the area and the people I was not willing to take a chance of William contracting either of the dreaded diseases. By the time we left several had died from typhoid. William felt so bad that the cause of our leaving was his health, but I didn't hesitate. The trip back to Iowa was not as exciting as our trip south, but we tried to keep our spirits up. William and I knew there would be other opportunities.

We were determined that someday we would find a place, and nothing could daunt that belief. We had healthy, wonderful children and we refused to let disappointments such as this mar our positive outlook. I must say I watched William like a hawk on our journey back. I knew what the symptoms were of typhoid and malaria. He couldn't cough or sneeze without me reaching up to feel his forehead. I didn't take any chances. I scrutinized the children each day to make sure they had none of the warning signs either. No one would dare to cough or complain of feeling bad or they would suffer my intense scrutiny. We were blessed and no one became ill. God was looking out for us.

When we finally arrived in Iowa, we rented a small place near Albia and near our families. The plot of land we farmed did not make much. I worked for neighbors as often as I could and canned all kinds of fruit and vegetables, even some beef. Our second baby girl, we named Blanche, was born in 1892. Our family was still growing and we felt so blessed.

Golden Earrings

When you have inquisitive and inventive youngsters they can think up the strangest things to do. Unknown to myself or their father, Frank, who was around nine or ten, told Winnie if she would let him pierce her ears he would buy her some gold earrings. He had worked for our neighbors, along with his older brother, and Frank had kept his earnings hidden. Winnie finally gave in and consented to this request. The thought of having gold earrings was quite tempting to her. Frank had shown her some tiny little 'gold' ball earrings he had bought in Albia some time earlier. He apparently knew he was close to getting her to agree to let him do it. He pierced her ears, unknown to either her father or me, with a darning needle and inserted the earrings. Little did these children know how important it is to keep the pierced area clean and apply alcohol on the holes several times a day until they were healed.

Frankly, I never noticed her wearing these little gold earrings until a few days later. Winnie's ears turned bright red and became so painful she finally came to me for help. We took the earrings out of the ears and applied alcohol and some home remedy salve we used on just about every open wound the family ever had. The ears did not heal in a few days. It seemed to take several weeks. In the meantime Winnie suffered much pain and a great deal of pus came out as they drained. She was so embarrassed she wouldn't let anyone see her. She stayed home and wouldn't even go to church. She didn't want anyone to see her bright red puffy ears. Frank was 'out of favor' with his older sister for some time. He finally admitted to her the gold earrings were too much money and he could only afford the ones made of brass. Oh my! I don't think Winnie ever wore earrings again.

A Democrat Through and Through

I was a staunch Democrat, as was my family, and whenever a political meeting was held in our neighboring area I made a point of attending. I had grown up in a Democratic home and my father always talked politics. In 1895 William Jennings Bryan, the Presidential Democratic candidate was running against William McKinley, the Republican candidate.

Bryan was traveling in our area and word came through our community that his train would stop in Albia. A large crowd of us had gone early so we would be there and see Bryant when the train came through. Hopefully I could get a glimpse of Mr. Bryan. Lo and behold, the train stopped and he came to the back of the train and gave a brief speech. He had a strong, commanding voice. I stood in awe amongst the crowd listening to what he had to say about our country and what he planned to do if we would help elect him as President of the United States. Bryan was the most impressive orator I had ever heard. I was thrilled to be in his presence.

I became an avid campaigner for Mr. Bryan. No one was safe from my speech on why we should elect William Jennings Bryan! Unfortunately when the election was held and the votes were counted the next President, the twenty-fifth, was William McKinley. Bryan ran for President three times and never was elected. I voted for him each time, but I guess it just wasn't supposed to happen. I was very disappointed.

Our third boy was born in 1897. I convinced William we should name our new son after him and William Jennings Bryan. William hesitated but I was so convincing he finally agreed. Our new baby's full name was William Jennings Bryan Long. It was quite a handle for a little kid like Will, but it never bothered him as far as I could tell. The name seemed to fit him. He was a talker and never seemed to meet a stranger. He was the most outgoing young-un we had. I always believed we had named him right.

Maybe he should have gone in to politics.

My dear, dear William was in poor health every winter. His ailments always went to his lungs and chest. The bitter cold always took its toll on him. He kept inside as much as possible and Lloyd, Frank and I took care of the outside chores. Money was scarce, but everyone in the family that was old enough helped as much as they could. Lloyd worked after school and was near graduating from high school. He always brought money home to help. Winnie helped in the kitchen and took good care of her little sister and brother. She could cook as well as I could, and often worked for the neighbors, too. Frank was young, but he did chores at home, when William couldn't. Once in a while someone in the community would have a job Frank could do. Thank heavens our children learned to work like their father and I had. I never once heard one of the children complain about chores or being asked to do a task.

Bethel Church was where we went on Sundays. One day I heard some people at church talking about a place in the far North Country where the crops were beautiful. "Golden wheat fields as far as the eye could see," said the man that had been there. It sparked my curiosity and when I inquired he told me that the farming in North Dakota was excellent, and people were moving there to farm because the Bonanza Farms had phased out a few years earlier.

I learned that Bonanza Farms that started around 1875. When the Northern Pacific Railroad sold vast acreages to their investors. The railroad had been granted the land to build their railroad line west. Since they didn't need all of the granted land, investors were eager to buy.

Most of the Bonanza Farms were mainly in the Red River Valley of North Dakota. Most of these investors were absentee owners, usually from Europe.

The Bonanza Farms were owned by corporations and were at least seven thousand acres or more, some as large as 35,000 acres. They farmed on a major scale with numerous plows and threshers, and they hired enough people to man them all simultaneously. In fact, many migrant workers moved in to help during the yearly harvest of wheat. Wheat was the main crop and when the weather was right they would reap a bountiful crop. Their success was due to the inexpensive price of land. New farm equipment had been invented in the 1870s, and the newly completed railroad to that area provided a way to get the harvested crop to the expanding eastern United States markets. These huge farms lasted until 1890 when the land had been exhausted and were no longer as profitable. The distant owners then offered their huge acreages, broken into small plots, to individual farm folk at reasonable prices.

North to Fargo

North Dakota had become a state in 1889, along with South Dakota, Montana and Washington. Opportunities in that region seemed to be what we, as a family, had been looking for and couldn't find in Iowa. The statement "golden wheat fields as far as the eye could see" certainly got our attention. North Dakota was the second largest state in wheat production with almost sixty million bushels per year. No state exceeded them, except Minnesota. Iowa produced only about 25 million bushels.

I was still determined to find a place where William would feel better than he did in Iowa. Once more time we loaded up our belongings, our five children, and this time we headed north. It was late fall of 1898. This time, however, we went by train, which was a wonderful experience for us, and especially for the children. Our wagons loaded with supplies were placed in a boxcar and our horses were put in a cattle car with other stock being shipped.

We arrived in Fargo, North Dakota, and it didn't take very long to get settled. We found a small farm not too distant from town. The people who owned the land leased it to us. They understood we had very little money, but said if we would pay them one-third of what we got for the crop we would yield at harvest time, we could live there. They were also willing to sell us the land when we got financially able to buy.

The price of wheat was respectable and what we had been told of the yield meant we would still make good money for our crop, even giving a third to the landlord. We had planned to bring grain from Iowa but before we left we discovered the wheat that made the best yield in North Dakota was spring wheat, a different variety than we had been growing in Iowa. There was a small house on the property, where migrant workers had stayed, and with some carpentry which Lloyd and Frank quickly completed, we settled in quickly. William and the boys often helped the neighbors and we felt a part of the community within a very short time. To the children, a new place was always an adventure and they loved discovering new things. Lloyd helped his dad, while Winnie, Frank and Blanche attended a small school nearby. Winter was chilly, but our little house was built well, with no cold air 'sneaking' in, and we had plenty of firewood. It was a lot like our Iowa winter.

Our blessed family was growing so fast. It helped Will and I so much to be able to ask the older ones to assist us, especially Will. Even William Jennings Bryan and Blanche were helping with easier chores. We thanked God for all the riches he had given us.

The rains came just at the right time and early May our small acreage was planted with spring wheat. Soon the crop began to sprout. It was beautiful. We could look out our front window and see our future crop as it grew. At first the field was a bright green, with no bare spots. As it grew taller and taller the heads of the wheat, which were filling with grain, became lush and full. Then slowly it turned from green to yellow and then to a golden color. Our little ones loved to go to the edge of the field and measure the height of the wheat against their own height as it grew.

"It's up to my knees," said Blanche.

Later, "It's past my shoulder," she squealed.

The beards on the shafts of wheat shimmered in the gentle breeze. Harvest was just around the corner. We were so excited by mid-summer all of the conversation between William and I was about the good yield it would make. Why we even thought we could see a substantial profit in the lush field.

The rains had stopped by early June. The closer we got to harvest the heat soared up past 90 and even past 100 degrees. The early rains we had enjoyed and made the wheat grow so quickly were gone. It was just plain hot. 111 degrees one day, and another day it was reported to be 114 degrees. The breezes became strong winds. So hot they were stifling. The kernels started to shrivel, and the fields began to crack.

By late August the tallest wheat began to bend in the wind and did not return to its tall upright position. The winds rarely ceased. I thought it would never stop. Then we got more hot wind, but it was followed by a huge rain storm and hail. When the storm ended our crop, or what was left of it, was totally destroyed.

This time the disappointment was almost more than we could bear. I watched William walk from the field back to the house. His shoulders, which were usually straight and strong, were bowed with fatigue and failure. We had no monies in reserve. Our landowners had suffered the same damage to their fields. They said it was such a freak of nature. In all their time in North Dakota they had never seen anything like it. The wind, then the rain and hail, had destroyed crops in a huge area of the state.

The entire family was so disappointed. We sadly packed up our belongings and headed back to Iowa. Oh what a dejected group we were. Blanche and the baby, William, cried, and so did I. The seven of us had put all our hopes in this venture. What made it even more painful is that we were within days of harvest. All our prayers were going to be answered. And to top it off, William had not had one bout of illness while we were there. Our trip home, in our crowded wagons, was slow and silent.

Iowa, Once More

After returning to Mahaska County, we found a place to rent and life resumed with William, Lloyd and Frank working for neighboring farmers. Winnie worked in the area, too. It took us awhile to get our spirits up. But we still had so much to be thankful for. Our children were healthy and we knew, in spite of our disappointments, we were blessed.

Lloyd our oldest son, married a few years later. She was a lovely girl, Ollie Maud Finley. They had two boys, just a year apart. Just before their first boy was born William and I had our sixth child, a boy we named James. Lloyd and family lived not far from us, and we often got together. What fun to have three little boys all around the same age. We talked about them growing up and playing together.

Then tragedy struck Lloyd's little family. His wife, we called Maud, became ill and died in a very short time. She was only twenty-four years old and they were only married five years. The boys were just three and four when they lost their mother. Lloyd was devastated, but he hardly had little time to grieve with the two little boys. We helped as much as we could. Lloyd's brothers and sisters also helped him as much as they could. Winnie had married Jess Hughbanks a few years earlier and they would take the boys, when I couldn't.

Lloyd came to us one day and told us he had been offered a good job by the Burlington Railroad. We were so pleased for him. There wasn't much employment available at that time. Then he told us the job was in northeastern Colorado. We hated to see him leave and take the boys because we all had been helping him with their care.

Four generations. Top row: William Long. Sitting, left to right: son, Lloyd, holding grandson, Vern, with William's father, Lemuel. *Photo courtesy of the author.*

We helped him pack and there was little to be said. It was an important opportunity for him and we knew he couldn't pass it up. He had to make a good living for his two little boys. We went to the depot and waved goodbye as they boarded the train west. We knew Lloyd was much like his dad and I, and always saw a move elsewhere as a great adventure. He was as sure as we had been, every time we had moved, it was the right thing to do. We couldn't help but agree with him. After all, look where we had gone. You never know until you try.

We received a letter from Lloyd, a month or so later. He had found a place in Sterling to live. He had hired a lady to care for the boys when he was working. He went on to say the boys were doing well and seemed to have adjusted to their new life. He did admit they missed us, and the rest of the family.

A few weeks later we received another letter from Lloyd. He said he had claimed a homestead near Willard, a small community about twenty miles west of Sterling. We knew what it was to 'prove up' on a homestead, and wondered if it was possible for our son to hold an important job with the railroad, raise two boys, and qualify his homestead. He truly had his hands full.

The Homestead Act required a person making a claim to 'prove up', which was a term the government used meaning the homesteader must improve the land within a period of two years of declaration. This means building a house, or a barn, building corrals, etc.

The next letter we received told us he had married a woman by the name of Florence Graves, from Sterling. I was pleased to know he had been able to move on, after the death of his wife and mother of his children. He went on to tell us that Florence was unable to stay on the Willard homestead. She owned a hotel in Sterling and had to stay in town to run it. He did say he had built a very small house on the land at Willard. When he was working on the railroad there was still no one to help him care for the boys unless he took the boys to Florence's. She kept so busy with her hotel he knew it was a major inconvenience. Shortly, thereafter, our second oldest son, Frank, decided to go to Sterling and help Lloyd with his homestead and boys.

One day we received a letter from Lloyd, and he wrote:

Dear Mother and Dad,

I have no one to take care of the boys when I am working for the railroad. I'm running out of time to prove up on my place. Frank has taken over a relinquishment that is right next to my land, and he has done all he can for me. Would you be willing to come to Willard and help me? I hesitate to ask because I know dad is not well. I don't have much choice. There is definitely land in the area that you could homestead if you chose to do so.

Your loving son,
Lloyd

Although William worked when he could, we knew his lungs were weak and the smallest cold would go to his chest. For the first time in my life I had to stop and think about the offer. If we had been younger, and William had been in better health . . .

"We just can't go, William — can we," I asked hesitantly?

William disagreed with me, in spite of his health. He felt that this request from our son was God giving us one more chance to find a place of our own. I prayed to God for guidance morning, noon and night. We still had three young-uns living at home and we still paid rent and didn't own any land.

Back to Colorado

One morning I awoke to discover William awake, lying next to me. "I know I'm not much help, most of the time, but I want to move to Colorado," he said with so much determination in his voice there was no way I would argue with him. I could see it in his eyes. I knew God had answered our prayers and our decision was made. I wrote Lloyd and told him we would be there just as soon as we could make arrangements. We were sure he would lose his job with the Burlington if he didn't let them know he had a solution in the works. He notified the railroad headquarters and they made arrangements for us to travel by train. This made our second trip to Colorado much easier and shorter than the first trip we made some thirty years before.

Winnie, and husband Jess, had a young son, Guy, not much younger than our youngest. They had been talking of moving to Canada as they had heard that jobs were plentiful there. Since there was no land to purchase to farm, about the only other job available around our part of Iowa was mining coal. Jess had told Winnie he was not going to work below the surface of the earth, and that was final.

We said our goodbye's to Winnie and her family, plus the rest of our families once more. William and I, and our three youngest boarded the train. Blanche was nearly seventeen; William Jennings Bryan was thirteen; and young Jim was six.

We arrived in Colorado in the fall of 1910. Lloyd and Frank met us at the railroad station and loaded our belongings and we went west to Lloyd's homestead and Frank's place, just across the road. Everyone helped us get settled. It was early spring and there was still a nip in the air. You could see for a great distance as there was not a tree in sight. The prairie seemed so private and vast. But both William and I liked what we saw. We had liked it thirty years earlier when we had been here. It felt like home.

It was evident the two room house Lloyd and his boys had been living in was not big enough for all of us. It was probably no more than twelve feet wide and twenty four feet long. The boys all slept upstairs, which was reached by a ladder on the outside of the house. Temporarily William and I, and Blanche, slept at Frank's house across the road.

The boys had a plan to build a barn as quickly as possible. The main reason buildings were slow to be built in this part of the country was the lack of lumber. There were very few trees and lumber was not only scarce but cost a pretty penny at the lumber yard. Lloyd and Frank were all ready gathering lumber from various places around the country, hoping to keep the cost of building as low as possible. We knew we'd have to 'make do' until we could collect enough lumber to build. Some homesteaders had built their homes out of sod, but everyone in our family decided we'd wait until we could find enough lumber.

Meanwhile William, with the help of Lloyd and Frank, designed the barn. It would have stalls for four horses on the north side, and on the south would be one large area for milking and to keep a few cattle out of the weather and a bin in the corner for feed for the stock. There would be a loft above it to use for storage and hay.

Our sons and William enjoyed this project so much that when they finished the design of the barn they began talking about the house they would build for William and me. It was decided we should have two bedrooms with a storage closet between the bedrooms, a large kitchen and living room. The front porch, off the kitchen, would face the east. A windmill and water tank for the stock, set just east of the location we had picked out for the new house. Also a hand pump which we used to haul water to the house was there, too. We were lucky to have a well as water sources were scarce in this part of the country. We learned that many of the homesteaders around Willard had to get their water from the well in town which was used by the Burlington Railroad to fill their steam engine. All the men in the family kept so much activity going it was hard to keep track of all that was happening.

Will and Frank kept the outside work done, but Lloyd had to be gone much of the time. He was either working for the Burlington or helping Florence with the hotel in Sterling. I took care of his boys, as well as our three young'uns. When I wasn't patching up skinned knees or fixing a meal for our 'brood' I kept the houses clean the best I could. Blanche was such good help with the cleaning. I always had laundry to do with such a wild bunch of boys. I'd barely get it on the line and it would be dry in no time with the

Colorado sunshine and breeze that always seemed to blow. Humidity was gone out here on the prairie, and as far as William and I were concerned we loved this new found weather.

Lloyd and Frank showed us land adjacent to theirs that had not been claimed and we went to Sterling and filed on it for our homestead. William was working a field on our claim as soon as the ink was dry. I never saw a man work as hard as he did, in spite of his health. I was so proud to call him my husband. His breathing was so labored, at times, but he never complained. Everything seemed to fall in to place and it was as if we were destined to call this place home. Winter set in and before we knew it the snow flurries had vanished and spring was upon us. The pastures were sprouting wild lilies, which the boys would pick and carefully bring to me. I always put them in a saucer of water and put them on our dinner table. They never lasted very long, but the boys knew how much I loved to have flowers on the table.

Blanche Moves On

Blanche was offered a job on the Propst ranch in the neighboring community of Merino. She was to help the ranch-owner's wife, cook and clean, during spring roundup. After the roundup was over, Mrs. Propst came to our house and asked if Blanche could stay with them on a full-time basis. She was so impressed with Blanche's work and said she knew she couldn't do without her. I took Blanche aside and asked her what she wanted to do. She assured me she was excited about the opportunity. She thought a great deal of Mrs. Propst. William and I gave her our blessings. Mrs. Propst said she would make sure she came home for holidays. She really wasn't that far away. Meanwhile William farmed and took care of the cattle. My life was full of boys, boys, and boys. They were a handful, but I enjoyed every minute of the day with them. Even the occasional scolding they required. After all they were rough and tumble boys.

It was a breezy summer day and William had been in the field. He spent most days in the field. He came in for dinner, our main meal, at noon. He still had a cough. He always had a cough these days and I guess we just became accustomed to it. It was a warm day. I noticed when picking up the dishes he hadn't eaten much, but often these days he would leave half his meal and say he was full. After dinner he always went in to the living room and lie down on the floor and take a short nap. The breeze coming through the front door brought a small reprieve from the hot Colorado sun. A short nap was William's routine, then he'd get up, refreshed and back to work.

After half an hour I had finished the dinner dishes and I noticed he was still sleeping. I gently shook his shoulder. "William, wake up," I said. He did not respond. I shook him a little harder and when he didn't move I slumped to the floor beside him.

"Oh William, please wake up," I cried. It was then I realized my dear husband was gone.

I'm not sure what happened then. One of the older boys was summoned and the rest is a blur. William was buried among the elm trees, not far from the Platte River near Sterling, in Riverside Cemetery. I was exhausted, drained, and my heart was broken. I loved him with my very being. I always knew he loved me the same way. We seldom talked about our feelings for one another but the evidence was in our actions. Our life together was pure joy, regardless of the hardships or disappointments. We always knew we had each other and could endure what ever we were given. When that was taken away it made me wonder if I had the strength to go on.

When we left the cemetery and headed back home I became aware of my boys. The grown boys were solemn but in charge. The little ones looked so sad. I realized I had to be strong. William would want me to put aside my grief and do what was best for the family. Our family was our purpose in life, and that had not changed.

Although my dear William was gone I knew in my heart what he would want me to do. He and I had done everything we could to try and find a better place to live. Where we could own land and hopefully the climate would allow his health to improve. We had moved west to the Colorado Mountains, south to Oklahoma, north the North Dakota, and had always been forced to return to Iowa. Now here we were in Colorado again. I knew this move was what we had been looking for all those years. My family was here. I told myself I would never leave this place. We had finally found our home and William would want me to stay.

My children all worked toward making our homesteads successful. It was a joint effort and we all knew we could call on one another when ever necessary. I took care of Lloyd's two boys, our two youngest, Billy and Jim, and eventually Winnie's son, Guy, joined the brood. Oh those boys could get in to mischief so easily. But they were good boys. We always laughed a

Family gathering (left to right) Jess Hughbanks, Margaret Long, Winniie Hughbanks, Wilma Long, Adeline Long (in chair), Frank Long, Sr. and Frank Long Jr. Late 1920s.
Photo courtesy of Paula Burton, great-granddaughter.

lot and enjoyed life. They did much of the field work, but often I would too. I loved the outdoors and being able to watch the birds and little creatures scurry across the pastures was sheer delight!

My house was finally built, but it was at least four years before we had enough lumber. It also had to be done when the boys could build it. It was built to the exact design William had suggested. It had two bedrooms, a nice sized living room, and a large kitchen. I loved to cook and spent many hours in my kitchen. The way my 'brood' reacted at meal time I knew my cooking was appreciated. My favorite time of the day was when I had prepared a meal, and it was on the table, surrounded by the whole family. That was pure contentment to me.

The front porch faced the east and it was a perfect place to sit and watch the sun rise. The water tank by the well was always a 'gathering place' for our cows and horses. The meadowlarks, magpies and other native birds also came to get a drink. Often I sat on the porch and remembered the life I shared with William. I could hear his laughter and the quiet way he would always calm me when I needed him. I could only be grateful that I had found my soul-mate. We had 31 years together. We worked hard but we

Adeline, on right, with sister, Ella Powell.
Photo courtesy of author.

could laugh about the silliest thing. We had such pride in our children. Oh how I missed him. He would have been so happy to sit on the porch and watch the sun come up over the prairie.

Eventually Lloyd left his homestead and the Burlington moved him to Denver. Frank married Dora Harris and they had four children. They decided to move to California. They weren't gone long when they returned to northeastern Colorado as Frank was called back to be a lawman. He eventually became sheriff of Logan County; a position he held for many years. Winnie, and her husband Jess, took over the land our family had homesteaded and raised free-range turkeys. They lived across the road in the house where Frank's family had lived. Blanche married Kiah Brown, from Merino, and lived not fifteen miles away. They had two children, Edna Mae and Richard.

You may think my life was a series of failures and disappointments, and you may be right. I don't choose to think of it that way. I found a man I loved dearly and he loved me. I thought he was the most handsome man I had ever seen, and think so to this day. William wasn't as healthy as we had hoped he would be, but he worked hard and did his very best. Every experience we had was a lesson learned and an adventure that became wonderful memories, as we grew older. William died too young, that is true. He was only 53. We had six wonderful children that always made us proud. They did not become rich or famous, and some had tragedies and hardships in their life, but they lived life with good morals, good character and were proud Americans. We liked nothing better than to spend a Sunday or holiday together. Everyone shared in planning a family meal and sat down together to enjoy it. We watched the grandchildren and great grandchildren growing and each one developed their own personality. We came from good stock. What more could I have asked for?

Suzana Adeline Powell Long died December 28, 1936, at Sterling, Colorado, and was buried in Riverside Cemetery, next to her husband William. She is the author's great-grandmother. The author is convinced some of her own tenacity, courage and determination came from Adeline. Although Adeline died when the author was only six months old, she was raised hearing her family tell stories of this woman who was highly respected and revered by her family and friends for all she strived to accomplish and achieve. Adeline was not a 'woman's libber'. She held the role like most women of her day. But she never hesitated or quit venturing into the unknown, in search of a better life for her family. In her era to travel with a husband who was ill, and six children, was no easy feat. She did it without hesitation. Even when the destination proved unsuitable, and they were forced to return to family in Iowa, she always regained her 'try'. She truly dared to be different!

Her granddaughter, Edna Mae Brown Dean, age 95, who was sixteen the day before Adeline died, recollects this about her, "I remember her as stately, and every one had the greatest respect for her. She knew how to calm 'the waters' when things got rocky in the family. She always said Grandpa William had created the farm for her. There were always irons (the ones you iron with) on the back of her cook stove. She had an old-fashioned pump organ. Everything in her home was spotless."

Adeline's granddaughter, Margaret Long Dickerson, age 97, remembers, "Grandma Long always fixed the best meals. Everything was so tasty. She had all those boys to take care of, but every meal she would have was wonderful. Most every meal she made pudding for dessert. The family always ate well. I remember when she was ill, and we lived across the road. My folks would have me, or my sister, stay with her at night. In case she needed help. She would get nose bleeds and often could not get the bleeding to stop. One night when I was with her, her nose would not quit bleeding. She asked me to run up to my folks house, and get someone to come help. It was cold, so I put on my coat, and tried to run up that hill. My legs felt so heavy I didn't think I could make it. I was so scared. I thought I'd never get there."

Pauline Woodward Long, (deceased) wife of William Jennings Bryan Long, Adeline's son, always said, "You could eat food off Grandma Long's floor. It was spotless. She mopped every day."

In spite of all the disappointments she encountered throughout her life she never gave up looking for the place she could raise her family and have land. Adeline Long did dare to be different.

REFERENCES

Chapter 1 – Polly Burson

Interview with Polly in Oxnard, CA October, 2003
"The Perils of Polly" by Lila Finn and "Polly" by Henry Wills and Frank Pawluc for United Stuntwomen's Association & Burbank Elks Club honor Polly Burson, March 15, 1986
"The Life and Times of Polly Burson" by Annie Lambert, for April 1999 *Western Horseman*
Telephone conversation with May Boss, trick rider, stuntwoman
IMDb Earth's Biggest Movie Database Polly Burson Filmography
Archives, National Cowboy & Western Heritage Center, Oklahoma City, OK.

Chapter 2 – Temple Grandin

Interviews with Temple by phone, Spring and Summer, 2013
Thinking in Pictures, My Life with Autism, by Temple Grandin. Published in 1995, 2006 by Vintage Books, A Division of Random House, Inc.
Animals in Translation, Using the Mysteries of Autism to Decode Animal Behavior, by Temple Grandin and Catherine Johnson. Published in 2005 by A Harvest Book.
A Thorn in My Pocket, Temple Grandin's Mother Tells the Family Story by Eustacia Cutler. Published in 2004 by Future Horizons, Inc.
The Way I See It, A Personal Look at Autism & Asperger's by Temple Grandin, Ph.D. Published in 2011 by Future Horizons, Inc.
The Autistic Brain, Thinking Across the Spectrum by Temple Grandin and Richard Panek, Published 2013 by Houghton Mifflin Harcourt.
Attended Program on Autism by Dallas Museum of Art featuring Temple Grandin, May 10, 2013
Ingenious Brains, television program featuring people with unique talents that have some form of Autism, Sept 14, 2013

Chapter 3 – Connie Douglas Reeves

Numerous personal interviews with Connie from 1993 to 2003
I Married a Cowboy by Connie Reeves, published 1995 Eakin Press
Equestrian and Nonagenarian is a Nineties Kind of Gal article by Gail Woerner in *American Cowboy Magazine*, January/February issue 1996
Local Woman among Texas Women of the Century by Rhonda Lashley, *Kerrville Daily Times*, November 17, 1999
Legendary Cowgirl Connie Reeves dies at 101, article in *San Antonio Express-News*, August 20, 2003.
Letters of correspondence to author from Connie Douglas Reeves

Chapter 4 – Imogene Veach Beals

Boors & Saddle column in *The Ranchman Magazine*, published in Tulsa, Oklahoma from 1953 to 1958
Boots & Saddle by Imogene Veach Beals, published in 1994 by Siloam Springs Publishing (A compilation of Imogene's columns published in *The Ranchman Magazine*)
Interview with Donna Clark, daughter of Imogene, 2009
Interview with Letty McAlister, sister of Imogene, 2009
Interview with Peggy Robinson, sister of Imogene, 2009

Chapter 5 – Patricia Wolf

Personal Interviews with Patricia Wolf, Summer, 2013
Some Turtles Have Nice Shells by Roger D. Beck, Published by Trucking Turtle Publishing, 2002

Chapter 6 – Claire Belcher Thompson

Numerous phone conversations with grand-nieces, Doreen Alfonso & Ellie Baldwin
Research material from grand-nieces, Doreen Alfonso & Ellie Baldwin
Billboard Magazine, The Corral Column, from 1926 through 1942
Hoofs & Horns Magazine, re: career and All Girl Rodeos, 1938 through 1954
Cowgirls of the Rodeo by Mary Lou LeCompte, published by University of Illinois Press, 1993
The Cowgirls by Joyce Gibson Roach, published by University of North Texas Press, 1990
The Ketch Pen, Autumn 2008, Number 3, Volume XXIV
The Oshkosh, WI Northwestern, July 7, 1936, page 13
Boston Post, Nov. 1, 1936
The New York Times, July 7, 1934
Sunday Times Advertiser, Trenton, NJ, Aug. 4, 1930; July 26, 1931

Chapter 7 – Violet Hnizdil Christopherson

Author lived in the area near subject during their childhood and school years.
Personal Interview with Violet Christenson, July, 2012
Article by Kevin Christopherson re: World Record in Wyoming #3, in *Hang Glider Magazine*, October, 1989

Chapter 8 – Anna Lindsey Perry-Fiske

Hawaii's Incredible Anna by Ruth M. Tabrah, published in 1987 by Press Pacifica
Visit to Anna Ranch and interview with Director, August 2008
Interview with Dr. Billy Bergin, 2008
Telephone Interview with Pudding Lassiter, 2010

Chapter 9 – Lois Herbst

Personal Interviews with Lois Herbst, 2005, 2013
"WBCIA Commercial Producer of the Year, Herbst Lazy TY raises genetically proven cattle for the next generation", by the Roundup Staff, article in the *Wyoming*

Livestock RoundUp, 1996 Performance Edition.
A Cowgirl Takes the Reins by Gail Woerner, in American Cowboy Magazine, Nov./Dec. 2005
Herbst to Challenge Campbell for House District 34 Position article by Martin Reed, *The Ranger*, Riverton, WY., April 27, 2012.
Telephone interview with Liz Cheney, September 3, 2013

Chapter 10 – Adeline Long

History from an unpublished manuscript, *Long on Spirit* by Gail Hughbanks Woerner
1890 Census for Oklahoma Territory
Converation with granddaughter, Margaret Long Dickerson 2011
Conversation with granddaughter, Edna Mae Brown Dean, 2012

INDEX

Symbols

100 Years of Stock Contracting 104
101 Wild West Show 139

A

Abba 124
Aber, Doff 23
Adams, Roy 145
Albia, Iowa 216
Alfonso, Doreen 152
Alma, Arkansas 143
Alma, Colorado 222, 227
Almeda County 11
American Heart Association 193
American Legion 88
American Quarter Horse Association 91
American Society of Agricultural Consultants 51
Amon Carter Museum 79
Andrea Doria 29
Andrews, Julie 31
Animals in Translation, Using the Mysteries of Autism to Decode Animal Behavior 55
Anna and the King of Siam 31
Anna Ranch 189
Anna Ranch Heritage Center 180, 194
Arizona Farmer-Ranchman 48
Arizona State University 48, 198
Arlington, Virginia 82
Armstrong, Ann 78
Arness, James 27
Ashland, Kentucky 197
Aurania 144
Aurora, Illinois 140
Austin, Texas 60, 73, 104
Austin, Tex 140, 144, 145
Australian Outback 133
Awini Land and Coffee Company 186

B

Babbitt, Bruce 209
Baldwin, Ellie 152
Bandera, Texas 152
Bangkok, Thailand 31
Barnes, Mabel 150
Barrasso, Dr. John 164
Baxter, Ann 36
Bay Meadows Race Track 19
Beal, George Brinton 153
Beals, Charley 88-107
Beals, Faye Jones 101
Beals, Imogene Veach 85-109
Beals, Donna Kay 89
Beck, Roger D. 129
Belcher, Bob 139, 141
Belle Fourche, South Dakota 140
Bell Telephone Company 124
Belvedere Hotel 21
Bennett, Tony 123
Big Horn Mountains 166
Birmingham, Alabama 207
Blessing, Faye 22
Bluff Creek Post Office 226
Bonam, Dr. Claud 150
Bonanza Farms 233
Bond, Paul 103
Bonham, Texas 149
Boot & Saddle Makers RoundUp 103
Boots & Saddles 98
Boss, Claytie 34
Boss, May 34
Boston Garden 67
Boston, Massachusetts 38
Boston Sunday Post 147
Bowman, Everett 147
Bowman, John 147
Boysen Reservoir 200
Brady, Buff 17
Breakfast at Tiffany's 124

Brecheen, Ann 43
Brown, Alta 86
Brown, Charlie 197
Brown, Clara 75
Brown, Edward F. 195, 197
Brown, Harold 197
Brown, Jake 196-197
Brown, Mary 197, 201
Brown, Rosemary 197-198
Bryan, William Jennings 232
Brynner, Yul 31
Buckboard 99
Burch, Lindy 75
Bureau of Land Management 209
Burlington Railroad 240
Burnet, Texas 103
Burns, Frankie 19
Burson, Polly 7-36
Burson, Wayne 22, 30
Burton, Paula 243
Burwell, Nebraska 143, 149
Buschbom, Jack 95
Bush, Barbara 78
Bush, George W. 214

C

Cabo San Lucas 33
Calgary Stampede 167, 194
Campbell, Bonnie Lou 83
Camp Verde Cemetery 82
Camp Waldemar 60, 61, 66, 71, 74-75, 81, 83
Cannon, Jan 80, 83
Capital University 198
Cardiff, Wales 101
Carmelite Cloister 116
Carnation Governor Imperial 188
Carpenter-Trent Drilling Company 198
Carr, Clay 16
Carter, A. W. 181, 185
Casper Wyoming 161, 164, 166, 212
Catholic Nazareth Hospital 113
Cheney, Liz 214
Cheney, Vice President Dick 213
Chester A. Reynolds Award 76, 78
Chester Springs, Pennsylvania 114
Cheyenne Frontier Days 19, 88, 100, 103, 107, 178, 214

Cheyenne Wyoming 85, 107, 164, 204
Chicago, Illinois 65, 67, 143
Chicago Tribune 140
Chillicothe, Ohio 198
Christmas Island 34
Christopherson, Kevin 161, 163-167
Christopherson, Phil 161-162
Christopherson, Phillip 161
Christopherson, Violet Hnizdil 154-169
Churchill Downs 93
Civil War 196
Claire, Sister Saint 119
Clancy, Foghorn 140
Clark, Bobby 105
Clark, Derek 100, 103, 107, 109
Clark, Donna 92, 94-97, 100-106
Clark, Doug 100, 108
Clark, Drew 100, 107
Clark, Duke 97, 100, 102, 104, 106
Clark, Phyllis 105
Clarksville Texas 146
Clemens, Bill 16
Clyde S. Miller Wild West Show 88
Colborn, Everett 21
Colcord, Oklahoma 100, 104
College of Industrial Arts 64
Colonel W. T. Johnson's Centennial Rodeo 147
Colorado State University 37, 53, 56
Columbus, Ohio 198
Connie's Song 81, 83
Cook, Captain 171
Corral Industries 48, 49, 50
Cowboys' Turtle Association 88, 148
Cow Country 208, 211
Creature from the Black Lagoon, The 27
Crosby, Bob 145, 146
C & S Trucking Company 161
Cutler, Ben 43

D

Dallas, Texas 147, 204
Danger Boy 83
Davis, Linda 76
Dayton, Ohio 198
Dean, Edna Mae Brown 245
DeCarlo, Yvonne 27, 36
DeFriest, Babe 24

Denton, Texas 64
Denver, Colorado 97, 161, 163, 198, 202, 205, 208, 221
Denver Post Relay Race 19
Denver University 198
Dickerson, Margaret Long 245
Dickinson Research Center 18, 22, 24
Diller, Phyllis 123
Dillon, Matt 27
Doherty, Ron 99
Dossey, Bernice 20, 22
Dougherty, Red 88
Douglas, Ada 63
Douglas, William 63
Drayer, John 13, 16
Dr Pepper 80, 81, 82, 83

E

Eads, Colorado 86
Eagle Pass, Texas 63
Eakin, Ed 74
Eakin, Lou Ann 160
Eakin Press 73, 74
Earthquake 35
East Bay Hills 11
East Central High School 98
Elliott, Verne 30
Ellis, Phillip 211
Elmore, Marsha 76, 80, 82, 83
El Paso, Texas 17
El Paso (TX) Ranchmen's Reunion & Rodeo 142
Emmons, Florence 137
Emmons, Gladys Rogers 137
Emmons, Henry 137
Encampment, Wyoming 92
Erye, John 208
Estelle, Mother Marie 121
Estes, Bobby 27, 32
Estes Park, Colorado 161
Evans, Dale 25

F

Fairmeadows Race Track 105
Faulk, Bob 165
Fay, Jim 172
Fay, Ka'ipukai 172
Fay, Mary 172

Fender, Mary 199
Finley, Ollie Maud 236
Firefly 147
Fisher Ranch 190
Fleming, Rhonda 36
Fog Horn Clancy Wild West Show 86
Fort Collins, Colorado 56
Fort Riley, Kansas 86
Fort Worth Science and History Museum 79
Fort Worth, Texas 75, 143, 149
Frank Hafley's Wild West Show and Rodeo 142
Franklin Pierce College 47
Fred Lowry Roper Saddle 87
Freedom Forum 82
Fulkerson, Jasbo 91
Fuller, Jimmy 94
Furlong, William Harrison 138
Future Farmers of America 203

G

Gasche, Frances 92
Gatlin, Jerry 33
George, Bill 91
Geringer, Governor Jim 207
Gilbert, Melissa 77, 78
Gillig Manufacturing 126
Girls Rodeo Association 152
Glenclif Dairy 94
Golden Boot Award 35
Golden Gate Bridge 129
Golightly, Holly 124
Goodacre, Glenna 78
Good Year Atomic Corporation 198
Gottschee Austria 200
Grandin, Eustacia Cutler 38
Grandin Livestock Handling Systems 37
Grandin, Richard 38
Grandin Stockyard Systems 53
Grandin, Temple 37-58
Grant, Jack 23, 25
Grateful Dead 126
Graves, Florence 238
Graves, Peter 27
Gray, Bonnie 16
Gray, Tom 90, 93
Green Township High School 197
Gress, Marie "Mary" Keen 75

Griffith, Dick 17, 20, 149
Grimes Funeral Chapel 82
Guadalupe River 60
Guthrie '89er Days Rodeo 91

H

Hamilton, Harry 65, 66
Hampshire Country School 42, 47
Happy, Bonnie 36
Harding, David 137
Harding, Frances Rogers 137
Harris, Dora 244
Harrison, President Benjamin 226
Harvard University 43
Harvard University Houghton Library 153
Hastings, Fox 141
Hastings, Mike 141
Havana Cuba 142
Hawaii Preparatory Academy 189
Hawkins, Johnny 95, 99
Hayes, Bonnie 160
Hayes, Kansas 161
Hayward, California 11
Hayward, Susan 27
H. D. Lee 96
Hefner, Hoytt 91
Henryetta, Oklahoma 96, 98
Hepburn, Audrey 124
Herbst, Bill 199-202, 204-206, 208
Herbst, Emma 210
Herbst, Emma Ruth 207
Herbst, Frank 200, 202-203, 206-207, 210
Herbst, Jean 209-210
Herbst, Karen 201, 203-204, 212
Herbst Lazy TY Cattle Company 206
Herbst, Linda 201, 203-204
Herbst, Lois 195-215
Herbst, William 207, 209-210
Hermosa Beach, California 124
Heston, Charleton 78
High School 65
Hill Air Force Base 198
Hilo, Hawaii 170, 176-178, 181
Hilo Jockey Club 179
Hilo Meat Company 185
Hilo Women's Club 179
Hipp, Henry Lai 176-179
Hnizdil, Adeline 154-155

Hnizdil, Anna Lee 154-156
Hnizdil, Blanche 155-156
Hnizdil, Charles Wayne 156
Hnizdil, Frank 155-157, 169
Hnizdil, Paul 155
Hnizdil, Vernon 154-155, 157-158
Hog Eyes 145, 150
Hollywood, California 65, 77, 78
Hollywood Disney Studio 80
Hollywood Stuntman's Hall of Fame 35
Holthusen, Kitty 160
Honey 15
Hong Kong 32
Honolulu Hawaii 173, 177, 185-186, 188, 191
Hoofs & Horns 99, 148
Houston, Texas 21, 67
Houston, Jim 95
Houston Stock Show and Rodeo 134
Howard, Duane 99
Howdy Doody 41
Hoy, Bob 36
Hughbanks, Grandmother 6
Hughbanks, Grandpa 5
Hughbanks, Jess 243
Hughbanks, Winniie 243
Hunt, Texas 60
Hurley, Wilson 77
Hutchison, Kay Bailey 76
Hutton, Betty 25, 36

I

I Married A Cowboy 72, 74, 75, 83
International Vietch-Veatch-Veach-Veech Reunion 100
Ironton, Ohio 195
Ivory, Buster 21, 104
Ivory, June 104

J

Jackson Hole, Wyoming 134
Jayhawkers 33
Johnson, Colonel W. T. 66, 68
Johnson, Lady Bird 78
Jordan, Barbara 78
Junction, Texas 68, 72

K

Kaala, Hawaii 179
Kalispell Montana 167
Kamehameha, King I 172
Kamehameha, King III 172
Kanner, Dr. Leo 39
Kansas City, Missouri 77
Kawaihae Hawaii 173, 188
Kaycee, Wyoming 167
Keenan, Little Tin Horn Hank 13
Keenan, Tin Horn Hank 13
Kellog, William 196
Kentucky Derby 93
Kerr, Allison 81, 83
Kerrville Texas 72-74, 82
Kimura, Yutaka 187
King Merritt Steer Roping 92
King Ranch 94
Kiowa, Kansas 140
Kiowa, Oklahoma 98
Kirby, Sumner Barton 138
Kirksville, Missouri 140
Kirkwood, Faye 149
Knight, Harry 30
Koehnen, Kate 187
Kohala Girls School 173

L

Ladislaw, Sister 174
LaGuardia, Fiorello "Little Flower" 22
Lake City, Florida 152
Laramie, Wyoming 23, 92, 94
Laredo, Texas 138
LaSalle Junior College 138
Lassiter, Pudding 191
Las Vegas, Nevada 103
Lenapah, Oklahoma 87, 92
Leone, France 28
Lethbridge, Alberta 194
Levi Strauss 130
Lewallen, Nita Brooks 75
Liliuokalani, Queen 175
Lincoln, George Washington 174
Lindsey, Bill 170, 180
Lindsey, Charles 170, 177, 182
Lindsey, Edwin 186
Lindsey, Florence 177
Lindsey, George Kingston 173
Lindsey, John 91
Lindsey, Mary 170, 182
Lindsey, Mary Fay 173
Lindsey, Richard 177, 179, 183
Lindsey, Thomas 173
Lindsey, Thomas Weston 172
Lindsey, Vivian 188
Lindsey, William 170
Lisbon. Portugal 28
Lohre, Frank 152
London England 27, 144
Lone Ranger, The 24
Long, Adeline 6, 216
Long, Billy 242
Long, Frank, Jr. 243
Long, Jack 59, 65
Long, Jim 242
Long, Lemuel 237
Long, Lloyd 226, 227
Long, Margaret 243
Long, Pauline Woodward 245
Long, Suzana Adeline Powell 216-246
Long, Vern 237
Long, William 217, 236, 237
Long, William Jennings Bryan 245
Long, Wilma 243
Long, Winnie 226, 227
Lorain, Ohio 197
Los Angeles, California 23
Louisville, Kentucky 93
Low, Eben 177, 178
Lowry, Fred 87, 94
Lowry, Kate 92, 93, 94
Lubbock, Texas 5
Lucas, Tad 17, 22, 149

M

Macho 62
Madison Square Garden 19, 20, 67, 97, 143, 147
Madison Square Garden Rodeo 20, 22, 70, 92, 140, 142, 148
Magdalene, Sister Mary 115, 117
Maggie Mae 9, 11
Magnolia, Texas 130
Mahan, Larry 95
Main Avenue High School 64

Malone, Dorothy 36
Mansfield, Massachusetts 137, 152
Marseilles, France 28
Marshall, George 26
Matthew, Sister John 118, 119
Maui, Hawaii 178
Maui Parrot 178
Mayo Clinic 94
Mazatlan, Mexico 33
McDonalds 54
McEntire, Clark 98
McEntire, Jackie 98
McEntire, Reba 98
McGinnis, Homer 15
McGinnis, Vera 14
McKinley, William 232
Meeker Massacre 227
Mendoza, Johnny 83
Merino, Colorado 160
Merino High School 160
Merritt, King 23
Merritt, Sis 23
Middleground 93
Midland, Texas 162
Milan, Italy 28
Miller, Clyde S. 87
Miller's 101 Wild West Show 140
Mills, George 18
Mills, Hank 19
Minick, Pam 80
Missouri River 220
Missouri, Trenton 90
Mixer, Orren 91, 107
Mobil Oil 97
Monterrey, California 171
Monte Vista, Colorado 143
Monte Vista (Colorado) Tribune 142
Montez, Maria 27
Moore, Clayton 24
Moore, Frank 19
Moore, Mary 24
Morrell, Dorothy 16
Mount Isa Rotary Rodeo 102
Mount Pilgrim Church 134
Munroe, Jimmie Gibbs 79, 80
Murphy, Audie 30
Murphy, Eddie 36

N

National Cattlemen's Beef Association 208-209
National Cowboy Museum and Hall of Fame 77
National Cowboy Symposium 5
National Cowboy & Western Heritage Center 18, 22, 24
National Cowboy & Western Heritage Museum 103, 104
National Cowgirl Hall of Fame 35, 58, 75, 76
National Finals Rodeo 104, 109
National Press Club 82
National Tube Company 197
Nebraska, Burwell 146
Nesbitt, Jimmy 19, 149
Newcastle, Colorado 5
New England Conservatory of Music 138
New Haven, Connecticut 98
Newton, Iowa 88
New York City 20, 21, 43, 65, 67, 70, 97, 143
New York Times 140
Niagara Falls, New York 65
Nielson, Fanny 147
Nogales, Arizona 103
Norpramin 52
Norris, Bascom 152
Norris, Dr. Frank 150
Northern Pacific Railroad 233
North Guadalupe River 60
Norton, Debbie 83
Nowata, Oklahoma 87

O

Oahu, Hawaii 173
O'Donnell, Rosie 79
Ogden, Utah 198
Ohio University 198
Oil Capitol 93
Oklahoma City, Oklahoma 22, 24, 77, 103, 104
O'Leary, Pat 34
Omaha, Nebraska 156
Ontario, Canada 7

Osorio, Judge 181
Ott, Amy 111
Ott, Bernice 110
Ott, Bill 111
Ott, Christine 111
Ott, Denise 111
Ott, Joan 111
Ott, John 110
Ott, Matthew 111
Ott, Patricia 110
Oxnard, California 35

P

Pacific Ocean 11
Paddy 83
Palace of Sports 28
Pan American Airlines 33
Paramount Studios 25
Paris, France 27
Paris, Texas 149
Park City, Utah 130
Park County Bulletin, The 223
Parker Ranch 170, 176, 181, 182, 183, 185, 188
Parks, Mary 22
Patricia Wolf Company 135
Pawluc, Frank 36
PC Transport 161, 163
Peaches 5
Peacock, Gene 91
Pearl Harbor, Hawaii 197
Peebles, Scotland 101
Pendleton Oregon 85
Pendleton Round-Up 16, 100, 108, 142
Perils of Pauline 25, 27
Perry-Fiske, Anna Lindsey 170-194
Perry-Fiske, Lyman 186
Philadelphia Pennsylvania 65, 110, 132
Pierre, South Dakota 17
Pine Ridge Reservation 165
Pipkin, Catherine 83
Plains Hotel 107
Plantersville, Texas 131
Platte River 242
Pohl, Liz 83
Porter, Willard 99
Portwood, Jerry Ann 79
Portwood, Jerry Taylor 80

Powder Puff and Spurs 152
Powell, Ella 244
Powell, James 216
Powell, Mary Jane (Hornaday) 216
Powell, Suzana Adeline 245
Prairie Schooner 128-132, 135
Professional Rodeo Cowboys Association 214
Professional Rodeo Stock Contractors Association 104
Providence Minerals LLC 204
Pruitt, Gene 97
Pruitt, Jean 97
Purdy, Ikua 178
Purple Monster Strikes, The 24

Q

Quarter Horse Journal 142
Quiet American, The 30

R

Rambo, Gene 21
Ranchman 98
Randall, Jean 207
Reagan, Maureen 78
Reagan, Ronald 78
Red Bluff California 13
Red Feather Lighthouse Camp 114
Reeves, Connie Douglas 59-84
Reeves, Jack 60, 68
Regan, Johnny 65-66
Renton, Washington 89
Republic Pictures 23
Republic Studios 25
Reynolds, Chester A. 77
Rhonda Hole Photography 58
Richards, Lucyle 17
Richter, Mary Margaret 58
Riley, Mitzi 149
Riverside Cemetery 242, 245
Riverton Chamber of Commerce 209
Riverton, Wyoming 205, 212
Robbery Under Arms 103
Roberts, Bertha 92
Roberts, Clyde 92
Robin Yates Western Saddlery 102
Rochester, New York 94
Rocky Mountain National Park 161

Rocky Mountains 222
Rodeo Cowboys Association 97, 99, 104
Rodeo Historical Society 35, 100, 103, 104, 109
Rodeo Sports News 97, 99
Rogers, Roy 23, 57
Rohrer, Tom 50
Roman, Ruth 29, 36
Roscoe, California 15
Rose Bowl Parade 193
Ross, Douglas 63
Rowell Ranch Rodeo 11
Royal Canadian Mounted Police 192
Royal Hawaiian Hotel 191
Royer, Adelaide Moncrief 58
Rumsey Electric Company 117
Rutledge, Moey 83
Ryder, Thomas J. 215

S

Sacred Heart Academy 173
Saigon 31
Saint Hubert High School 114
Saint Matthew Parish School 113
San Antonio 65, 69
San Antonio Express-News 82
San Antonio Texas 59, 63, 198
San Diego 34
San Francisco 12, 18, 129, 190
Scherer, Albert 195
Scherer, Pauline Anastacia 195
Schossow, Reverend Lyle 160
Screen Actors Guild 23
Sea of Cortez 33
Searle, Lucy 175
Seattle 188
Sevit, Blanche 156
Shelton, Marvel 10
Shoshoni Wyoming 199
Shoulders, Jim 95, 96, 98
Shoulders, Sharon 98
Sicking, Georgie 6
Sidney Iowa 88, 149
Silicon Valley California 57
Silva, John 189
Singapore 32
Ski-Hi Stampede 143
Smart, Thelma Parker 183

Smith, Carol 160
Smithville Texas 131
Some Turtles Have Nice Shells 129
Sound of Music 121
Spartan Aircraft Company 90
Spring Brook Cemetery 152
Springtown Texas 143
Sr., Frank Long 243
Stahl, Jesse 13
Stanwyck, Barbara 36
Star Trek 52
Stearns, Rhonda Sedgwick 5
Sterling Colorado 155, 238, 245
St. Petersburg Times 152
Stuntwoman's Association of Motion Pictures 35
Sweeney, Tom 124
Swift Meat Packing 50

T

Tad Lucas Memorial Award 35, 109
Taps 83
Tempe, Arizona 48
Ten Sleep Ranch 168
Texas Women's University 64
Therafin Corporation 46
The Ranger 213
The Territory 133
Thinking in Pictures 44, 49, 56
Thomas Jefferson High School. 64
Thompson, Claire Belcher 137
Thompson, Mrs. Jack 'Red' 143
Thompson, Red 146, 153
Thompson, Stelzer Jack 'Red' 143
Tibbs, Casey 95, 98
Tiny 15
Tofranil 52
Tompkins, Harry 95, 98, 105
Torrington, Wyoming 206
Toulouse, France 28
Trans World Airlines 124
Trenton High School 86
Trenton, Missouri 85, 90, 97
True West Magazine 135
Tulsa, Oklahoma 90, 98, 101
Tulsa World 93

U

Unflinching Courage: Pioneering Women Who Shaped Texas 76
United Stuntwomen's Association 36
University of Hawaii 189
University of Texas 64
University of Wyoming 204
Uvalde, Texas 138, 144

V

Vancouver, Lord George 171
Vaughn Krieg's All Cowgirl Rodeo 149
Veach, Alta Brown 85
Veach, Ben 85
Veach, Billie 85, 97
Veach, Letty 85, 104
Veach, Mary 85, 104
Veach, Monroe 85, 101, 104
Veach, Nora 87
Veach, Peggy 85, 91, 104
Veach Saddlery 87, 94, 99
Veach Saddlery Company 101
Veach Saddlery Company of Tulsa 90, 101
Veach Saddlery/Drew Clark Custom Saddles 100
Veitch Historical Society 101
Venice, Italy 28
Vertigo 33

W

Wagon Wheel Bar 199
Waikiki Beach 175
Waimea, Hawaii 170, 173, 177, 185
Wakely, Jimmy 23
Washington, D. C. 65, 82, 197, 211
Waterloo, Iowa 88
Wayne, Oklahoma 107
Webster, Mevelyn 86
Webster, Shoat 92, 94, 98
Western Heritage Awards 77
Whiskey Peak 165
Whistler 34
White City Stadium 144
Whiteman, Hub 146
Whole Foods 132
Wilford Hall Medical Center 82
Willard, Colorado 156, 158, 238
Williams, George 102
Williams, Jackie 14
Willingham, William 31
Willoughby, Ellen 102
Will Rogers High School 96
Will Rogers Stock Show & Rodeo 79
Wills, Henry 36
Winnisky, Emil 49
Withers, Jane 65
Witmer, Nancy Bragg 75
Woerner, Cliff 83
Woerner, Gail Hughbanks 74, 160, 168
Wolf, Bill 125
Wolf, Indio 127-128, 130, 134
Wolf, Patricia 110-136
Wolf, Sam 126-134
Wolf, Zachary 127-128, 132, 135
World War I 10
World War II 30, 34, 89, 149
Worthington Hotel 75
Wrangler National Finals Rodeo 134
Wright Patterson Air Force Base 198
Wurabarra, South Australia 102
Wyoming Agriculture Hall of Fame 209
Wyoming Beef Cattle Improvement Association 207
Wyoming Beef Council 207
Wyoming Game and Fish Department 215
Wyoming Stock Growers Association 208

Y

Yale University 43
Yates, Robin 102
Yellowstone Drug Store 201
You are My Sunshine 83
Youren, Jan 80

Z

Zipperlen, Mrs. 198

Author Biography

Gail Woerner was born and raised on a ranch in northeastern Colorado and worked with cattle and broke horses with her grandfather. She has written five books on the history of rodeo, a children's book on rodeo and numerous articles in various western-related magazines and periodicals including magazines in France, Canada and Australia. She presently writes a column on the website: www.rodeoattitude.com called *Behind the Chutes & Elsewhere* which tells about rodeo cowboys and cowgirls of yesteryear. She also reviews other writer's books several times a year, and continually answers questions about rodeo from e-mail queries from around the globe.

Gail is the Chairman of the Oral History Project for the Rodeo Historical Society and interviews senior cowboys and cowgirls and those being inducted in to the Society's Hall of Fame. These videos and vocal recordings are housed in the archives of the National Cowboy & Western Heritage Museum in Oklahoma City.

Gail is the Chairman of the Rodeo Clown Reunion which is held at various rodeos across the nation and generally has forty retired laugh-getters, bullfighters and barrelmen attend. They don their familiar makeup and costumes and sign autographs and entertain the fans. She also writes a newsletter to numerous retired rodeo clowns and their widows monthly.

She received the Academy of Western Artists Will Rogers Medallion-Award for Western Nonfiction for her book entitled, *Rope to Win, The History of Steer, Calf and Team Roping* in 2008. She received the American Cowboy Culture Award for Western Writing at the National Cowboy Symposium held in Lubbock, TX, in 2009. She received the Western Heritage Award at the Texas Rodeo Cowboy Hall of Fame in 2012.

Gail lives near Austin, Texas, with her husband, Cliff.

More Books by Gail Hughbanks Woerner

Belly Full of Bedsprings: The History of Bronc Riding
ISBN 9781571682093 .... Paperback ..... 250 pages $24.95

Cowboy Up! The History of Bull Riding
ISBN 9781571685315 .... Paperback ..... 322 pages $24.95

The Cowboys' Turtle Association: The Birth of Professional Rodeo
ISBN 9780981490366 .... Paperback ..... 358 pages $24.95

Fearless Funnymen: The History of the Rodeo Clown
ISBN 9781571682826 .... Paperback ..... 240 pages $19.95

Rope to Win: The History of Steer, Calf, and Team Roping
ISBN 9780978915025 .... Paperback ..... 277 pages $24.95

Available From Your Favorite Retailer
or

Wild Horse Media Group
PO Box 331779
Fort Worth, TX 76163
www.WildHorseMediaGroup.com

www.ingramcontent.com/pod-product-compliance
Lightning Source LLC
Chambersburg PA
CBHW070609170426
43200CB00012B/2639